CYBER SUFIS

Islam in the Twenty-First Century

Series Editor: Omid Safi

About the Author

Robert Rozehnal is Professor of Religion Studies and Founding Director of the Center for Global Islamic Studies at Lehigh University. He is the author of *Islamic Sufism Unbound*, the editor of *Piety, Politics and Everyday Ethics in Southeast Asian Islam: Beautiful Behavior*, and numerous articles. He previously served as the national co-chair of the Islamic Mysticism program unit at the American Academy of Religion.

CYBER SUFIS

Virtual Expressions of the American Muslim Experience

ROBERT ROZEHNAL

ONEWORLD
ACADEMIC

Oneworld Academic

An imprint of Oneworld Publications

Published by Oneworld Academic, 2019

ISBN 978-1-78074-758-3
eISBN 978-1-78607-535-2

The screenshots herein are reproduced with
kind permission of the Inayati Order

Typeset by Siliconchips Services Ltd, UK
Printed and bound in Great Britain by
Clays Ltd, Elcograf S.p.A.

Oneworld Publications
10 Bloomsbury Street
London WC1B 3SR
England

Contents

Acknowledgements

The inspiration for this book emerged from my previous monograph, an ethnography of a contemporary Sufi community in Pakistan (*Islamic Sufism Unbound: Politics and Piety in Twenty-First Century Pakistan*). During my time living and traveling with members of the Chishti Sabiri Order, I documented their initial experiments with digital media as a tool for internal communication, spiritual pedagogy, and public outreach. For the past decade, my thinking has been further shaped by courses I teach at Lehigh University that in various ways explore digital religion, Internet Islam, and Cyber Sufism. It goes without saying that today's Generation Z students swim in digital media as naturally as fish in water. To meet them where they are, I quickly discovered the utility of Internet resources as supplementary teaching 'texts.' This immediately led to other, more humbling realizations: that while I am no Luddite, my tech talents lag far behind my undergraduate students; that while most students are enthusiastic technophiles, they often lack the critical skills required to 'read' and interpret digital sites and spaces; and that what I really needed in the classroom was an introductory road map to guide us all through the virtual jungle. That book did not exist, however. This study is an attempt to help fill that lacuna.

The research for this project was funded by generous institutional support from the Department of Religion Studies at Lehigh University, a summer grant from Lehigh's Humanities Center, and a two-year "New Directions Fellowship" from Lehigh's College of Arts and Sciences. I wish to thank Ryan Stillwagon who helped launch this project as a student assistant in the early stages. I owe a special debt of gratitude to my department colleagues and, in particular, Anna Bigelow of North Carolina State University for their friendship, collegiality, and careful readings (and insightful critiques) of the book's multiple drafts.

As an Islamicist with specialized training in South Asia, this book represents a new trajectory for my own scholarship. My analysis draws liberally on a diverse range of resources in order to situate Sufi digital media within the extant scholarship on digital religion and Islam in America. I am deeply indebted to every scholar whose name appears in the endnotes and bibliography. In the interest of accessibility for non-specialist readers, I have minimized the use of diacritics for all transliterated terms (Arabic, Persian, Turkish) throughout the book.

Over the past several years, I presented versions of this work in a variety of academic settings. These included public lectures at Rutgers University, Franklin and Marshall College, Lafayette College, Bard College, Duke University, Emory University, and the Ecole des Hautes Etudes en Sciences Sociales (EHESS) and Institut d'etudes de l'Islam et des Societies du Monde Musulman (IISM) in Paris. I also presented various iterations of this research at several international conferences, including the 2012 International Conference on Digital Religion at the University of Colorado's Center for Media, Religion and Culture; the 2014 Conference of the International Society for Media, Religion and Culture, University of Kent, Canterbury, UK; the 2015 Eighth Global Studies Conference, "Power and Participation in the Age of Globalized Information Webs and Big Data," at Imperial College London; and a 2017 conference in honor of Professor Carl Ernst at the University of North Carolina, Chapel Hill. I am immensely grateful for the provocative questions and constructive criticism I received from colleagues, students, and audience members in each of these forums. In the end, however, I am solely responsible for the analysis and interpretations—as well as any omissions and mistakes—expressed in this book.

Finally, I offer heartfelt thanks to Novin Doostdar and Omid Safi (Series Editor) of Oneworld Publications for their wisdom, encouragement, and boundless patience—and to Jonathan Bentley-Smith, Laura McFarlane, and the entire Oneworld editorial team for their assistance, advice, and expertise.

Introduction

Cyber Sufis in the Digital Age

In the twenty-first century, global religions survive and even thrive within the digital ecosystem of the World Wide Web. As a study of digital religion in practice, this book explores cyberspace as an alternative media platform for tech-savvy Muslims who seek to root (or reboot) their faith within the complex religious topography of the United States of America. The focus of my inquiry is the Sufi tradition. Sufism—'Islamic mysticism'—is a spiritual path deeply embedded in the long and storied history of Islamic civilization. At its heart is the intense and intimate relationship between a disciple (*murid*) and a teacher (*shaykh*). In Sufi pedagogy, inner, intuitive, experiential knowledge (*ma'rifa*) is cultivated through routinized and rigorous ritual practices. Both past and present, a panoply of Sufi institutional orders (*tariqa*, plural *turuq*) are found in diverse Muslim communities across the planet. Wherever and whenever they traveled, Sufis adapted to new social milieus by adopting local languages and embracing vernacular cultural traditions. Time and again, Sufis also proved adept at utilizing media technologies to amplify their message, to reach new audiences, to answer their critics, and to facilitate social interactions. In this sense, the ongoing transplantation of Sufism onto American soil and across the virtual continuum of the Internet represents a new chapter in an old, ever-evolving story.[1]

From Morocco to Malaysia, from Bethlehem (Palestine) to Bethlehem (Pennsylvania), Sufis have gone global and viral in the new millennium. Today, Sufi teachings, poetry, music, and ritual performances are available to a worldwide audience via an astounding array of digital media. With a click of a button, cybernauts can access translations of the ecstatic Persian love poetry of the renowned thirteenth-century Sufi luminary, Jalal ad-Din Rumi; experience the raw emotion and vocal mastery of the female Pakistani Sufi singer, Abida Parveen; view streaming YouTube clips of members of a Tijaniyya *tariqa* in Senegal immersed in a late-night session of meditative chanting (*dhikr*); and download the latest video of the American Muslim convert, poet, and hip-hop artist, Baraka Blue, performing his Sufi-inspired song, "Love and Light," against the backdrop of the medieval city of Fez, Morocco. A more nuanced understanding of Sufi piety in practice, however, requires more than casual web surfing. This study offers a multidimensional exploration of Cyber Sufism, spotlighting a prominent transnational Sufi community based in the United States: the Inayati Order. As the stories in this book demonstrate, today's Cyber Sufis deploy online multimedia to expand networks, rethink tradition, and refashion identity amid the raucous spiritual marketplace of contemporary American religious life.[2]

MUSLIM NETWORKS AND THE DIGITAL UTOPIA/DYSTOPIA

From its foundations in seventh-century Arabia to its twenty-first-century global reach, the rise and spread of Islam can be mapped as an intricate web of interdependent *networks*.[3] For fifteen centuries, key nodal points within Islam's complex civilizational matrix have united Muslims across the globe with an enduring sense of collective identity, shared experience, and social cohesion amid the immense diversity of their lived, localized cultural realities. Among the worldwide community of believers (*umma*), a constellation of prophets, moral exemplars, and pious heroes—from Adam, Abraham, Jesus, and Muhammad to a host of scholarly and spiritual luminaries—offers a universal blueprint for Muslim subjectivity, ethical practice, and social etiquette (*adab*). Paradigmatic texts—first and foremost the Qur'an, but also the *hadith* (the traditions of the Prophet Muhammad), the canons of theology, philosophy, and law, and the teachings of Sufi masters—communicate knowledge, clarify, orient, and inspire. Prominent institutions (family and tribal affiliations, political dynasties, schools of law,

Sufi orders) shape the dynamics of Muslim social relations and the contours of Islamic tradition. Ritual performances—daily prayers, Ramadan fasting, and Hajj pilgrimage—transform personal Muslim faith into embodied public practice. And the geographic centers of Islamdom—cities and sacred sites across the planet, connected by commerce and trade, empire and conquest, pilgrimage and scholarship—bind Muslims within a cosmopolitan ecumene that spans a vast spatial, temporal, and cultural landscape. Together, the tentacles of these interlocking, symbiotic networks anchor Muslim memory, identity, and piety, linking the past to the present while shaping the direction of Islam's global future.

Today, cyberspace constitutes an entirely new and rapidly expanding Muslim network. During the past quarter century, digital technologies have exploded onto the scene. With astonishing speed, virtual spaces have opened up alternative sites for communication, collaboration, commerce, education, entertainment, identity-making, politics, and polemics. At the same time, the massive paradigm shifts of the globalized, hypermediated Internet Age have unsettled and upended established patterns of social life. As Bernie Hogan and Barry Wellman note:

> A funny thing happened on the way to the embedding of the internet in everyday life. The nature of everyday life changed for many people, from group-centric to network-centric. Much social organization no longer fits the group model. Work, community, and domesticity have moved from hierarchically arranged, densely knit, bounded groups to social networks. In networked societies boundaries are more permeable, interactions are with diverse others, linkages switch between multiple networks, and hierarchies are flatter and more recursive. The shift to a ubiquitous, personalized, wireless world fosters personal social networks that supply sociability, support, and information, and a sense of belonging. Individuals are becoming switchboards between their unique sets of ties and networks.[4]

Digital networks have the potential to radically reconfigure the everyday experience of both space and time. With streaming downloads, spontaneous interactions, and the instantaneous exchange of words, images, and sounds, virtual reality transcends the solid, fixed boundaries of territory and temporality. Via web pages, blogs, dating sites, podcasts, wikis, chat rooms, and myriad social networking platforms (Facebook, YouTube, Twitter, Skype, Snapchat, WhatsApp, Telegram) today's Muslim netizens encounter novel pathways to meet, interact, build communities, and reshape ways of thinking, acting, and being in the world.

With more than ten billion gadgets—from desktops, laptops, and cell-phones to cars and refrigerators—now connected to the Web, the 'Internet of things' is no longer a science-fiction fantasy. With each passing year, the avalanche of digital information and electronic communication accelerates. Coupled with the integration of cloud-based computing on ever-faster, cheaper, and more accessible mobile devices, the growth curve of online multimedia usage continues to expand exponentially. "Soon everyone on Earth will be connected," proclaim Jared Cohen and Eric Schmidt—the former executive chairman of Google and its parent company, Alphabet—in their best-selling book, *The New Digital Age: Transforming Nations, Businesses, and Our Lives.*[5] But how soon is "soon" and just how capacious and inclusive is this conception of "our lives"? Amid the drumbeat of such triumphalist and utopian predictions for humanity's digital future, the promise of seamless, universal global connectivity remains a distant dream. In the end, the fundamental materiality of technology means that cyberspace always and everywhere remains embedded in (and limited by) the particularities of local contexts.

In the early decades of the twenty-first century, a deep and pervasive 'digital divide' persists, with a stark bifurcation between the world's techno-logical 'haves' and 'have nots.' Profound structural inequalities continue to segregate Web usage along the fault lines of class, race, gender, literacy, and geography. According to a 2013 McKinsey & Company report, the global population with Internet access grew to just over 2.7 billion at the dawn of the twenty-first century, with 1.8 billion joining the ranks just since 2004. "This growth has been fueled by five trends," the report asserts, "the expan-sion of mobile network coverage and increasing mobile Internet adoption, urbanization, shrinking device and data plan prices, a growing middle class, and the increasing utility of the Internet."[6] Yet even with this expansive and explosive development, approximately 4.4 billion people across the planet today remain *offline*. Of that staggering majority, 3.4 billion live in just twenty countries, most of them in the global south and many in Muslim-majority countries. Of those 3.4 billion human beings, 920 million are functionally illiterate. The 2013 McKinsey report predicted that an additional 500 to 900 million people would join the online population by the end of 2016. If that forecast was accurate, those potential gains would still leave up to 4.2 billion people on the sidelines. As these sobering metrics confirm, the digital revolution remains a vague and distant abstraction for much of humanity. Even in the United States, where per capita wealth equates with widespread Internet access, the digital pie remains unevenly divided. As Bruce Lawrence cautions, "The euphoria of Cyberspace may translate seamlessly into the lives of over-class Anglo-Americans, but it translates less evenly into the professional and personal future of immigrant Americans. Especially those who fall at the lower end of the socioeconomic scale of late capitalist global economy may never achieve the Cyberfantasy . . . of 'techgnosis.'"[7]

Once online, cyber surfers enter a virtual Wild West that, at first glance, appears to be an open and limitless (if chaotic and often anarchic) space. Even for the privileged minority with easy access to a computer or smartphone, a viable Internet connection, and the requisite cultural capital, however, utopian visions of the World Wide Web do not last long. The sense of unbridled freedom and endless possibility in virtual spaces is ultimately illusory. As a 2016 report from Freedom House documents, Internet freedom around the world has in fact steadily declined in the twenty-first century. More than two thirds of all Internet users today—including most of the world's Muslims—live in countries where criticism of the government, military, or ruling dynasties is subject to strict censorship.[8] And for all people everywhere, there simply is no escape from the long reach of the Internet's gatekeepers (media conglomerates and service providers, governments, militaries, and intelligence agencies) and the Four Horsemen of the neo-liberal Digital Economy: Amazon, Apple, Facebook, and Google.

Yet despite the barriers and restrictions to the increasingly corporatized, controlled, and surveilled digital landscape, cyberspace still offers fertile ground for imagination and invention, innovation and agency. As recent history attests, digital media have a proven track record of facilitating novel forms of individual empowerment, cultural expression, social organization, and political mobilization. In this sense, cyberspace now constitutes a distinct public sphere—though certainly not in the mode of Jürgen Habermas's vision of an open, democratic 'middle space' mediating between individual citizens and government authorities.[9] Unlike the coffee houses, public squares, street cafes, and print media of previous centuries, discourse on the World Wide Web is deterritorialized and diffuse. Moreover, digital communication is often anonymous and by definition not mediated via direct, face-to-face exchanges. If interpersonal interactions remain exclusively virtual, then cyberspace is ultimately a one-way street, a dead-end echo chamber. But we must always remember: the 'nowhere' of cyberspace is populated by real people who are embodied in concrete locations and embedded in local communities—and cyber networks can (and frequently do) circle back to the mundane realm of terrestrial life. In everyday practice, online encounters often lead to new offline relationships. People who meet in chat rooms often later meet for coffee. Virtual conversations frequently inspire individuals to attend community events in local neighborhoods. And even cybernauts who never meet their Internet 'friends' in the flesh still discover new ideas, attitudes, and desires online that impact their worldviews and alter their life trajectories. When true symbiosis between the digital and analog worlds occurs, the virtual is made real.

In the contemporary 'Muslim world,' cyberspace connects Muslims across a vast geographical, social, political, economic, and cultural spectrum.[10] Today, prominent religious institutions and authorities—*madrasas* (schools) and *'ulama* (scholars)—have joined the digital commons. Al-Azhar University, the renowned bastion of Sunni jurisprudence founded in the tenth century in Cairo, Egypt, maintains an elaborate website that is available in multiple languages.[11] In similar fashion, from his headquarters in Najaf, Iraq, Grand Ayatollah 'Ali al-Sistani (b. 1930)—the most influential cleric in Twelver Shi'ism—communicates with his followers around the world, issuing juridical opinions (*fatwas*) via his own multidimensional (and multilingual) web page and social media outlets.[12] At the same time, cyberspace also amplifies the voices of lay Muslims who speak and act beyond the purview of such traditional networks of authority and power. In recent years, a wide variety of social outsiders, outliers, and marginalized groups have learned to leverage the World Wide Web. For these tech-savvy Muslims, cyberspace has quickly proved to be a great equalizer—demonstrating a unique potential to upend the social status quo like no other form of mass media before it. I argue that the Internet's unique affordances, along with its underlying *messiness*, facilitate what Homi Bhabha calls a "contradictory and ambivalent space of enunciation," opening up new avenues for individual agency, social transformation, and the inversion of offline, 'real world' power dynamics.[13] The subversive potential of digital media is an outgrowth of its asymmetric power. Armed with the bullhorn of Internet access, the 'little guys' can punch above their proverbial weight, reaching vast audiences with a speed, focus, and volume they could never otherwise hope to attain.

Today, Muslims across the globe utilize the World Wide Web to circumvent fixed cultural taboos, traditional centers of religious authority, and entrenched political powers. Examples abound. In the United States, an array of Muslim advocacy organizations deploy digital technologies to promote human rights, gender equality, religious freedom, and racial justice[14]; create solidarity among African-American Muslims and Sufi women[15]; and amplify the critiques of media and popular culture by Muslim feminists.[16] Women in deeply conservative Muslim countries like Saudi Arabia—where access to public spaces is curtailed and opportunities for social relationships are proscribed—have also discovered a sense of empowerment and a place for social critique and community building via digital media.[17] During the tumultuous Arab Spring of 2010–2011, the adroit use of social networking tools such as Facebook, YouTube, and Twitter by political activists like Egyptian Wael Ghonim (b. 1980)—a former Google executive—played a salient (if over-hyped) role in catalyzing the spontaneous waves of popular protests and uprisings that swept across the Middle East and North Africa (Tunisia, Egypt, Libya, Bahrian, Syria, and Yemen).[18] As the subsequent brutal crackdowns by many Arab governments demonstrated, however, cyberspace can just as easily be weaponized as an intrusive instrument for state censorship and surveillance, propaganda and persecution, coercion and control.[19] And certainly no Muslims have proved more adept at exploiting digital media than militant *jihadi* groups. For al-Qaeda, the Taliban, Boko Haram, ISIS, and their myriad affiliates and offshoots, sophisticated and highly stylized YouTube videos (including 'martyr' testimonials, filmed executions, and live feeds of terrorist attacks), online magazines, websites, and social media campaigns provide an effective and affective platform for advertising and recruitment.[20] As all these examples illustrate, cyberspace is deployed, experienced and valorized by twenty-first-century Muslims in diverse ways to radically different ends. Its Janus-faced nature makes it a protean tool for both utopian and dystopian visions—equally effective for liberation and exploitation, for solidarity and division, for dialogue and demagoguery.

SUFI CYBERSCAPES IN THE LANDSCAPE OF LIQUID MODERNITY

In tracing the genesis, evolution, and impact of digital technologies, many scholars mark cyberspace as a key marker—for good or for ill—of contemporary global modernity. Like so many other terms (beauty, art, democracy, pornography), on closer examination 'modernity' proves to be a slippery signifier. Despite its common usage, in both theory and practice it remains an elusive and contested term, a problematic construct that is, as Dipesh Chakrabarty notes, "easy to inhabit but difficult to define."[21] This is not to say that scholars have shied away from the subject. Indeed, an ocean of ink has been spilled in a quest to delineate and deconstruct global modernity. Myriad academic studies have explored its genesis and genealogy, its causes and effects, from multiple theoretical and disciplinary perspectives.[22] While the sheer volume of this scholarly debate is remarkable, it has too often produced more heat than light.

While a consensus on terminology and definitions has proved elusive, scholars have tended to conceptualize modernity as a totalizing *system*. It is typically equated with a particular worldview and a discrete set of ideas, institutions, and social practices. These include such key post-Enlightenment concepts as "citizenship, the state, civil society, public sphere, human rights, equality before the law, the individual, distinctions between public and private, the idea of the subject, democracy, popular sovereignty, social justice, scientific rationality" and secularism.[23] The one common denominator underlying the normative genealogy of modernity is the looming presence of Europe. Conflating 'civilization' with 'the West,' the dominant narrative posits a singular process of social, political, and economic transformation. According to this logic, modernity comes prepackaged with a host of universal 'izations': Westernization, globalization, democratization, individualization, urbanization, bureaucratization, rationalization, scientific technicalization, and secularization.

With rare exception, the Eurocentric model of modernity has colored, coded, and ultimately distorted scholarly investigations of Islamic civilizational history. Drawing a sharp distinction between the West and the Rest, this dominant paradigm posits a universal teleology that obviates the particularities of local cultures and homogenizes Muslim experience. As Armando Salvatore argues:

> In this perspective, the relation between Islam and modernity can only be one of *deficiencies* (measured by Islam's alleged insufficient capacity to supersede traditions), *dependencies* (on Western modernity) and *idiosyncrasies* (in terms of distorted outcomes of a dependent modernization). Questions such as *What Went Wrong?* with Islamic civilization vis-à-vis the modern world hegemonized by the West inevitably come up as a result of static and unilateral views of tradition and modernity and their relations.[24]

In many scholarly and mass media accounts, the Eurocentric meta-narrative of modernity creates a straw man: a monolithic Muslim Other. Faceless and undifferentiated, Muslims are characterized as utterly different: exotic and irrational; pathologically prone towards patriarchy, misogyny, and violence; and mired in a medieval past, always and everywhere unwilling and unable to adapt to changing times. Such old, Orientalist caricatures reject the capacity of individual Muslims to reinterpret their pasts, reshape their own traditions, and remake their own lives. The end result is the erasure of Muslim history, agency, and humanity.

This book attempts to reframe the assumptions, parameters, and language of the debate. Drawing on the legacy of postcolonial scholarship, I reject the logic of historical teleology and the underlying assumption of a one-way street to modernity. I assert instead that in everyday experience modernity has no meta-narrative, no singular function, no universal form. It is neither monolithic nor hegemonic. In tracing the multiple vectors of American Sufi identity, I offer no grand theory to encapsulate modernity as an abstract, disembodied, decontextualized, catch-all concept. Echoing Katherine Ewing, I argue instead that the conglomeration of forces that together constitute the rubric of modernity—its ideas and institutions, its discourses and practices—are in fact encountered, defined, and shaped in myriad ways by individual social agents (real people) in specific historical moments (local places and spaces). "In order to avoid exaggerating its power, it is important to recognize that modernity itself is not a single force but rather the temporary conjunction of practices and ideologies that have diverse sources and divergent trajectories," Ewing notes. "Current technologies are, of course, taken up into Sufi practice, but they are transformed and encompassed in local circles of meaning. Sufism, itself a diverse phenomenon, thus has a historical trajectory that has been affected but not determined by the composite of forces that we call modernity."[25]

In an effort to map the shifting currents of contemporary American Sufism, I seek a more flexible and pliant approach to religious life on the Internet. One way to talk about the multivalent dynamics of twenty-first-century life without falling down the rabbit hole of ossified theoretical abstraction is to adopt a different vocabulary. To this end, the work of Zygmunt Bauman proves especially useful. According to Bauman, contemporary life now constitutes a new and distinct era of world history: the age of "liquid modernity." In sharp contrast to the "solid" and "heavy" stage of early modern history, he asserts, life in the present stage of late global capitalism is marked by its pervasive speed, volatility, and unpredictability. "Liquid modernity," Bauman insists, "is the growing conviction that change is *the only* permanence, and uncertainty *the only* certainty. A hundred years ago 'to be modern' meant to chase 'the final state of perfection'—now it means an infinity of improvement, with no 'final state' in sight and none desired."[26] While concepts like 'post-modernity' suggest a decisive break from the past, Bauman's taxonomy allows us to account for both historical continuity and change. Most importantly, his holistic model provides a crucial global perspective. Decentering the standard trope of Eurocentrism, liquid modernity identifies key social processes that increasingly impact humanity across the planet. Throughout the contemporary world, Bauman argues, capital and labor are mobile, politics is malleable, communities are fractured, identity is fluid, and communication is highly mediated.

In intriguing ways, Bauman's ideas are echoed and amplified by Arjun Appadurai in *Modernity at Large: Cultural Dimensions of Globalization.* As the book's subtitle suggests, Appadurai puts a bright spotlight on the dynamics of culture. In his view, the "new global cultural economy has to be seen as a complex, overlapping, disjunctive order that cannot any longer be understood" through the lens of standard interpretive frameworks.[27] For Appadurai, like Bauman, contemporary life is distinguished by a constant state of movement and fluidity. In an attempt to chart the flux and flow of everyday cultural dynamics, he posits a number of distinct yet symbiotic 'scapes': *ethnoscapes, mediascapes, technoscapes, financescapes,* and *ideoscapes.* In Appadurai's assessment, each of these 'scapes' constitutes a space in which individual identity and social life are first imagined and then inhabited. In his words:

> The suffix –*scape* allows us to point to the fluid, irregular shapes of these landscapes, shapes that characterize international capital as deeply as they do international clothing styles. These terms . . . also indicate that these are not objectively given relations that look the same from every angle of vision but, rather, that they are deeply perspectival constructs, inflected by the historical, linguistic, and political situatedness of different sorts of actors: nation-states, multinationals, diasporic communities, as well as subnational groupings and movements (whether religious, political, or economic), and even intimate face-to-face groups, such as villages, neighborhoods, and families. Indeed, the individual actor is the last locus of this perspectival set of landscapes, for these landscapes are eventually navigated by agents who both experience and constitute larger formations, in part from their own sense of what these landscapes offer.[28]

Appadurai's neologisms help us to chart the "perspectival constructs" of real human beings in specific cultural geographies, both large (global) and small (local). In my view, his notion of *mediascape* offers a particularly useful window for exploring virtual religious worlds on the World Wide Web. Why? Because it captures the potential of digital media as a powerful tool for self-imagining and self-formation. The sensual nature of cyberspace, its visceral displays of both images and sounds, allows for creative storytelling. And, in the end, it is through narratives that identity and subjectivity are most readily formulated, expressed, and experienced. Whatever its focus and wherever its location, questions of identity are invariably contextual: enmeshed in complex, interdependent webs of signification rooted in specific social, historical, and cultural contexts. In short, *who* we are depends to a great extent on the *where* and *when* of our location. Identity is neither a priori nor inherited. Instead, it is imagined, constructed, and then articulated in narratives: dynamic assemblages of stories about the self and its relation to others. Whether grounded in language, race, gender, sexuality, ethnicity, or religion—or a combination of them all—identity is invariably fluid and contingent. It is "relational and incomplete," always in process and under construction.[29]

Individuals and communities are free to stake their own claims to identity. Yet these narratives have immediate social consequences once they are communicated in public discursive spaces to a listening audience. "Narrative is not for all to hear, for all to participate in to an equal degree," notes Sudipta Kaviraj. "It has a self in which it originates, a self which tells the story. But that self obviously is not soliloquizing or telling a story to itself. It implies an audience, a larger self towards which it is directed, and we can extend the idea to say that the transaction of a narrative creates a kind of narrative contract."[30] The expression and embodiment of identity therefore constitutes a public, often political act. Individuals and communities draw boundaries, articulate who they are (and are not), and imagine who they might become through their stories. As Appadurai illustrates:

> Mediascapes, whether produced by private or state interests, tend
> to be image-centered, narrative-based accounts of strips of reality,
> and what they offer to those who experience and transform them is
> a series of elements (such as characters, plots and textual forms) out
> of which scripts can be formed of imagined lives, their own as well
> as those of others living in other places. These scripts can and do get
> disaggregated into complex sets of metaphors by which people live
> as they help to constitute narratives of the Other and protonarratives
> of possible lives, fantasies that could become prologue to the desire
> for acquisition and movement.[31]

Following Appadurai's lead, I envision the alternative narratives and networks enabled by digital technologies as virtual *Cyberscapes*. As a distinct genus of mediascape, Cyberscapes display a unique capacity for accessibility, immediacy, adaptability, and creativity. Fast and fluid, the malleability of the medium allows for the flexibility of its message.

Cyberscapes serve as powerful vehicles for the expression and experience of religious identity and community. This is demonstrably true for today's American Muslims.[32] In the Cyber Age, the exponential growth of digital media interfaces has opened up new pathways for Muslim community building, social networking, political participation, self-expression, storytelling, and meaning-making. Shaped by disparate blends of multiple identities—culture, ethnicity, class, gender, sectarianism, and political ideology—American Muslim Cyberscapes mirror the contemporary global *umma* in all its dazzling diversity, complexity and, at times, contradictions.

In the past several decades, the rapid expansion of electronic multimedia has empowered a new generation of Muslims to find their voices, to stand up, and speak out. At the same time, these new technologies have amplified and intensified intra-Muslim debates over the parameters of 'real Islam.' What is Islam? How are 'orthodoxy' and 'orthopraxy' defined? What is sacred, inviolable, and inimitable, and what can be modified or jettisoned in response to changing times and circumstances? Who exactly has the authority to speak for and interpret Islamic tradition? In the post-9/11 United States, such pressing questions persist amid an increasing cacophony of voices—and with rising social and political ramifications. As Nabil Echchaibi argues:

> This process has taken an unprecedented popular dimension in the last decade as new Muslim actors and protagonists of this dialectic of Islam and modernity have emerged on television and on the Internet, creating an interventionist public sphere where a new social imaginary of a religiously informed modernity is not only talked about but also performed. This social imaginary borrows from the toolbox of modernity and reconciles any tensions with a Muslim understanding of what constitutes a modern emancipated self.[33]

In order to keep pace with this volatile terrain, I argue that scholars need new tools to account for the heterodox, polycentric expressions of mediated Muslim subjectivities in the twenty-first-century United States.

Drawing on a bricolage of beliefs and practices, spiritual heroes, and (re)readings of sacred history, the American Sufi communities I examine in this book each display their own distinct versions of a hybrid religious identity that is simultaneously modern, Muslim, and mystic. They do so within localized religious environments where other Muslims, drawing on the same sources, imagine and enact markedly different models of Islamic normativity, subjectivity, and authenticity. It is important to recognize that this kind of heterogeneity is nothing new. From its origins, Islam has never been static, uniform, or monolithic. Throughout history, Islam has flowed through diverse social landscapes like water, adapting to the contours of local geographies and taking on the colors of local cultures. The transplantation of Sufi piety and practices into American society and across the virtual realm of cyberspace, therefore, repeats a well-established pattern of continuous accommodation, adaptation, and transformation.

BOOK OVERVIEW AND STRUCTURE

This book maps Sufi Cyberscapes in the United States in the early decades of the twenty-first century. My analysis interprets Sufi digital media as unique media formations: carefully crafted and authorized documents that reveal a great deal about the values and priorities, the networks and narratives, of discrete American Sufi groups. Since there is no single, universal, 'one size fits all' system of institutional authority in Sufism—no Church, no Pope, no formal ecclesiastical hierarchy—each Sufi order ultimately makes its own decisions about if, when, and how to engage digital media. In practice, the style and content of Sufi web pages and social media are typically shaped by each *tariqa*'s living Sufi master, often in consultation with senior disciples and tech-savvy (often younger) webmasters. As a result, every Sufi community's digital profile is different and distinct. Though influenced by past precedents and the gravitational pull of tradition, I argue that Sufi Cyberscapes demonstrate a remarkable capacity to facilitate new social connections and communal identities, alternative styles of affective and aesthetic experience, and diverse modalities of religious imagination, subjectivity, and expression.

For contemporary American Sufi communities, the words, sounds, and images communicated via digital media constitute descriptive accounts of the past and present, as well as aspirational visions of a desired future. A critical reading of these multidimensional sites therefore sheds light on how American Sufis see themselves. And because Sufi Cyberscapes are designed for public consumption, digital media also tell us a lot about how

Sufi communities seek to *re-present* their own history, beliefs, and practices to external audiences—Muslim and non-Muslim, domestic and global. While cyberspace offers a creative space for self-imagining, there is a symbiotic relationship between online narratives and offline practices. After all, digital media never operate in a vacuum; instead, they both shape and are shaped by the contingencies of everyday life. By reading against the grain (and by noting what is left unsaid), we can trace how American Sufis modulate their message to attract new disciples and potential allies, counter their critics, and adapt to changing social circumstances.

In thinking about Cyber Sufis, web pages and social media serve as my primary sources. Deviating from the standard definitions and methods in the field, I approach these digital documents as a distinct genre of *religious text* and a unique formation of *sacred space*. The challenge is to learn to read, interpret, and move through these sites. Why? Because these are strange kinds of texts and spaces: interactive, hyperlinked, and multisensorial. Moreover, they are projected into an anomalous sphere: a virtual world that is itself ethereal, non-material, and non-terrestrial, neither here nor there. Sufi Cyberscapes are also, by design, fluid and ephemeral. As living documents, websites and social media constantly expand, contract, and transform, leaving no trace behind. Even in the time it took to write this book, many of the sites I describe have morphed significantly. They are sure to shape-shift again and again, in a perpetual state of flux and flow. Given the intrinsic dynamism of digital religion, this study is perhaps best understood as a *screenshot* of digital Sufism in the United States at a particular moment in its continuous, unfolding evolution. All the digital resources that I reference and describe throughout the book were accurate and up to date as of March 2019.

This portrait of American Cyber Sufism emerges from my own online investigations. Given the distinctive spatial, temporal, and sensorial dimensions of the Internet, in many ways my methodology has more in common with ethnographic fieldwork than textual exegesis. After all, websites and social media are not static, linear, one-dimensional documents that can be read cover to cover. Instead, digital media are multidimensional and interactive mosaics of words, images, and sounds that are manipulated by maneuvering through multiple hyperlinked pages. Internet searches—and therefore Web-based research projects—are often random, extemporaneous, and even serendipitous. Because there is no convenient travel guide or ready-made road map for navigating cyberspace, the experience is also highly subjective. As Garbi Schmidt concludes in her own study of Internet Sufism, "Studies in cyberspace are always, one way or another, the results of 'jumping' investigations of certain bits of text, made within a certain timeframe and with a certain amount of available objects . . . In many ways searches in cyberspace are comparable to the process of anthropological fieldwork."[34] The unique nature of the medium necessarily shapes the academic study of digital texts and Cyberscapes. It also creates a vexing conundrum for scholars and students of digital religion: how to freeze the flowing river of digital media long enough to allow for observation and analysis, knowing full well that any interpretation will necessarily be contingent and short-lived?

The book's seven chapters contextualize Cyber Sufism in the United States through a number of lenses and from a variety of perspectives. The layout is as follows:

Chapter 1, "Mapping Digital Religion and Cyber Islam," provides an overview of prominent thinkers, theories, and methods within this rapidly expanding, interdisciplinary scholarly field.

Chapter 2, "(Mis)Interpreting Sufism," examines how the Sufi tradition has been understood—and misunderstood—by both outsiders (Orientalist scholars, Islamist ideologues, government agencies, Western media pundits) and insiders (Sufi masters and their disciples).

Chapter 3, "Sufism in the American Religious Landscape," locates living Sufism as a vital dimension of American Islam amid the pluralistic religious topography of the contemporary United States.

The next three chapters offer an extended case study of the oldest and one of the largest Sufi communities in the West: the Inayati Order. Founded by Hazrat Inayat Khan (1882–1927), this hybrid Sufi organization has undertaken a major institutional overhaul under the leadership of his grandson Pir Zia Inayat Khan (b. 1971). In my assessment, few American Sufi groups have pushed the boundaries of digital life with greater coordination, integration, sophistication, and bold ambition than today's Inayati Order. Through a deep-dive, thematic analysis of the multidimensional web pages and social media platforms of this dynamic *tariqa*, therefore, I aim to delineate many of the salient ideas, tropes, and trajectories that now shape American Sufism amid the tectonic cultural shifts of the Digital Age. In doing so, I attempt to construct a model and methodology for the study of Cyber Sufism around the world.

Chapter 4, "Narrating Identity in Cyberspace: Inayati Tradition and Community," explores how Inayati digital media communicate a story of both continuity and change, preserving the heritage of the past even as the order embarks on a comprehensive project of institutional transformation.

Chapter 5, "Virtual Practice: Inayati Rituals and Teaching Networks," charts how Sufi piety is learned, expressed, and experienced within today's Inayati community, both online and offline.

Chapter 6, "Bridging the Digital and Analog Worlds: Inayati Social Engagement," traces the symbiotic relationship between the Inayati Order's digital media outlets and its public outreach programs to diverse audiences in the United States and around the world.

In chapter 7, "Contextualizing American Cyber Sufism," I return to a wide-angle, meta-analysis. With brief vignettes of seven other prominent Sufi communities as a springboard, I search for shared patterns and resonant themes in the broader landscape of contemporary American Sufi digital media. Coming full circle, the chapter concludes with a speculative prediction for the possible futures of American Cyber Sufism amid the coming transformations of Web 3.0.

Since my analysis of Sufi digital spaces is largely descriptive, readers are encouraged to follow along online. Shifting between text and computer screen, they can move through the myriad links of these multilayered sites as I do—and then, more importantly, use these virtual footholds to launch their own investigations of this vast and largely unmapped terrain.

With its singular focus on Cyber Sufism in the United States, this book is the first scholarly intervention of its kind. As more and more Muslims plug into the virtual universe, and as the academic field continues to expand to keep pace, other studies will surely follow. There is certainly ample room for growth and abundant fare for future research. While this study breaks new ground, however, it is important to clarify from the outset what this book is *not*.

This book is not a comprehensive account of Cyber Sufis in the United States—to say nothing of the vast ocean of global Sufism and its myriad manifestations in diverse cultural settings (via multiple Islamicate languages) over time and across the globe. In researching this book, I compiled a vast amount of data on numerous American Sufi groups. I then had to make a choice: whether to pursue an encyclopedic survey of digital Sufism, or instead to explore a few paradigmatic examples in greater detail. I opted for depth over breadth. To that end, my analysis examines the English-language digital multimedia of a small (but representative) sample of Sufi Cyberscapes in order to create a snapshot of the complex digital expressions of twenty-first-century American Sufism.

In similar fashion, the three thematic case-study chapters on the Inayati Order are neither comprehensive nor exhaustive. My analysis does not include a longitudinal, diachronic survey of the Inayati community's complex institutional history, from its origin to its myriad offshoots over time and across the globe. Nor does it provide a detailed account of the voluminous writings and complex life histories of Inayat Khan and his spiritual successors. Instead, I intentionally narrow the analytical frame, focusing on the public profile of the North American branch of the Inayati Order as evidenced through its evolving digital multimedia productions.

Finally, this book is not a traditional ethnography. A full account of the impact and import of Sufism in cyberspace would require a different kind of research altogether, with extensive fieldwork interviews with the producers and consumers of these virtual spaces. In the present study, however, I follow a different path, approaching Sufi websites and social media as ends in themselves. As an ethnographer myself, I am fully aware that in doing so much of the 'real stuff' of living Sufism is marginalized or omitted entirely. The visceral, affective, and embodied experience of Sufi ritual practices. The subtle gestures, nuanced body language, and intimate conversations shared between a Sufi teacher and her/his followers. The daily, mundane interactions, discussions, and even disputes among Sufi disciples. The complex interplay between a Sufi devotee's spiritual life and the incessant, inescapable demands, intrusions, and doubts of everyday life (work, family, school, personal relationships, politics). All these things are muted, silenced, or erased in my narrow focus on Sufi digital media—virtual texts which are carefully designed and constructed to put on a good face, to communicate a crafted message, and to 'clean up' any private messiness, ambiguity, or anxiety for an external, observing, public audience. A detailed, granular ethnographic study of American Sufism in practice and 'on the ground' is research that I have tabled for a future project.

With those disclaimers in mind, the question remains: what then *is* this book?

To put it succinctly: this study is an experimental, introductory exploration of digital religion, digital Islam, and American Sufi Cyberscapes in practice. Drawing on a wide range of interdisciplinary scholarship, the book documents how select American Sufi communities attempt to harness the power of the Internet. Using specific examples to delineate larger trends, I argue that the World Wide Web now constitutes a new *virtual imaginarium* and *digital sensorium*: a parallel ecosystem where Muslim identity, community, and piety are increasingly envisioned, articulated, and enacted.[35]

The stories I tell contextualize American Sufism within the scholarship on digital religion and American Islam. My descriptions and interpretations of American Sufi Cyberscapes are shaped by a number of overarching, core questions that probe both the internal dynamics of these individual Sufi orders and the broader religio-cultural milieus in which they operate. Among many lines of inquiry, three key meta-questions guide my approach and inform my analysis:

- How do contemporary American Sufi communities from different social, ethnic, and cultural backgrounds harness the Internet to initiate conversations, debate issues, expand interpersonal networks, and explain their own distinct traditions to multiple audiences in the public sphere?
- In what ways do digital media either expand or dissemble established patterns of Sufi identity, institutionalization, authority, and spiritual pedagogy? To be more specific: how does cyberspace duplicate, complement, or alter the intimate relationship between a Sufi master and his/her disciples and the embodied ritual practices that are at the very heart of traditional Sufi piety?
- How does cyberspace facilitate (or impede) conversations and interpersonal encounters—within Sufi groups, between Sufis and other Muslims, and with external, non-Muslim audiences—across local, national, and global boundaries?

With these questions in mind, the following chapters engage multiple dimensions of the book's central thesis: that in the twenty-first century, Sufi Cyberscapes now serve as critical sites and alternative spaces for American Muslim narratives and networking, identity-making and community building, experience and expression.

1

Mapping Digital Religion and Cyber Islam

For American college students born at the dawn of the twenty-first century, life without digital media is utterly incomprehensible. Laptops, tablets, and cellphones, paired with seamless wireless networks and cloud-based computing, keep them plugged in and constantly connected, with round-the-clock access to an ocean of information and ever-expanding social networks always just a click away. In the classroom, asking my students to contemplate daily life without their digital devices provokes predictable reactions: from blank stares to lamentations of disbelief, mixed with sadness and horror, for their primitive ancestors doomed to such a cruel fate. For the youth of Generation Z it is quite simply an unimaginable past, as distant and disconnected from their daily experience as the Dark Ages. Their attitudes are a sign of the times. The digital world is now so integrated into every dimension of modern life that it is easy to forget the World Wide Web was invented in 1990 and that the iPhone, Android, and Kindle did not exist before 2007. Today, the everyday ubiquity of the Internet erases the perception of its newness and novelty. As Hogan and Wellman argue:

> The ethereal internet light that previously dazzled has now dimmed to a soft glow permeating everyday concerns. We have moved from a world of internet wizards to a world of ordinary people routinely using the internet. The internet has become an important part of people's lives, but not a special part. It has become the utility of the masses rather than the plaything of computer scientists. It has become the infrastructure for a variety of computer-supported communications

media, and not just the specialized conveyor of e-mail, Facebook, or any specific digital medium.[1]

Amid the torrential pace of technological change, digital media have been thoroughly domesticated as the 'new normal' of our wired lives.

From the printing press to cyberspace, the invention and dissemination of mass media technologies have continuously altered the ways in which human identity and social relations are experienced and expressed. Numerous scholars have explored the role of mass media in the formation of networks of community. In his groundbreaking work, *Imagined Communities*, Benedict Anderson documented the convergence of print technology and capitalism in the rise of the modern nation-state—an "imagined political community" bound together by a common "print language."[2] Pushing Anderson's conclusions even further, Armando Salvatore argues that the pervasive shift in media intervention marks "a deeper change in the very conditions of production, diffusion and consumption of discourse." He views this as a "transformation in the 'episteme' of an age," nothing less than a "type of change that potentially affects every discursive formation and influences the modalities themselves of defining the objects of knowledge."[3] The arrival and rapid dissemination of online digital multimedia resources has only accelerated this dynamic. Today there are more than one billion websites on the World Wide Web. In the age of liquid modernity, new electronic multimedia technologies—ever faster, cheaper, and ubiquitous—are radically reconfiguring the rules of economic consumption, social interaction, political discourse, and religious practice.

In recent decades, scholars have scrambled to map the tectonic shifts of the Digital Age. The expanding archive of Internet studies draws on multiple academic disciplines: media studies, communications, sociology, cultural anthropology, and, more recently, religious studies. Rather than reviewing all this voluminous literature, this chapter focuses on a particular subset of this scholarship: recent research on the impact of digital technologies on contemporary religious life. As background for our exploration of American Cyber Sufism, the following pages briefly spotlight some of the key thinkers, prominent models, and resonant themes in the academic study of digital religion and digital Islam.

KEY THEMES IN THE STUDY OF DIGITAL RELIGION

As the Internet continues to spread its tentacles wider and deeper, the impact of digital media has increasingly occupied scholars of religion. The field remains 'under construction,' however. At present, there is no unanimity among scholars on terminology, methodology, or theoretical approach. In the face of overwhelming evidence, what everyone seems to agree on is that the digital revolution is here to stay and that its influence on religious life is trending upward at an accelerating pace. "The important questions centering around the impact of new, personalized and interactive technology on an individual's religious experience and expression are still being formulated, much less answered," David Damrel argues. "Nor is that a phenomenon limited to a particular faith community: the proliferation of web-based resources, organizations and individual opinion sites is challenging our conception of how to interpret religions, spirituality and their social configurations."[4] Scholars of comparative religion are interested in how media digitalization impacts religious identity, community boundaries, and piety and practice— as well as the contours, definitions, and expressions of religious tradition, authority, and authenticity. Drawing on multiple interpretive frameworks, case studies that focus on diverse religious communities in the United States offer different perspectives on how religion is "being expressed, understood, and performed through digital media."[5]

The scholarship on the interface between religion and digital media can be divided into three distinct phases.[6] Beginning in the mid-1990s, early studies evaluated the emergence of religious cyber communities in bifurcated ways: from breathless, utopian visions to hyperbolic, dystopian predictions. This formative research tended to be heavy on description but light on explanation. As Gregory Price Grieve notes, "These first studies tended to be highly speculative, drawing heavily on researchers' own experience, and were triggered by the surprise of finding religion on the Internet. In a sense, the first wave of scholarship was caught up in the revolutionary qualities seen in digital media."[7] In the early to mid-2000s, a second wave of scholarship brought a new emphasis on critical reflection and methodological rigor to the field. The expansive growth of digital technologies at the dawn of the twenty-first century prompted scholars to rethink the importance and influence of online multimedia on religious life. In rapid succession, a number of important monographs and several groundbreaking edited volumes examined the cultural impact of digital media on religious identity and community from a variety of perspectives.[8] This work was complemented by the publication of a number of detailed studies that documented, delineated, and explained the appropriation of digital media by diverse religious groups across the globe.[9] Most recently, a theoretical turn has marked a third phase of research. In the past decade, a new wave of scholarship has explored the connectivity between online and offline religiosity. Drawing on a diverse range of theoretical models and focused case studies, these scholarly contributions aim to document how "authority, co-production, and convergence" transform both the 'virtual world' of digital religion and the 'real world' of everyday, terrestrial religious life.[10]

This rapidly expanding archive hinges on a few foundational questions that have elicited divergent responses from scholars. The first issue I label the 'chicken and egg' conundrum: namely, what is the key driver of this dynamic? Does media shape religion, or does religion shape media? Arguing for the prominence of the former, media and communications scholars such as Stig Hjarvard and Knut Lundby developed the 'mediatization of religion' thesis.[11] This model emphasizes the instrumentality of mass communication technologies as agents of social change and cultural transformation. "This approach retains the notion of separate spheres of media and religion," notes Stewart Hoover, "suggesting that the mediation of religion in fact changes religion."[12] The mediatization model insists that the medium shapes the message, arguing that, in practice, new media technologies fundamentally alter the structure and function of a variety of fields—from education, to business, to government and religion. In Lundby's assessment, "Mediatization is a more specific concept. That religion is defined by its practices of mediation does not imply that all religions are mediatized. A state or process of mediatization requires a context for the ongoing mediations: a media-saturated environment. . . . Mediatization, then, is characterized by the media-saturated context and, further, by the transformations this may imply—in our case, of religion."[13]

A contrasting paradigm disputes these central assertions, rejecting technological determinism, redirecting the focus to religion, and then tracing how new media do (or do not) transform it. In essence, the 'mediation of religion' model argues for a less structural approach. It views religion through the lens of practice and performance rather than doctrines or institutions. Led by cultural anthropologists such as Birgit Meyer, this school of thought insists that religions have always been mediated, and that emergent media technologies "simply introduce new forms through which religion is circulated."[14] Drawing on the work of Robert Orsi and David Morgan, this model privileges media's material forms and aesthetic capacities.[15] "To stress the multi-sensorial channels through which media address and shape religious subjects," Meyer writes, "I have coined the notion of 'sensational form.' Negotiated and authorized within religious traditions, these forms embed media into a distinct set of practices of mediation that is characteristic for a particular religious tradition. Sensational forms are central to generating religious sensations through which what is not 'there' and 'present' in an ordinary way can be experienced, over and over again, as available and accessible."[16] Adherents of this approach view the 'mediatization model' as too reductive and teleological—and reject the premise that media are the primary agent of religious change.

A second set of issues that shape the scholarship of digital religion centers on another fundamental question: what exactly is 'new' about new media? I think of this as the 'Goldilocks' conundrum: namely, is cyber religion an analog of offline religion, something entirely different and distinct, or a hybrid blend? In an oft-quoted 2000 article, Christopher Helland framed this debate by distinguishing between "religion online" (i.e., the religious use of the virtual environment) and "online religion" (i.e., the capacity of digital media to enable entirely new forms of religiosity).[17] Other scholars have since questioned Helland's binary, arguing that "this is perhaps too simple a way to look at things, that a range of different combinations of religious capacity, gesture, aspiration, and possibility are present in digital spaces."[18] In Stewart Hoover's view, "changes in media are actually changing religion, resulting in new forms, expressions, understandings, contexts of practice, and sources of authority."[19]

Hoover and Nabil Echchaibi—his colleague at the University of Colorado's Center for Religion, Media and Culture—posit that digital media increasingly constitute a unique and emergent "third space" for religious discourse, experience, and expression.[20] As a hybrid, liminal, 'in between' space, they argue, cyberspace is ambiguously located between the private and the public, the home and the workspace. In relation to religion, digital media offer a generative and reflexive space that extends "beyond established institutions (churches, mosques, denomination, faith groups) as the first space and individual practice as the second space."[21] Moreover, they assert, the Internet allows for a host of new affordances. It engenders new forms of community and novel networks of relationship. It promotes autonomy and self-reflexivity among users. Perhaps most importantly, it has the capacity to decenter entrenched modes and nodes of power and authority—so much so that even traditional, established religious authorities are compelled to employ electronic media to police boundaries, safeguard tradition, and defend their own positions. Hoover explains the concept of "the third spaces of digital religion" in this way:

> By this we intend to account for what appear to be the emergent normative practices of digital religion. Individuals today act as if these spaces are contexts from which they can articulate and advocate new ideas, in which they can circulate symbols and symbolic re-mediations, and in which they can form new communities and networks of common purpose. They do not necessarily imagine that these are practices that take place alongside of real or physical or structural contexts. Instead, they seem to imagine that new and elastic contexts and boundaries of practice and action are possible.[22]

By this account, digital media are potentially a total game changer. As a fluid, interstitial space of social practice, cyberspace offers an alternative playing field where entirely new visions of cultural power, religious imagination, individual subjectivity, and spiritual praxis can be articulated, shared, and deployed.

Heidi Campbell, one of the key architects of this emerging academic field, sees things somewhat differently. In a series of wide-ranging publications, Campbell calls for alternative theoretical and methodological models, grounded in detailed case studies, to chart how different religious communities practically engage new media. In 2010, she established The Network for New Media, Religion, and Cultural Studies: a website and online resource center for scholars and students in the field.[23] A related Facebook group, "New Media, Religion and Digital Culture," offers another important sounding board. Campbell labels her own model the "religious-social shaping of technology" (RSST). Her work spotlights the dialogic and symbiotic relationship between online and offline religion, and calls for "human-centered, rather than technology-centered, analysis to the study of digital media."[24]

A religious community's perception and appropriation of online multi-media, Campbell argues, are determined first and foremost by its *offline* social context, religious practices, and boundary markers. In her words:

> The religious-social shaping of technology approach seeks to give an account of the specific conditions influencing a user's negotiations with a technology, which can lead to changes in use or belief within a given social context. It also attempts to explain responses to new technology in socio-technological terms. In other words, the success, failure, or redesign of a given technology by a specific group of users is based not simply on the innate qualities of the technology, but on the ability of users to socially construct the technology in line with the moral economy of the user community or context. It recognizes that individuals and groups of actors within particular social situations see their choices and options constrained by broader structural elements of their worldview and belief system.[25]

In Campbell's view, religion leads and technology follows. This assertion, in turn, has immediate implications for scholarly methodology. Campbell argues that researchers need to look at four interdependent markers when analyzing how a particular religious community employs electronic media: the history and tradition of the community; its core beliefs and patterns related to media; the specific negotiation processes it undergoes with a new technology; and the communal framing and discourses created to define and justify their technology use.[26] In her monograph *When Religion Meets New Media*, she spotlights a number of case studies in order to delineate four modes of digital media usage by religious communities. In her assessment, online multimedia technologies can be used for: proselytizing and proclamation; to facilitate global networking; as a tool for agenda setting and to publicize beliefs; and to digitize religious rituals.[27] These taxonomies provide a useful road map to navigate in and between online and offline worlds. In my view, Campbell's research offers an important cautionary note—a theoretical 'reality check.' Her work reminds us that even if digital media open up an alternative 'third space' for religious meaning-making, networking, and praxis, the virtual landscape is invariably shaped by the ideological convictions and practical needs of flesh-and-blood human beings in the lived-in world of everyday life. The digital and analog worlds are, in the end, interdependent and symbiotic.

In the case studies for this book, I draw upon all of these interpretive models in an effort to map American Cyber Sufism as a particular manifestation of digital religion in practice. In chapter 7, I return to these specific theoretical and methodological questions in an effort to delineate the salient features and future trajectories of twenty-first-century Cyber Sufism.

SURVEYING CYBER ISLAM

For religious groups around the world, cyberspace offers an alternative platform for communication and community building. In the twenty-first century, a diverse range of American Muslims have joined the global digital revolution, integrating social media into every dimension of their lives with incredible speed and remarkable skill. As Zain Abdullah notes:

> The mushrooming of Muslim web sites on an array of Islamic topics illustrates the emergence of a 'Cyber Islam.' Muslims overwhelmingly participate in social networking, personal Web pages for scholars or bloggers, and institutional or group debates, which includes consulting online *fatwas* for questions about Islamic sexual mores, dating, raising children, *halal* (permissible) jobs choices, sports, diets, and Islamic financing. American Muslim (and transnational) online activities point to the increasing significance of virtual networks for discussing Islam and meeting Muslims in the twenty-first century . . . And along with these new venues, Muslim Americans have envisioned new identities that may have previously appeared incongruous with traditional beliefs.[28]

Amid this momentous paradigm shift, the challenge for scholars is to keep pace with the changing attitudes and practices of Muslim communities in the

United States (and across the globe) who increasingly deploy cyberspace in divergent ways to diverse ends.

When it comes to Muslims and media, the past is prologue. In myriad cultural locations and historical moments, Muslims have effectively leveraged the power of media as a tool to communicate their own distinct visions of religious identity, piety, and practice. Print technology was not established in the Islamic world until the nineteenth century, four hundred years after Gutenberg's invention of movable type facilitated the dissemination of Martin Luther's German translation of the Bible. Though late to arrive, it quickly spread during the colonial and postcolonial eras as a broad spectrum of Muslim political actors readily adopted print media to broadcast their messages.[29] These trends have expanded exponentially in the Cyber Age. Regardless of the medium, however, new articulations of Muslim faith, identity, and community are always built on the same bedrock foundations. As miriam cooke and Bruce Lawrence argue:

> The boundaries of digital Islam reflect the scriptural, creedal, and historical boundaries of Islamic thinking. There can be no Islam without limits or guideposts. You cannot have a straight path unless you know what is beyond or outside or against the straight path. Cyberspace, like social space, must be monitored to be effectively Muslim . . . The horizontal, open-ended nature of the Internet makes the boundaries of digital Islam at once more porous and more subject to change than those of its predecessors. There are still the same guideposts: the scripture (the noble Qur'an), the person (the Last Prophet), and the law (the *shari'a*, or broad path, with the *'ulama*, or religious specialists, as its custodians). Each term—the book, the prophet, the law—has to be defined historically and then redefined in cyberspace in order to reflect the diversity of resources and worldviews within the *umma*.[30]

Given the persistence of tradition, what exactly is 'new' about the contemporary Muslim media landscape? Beyond the obvious affordances of digital technologies (speed, cost, access), cyberspace has upended entrenched social hierarchies and power dynamics. In the twenty-first century, amid a cacophonous—and at time combative—competition over the mantle of Islamic authority and authenticity, Muslim religious leaders and laypeople alike employ electronic multimedia platforms to speak for Islam. Access to canonical religious resources (the Qur'an, *hadith*, and the sources of Islamic jurisprudence) is no longer the exclusive monopoly of religious scholars and the educated elite. Neither are claims to the right to interpret Islamic tradition. In everyday practice, the increasing volume and intensity of public debate via digital media has only accelerated the fracturing of traditional modes of communal identity and social cohesion. The participation of new Muslim social actors has also radically reconfigured the dynamics of the public sphere, both locally and globally. As Dale Eickelman and Jon Anderson note, "This combination of new media and new contributors to religious and political debates fosters an awareness on the part of all actors of the diverse ways in which Islam and Islamic values can be created and feeds into new senses of a public sphere that is discursive, performative and participative, and not confined to formal institutions recognized by state authorities."[31] In the Digital Age, new media facilitate new messages and empower new messengers.

Though relatively limited in scope and scale, scholarship on Cyber Islam has made important theoretical, methodological, and ethnographic contributions to the broader field of digital religion. Research in this sub-field began in the late 1990s with the groundbreaking work of anthropologist Jon W. Anderson. In a series of wide-ranging articles, Anderson charts how a diverse array of Muslims in the Middle East and the global diaspora employ digital media. These Muslim netizens include students (in both traditional *madrasas* and modern universities), religious scholars (*'ulama*), middle-class technocrats, labor migrants, government gatekeepers, corporate workers, Islamist ideologues, as well as members of established religious institutions.[32] "They range from political activists to Sufi orders, from mobilization to witness," Anderson argues. "They both recruit and propagandize, bringing their issues into a wider, already public sphere in some cases but in others carving out a new one that encompasses or repackages existing ones, compelling dialogue by leveraging forms of communication that reshape the social field . . . Islam on the Internet is first a story of new interpreters, newly emboldened by confidence in and command of the channel."[33]

As Anderson documents, the development of Cyber Islam in the West began during the 1980s, led initially by Arab university students studying in the burgeoning IT fields. These diasporic Muslim techies endeavored to build nascent online communities and services by creating experimental websites that included scanned copies of the Qur'an and *hadith* collections "as pious acts of witness for Islam in cyberspace."[34] During the mid-1990s, groups such as Muslim Student Associations on North American college campuses followed their lead, developing more sophisticated web pages and online discussion forums in the absence of local networks of *'ulama* and US-based *madrasas*. Since the late 1990s, a wide range of established Muslim leaders and institutions with varied agendas and interpretations of the faith have joined this expanding Cyber Commons. As Anderson illustrates, these new virtual Muslim voices include conventional religious institutions, publishing houses, government agencies, Islamist and *jihadi* groups, and Sufi orders.

Anderson divides Muslim digital entrepreneurs into three distinct group-ings: 'creole' pioneers, activists, and 'officializing' interpreters.[35] Collectively, these hybrid and polyvalent groups represent competing voices, multiple claims to authority, and contested assertions of legitimacy. They employ divergent intellectual techniques to forge new linkages and social networks while occupying "intermediate social space that they in part define and help to build."[36] In Anderson's view, digital media facilitates Muslim agency by providing entirely novel avenues for communication and community. At the same time, this democratization of knowledge and discursive power disrupts and fragments established nodes of religious power and authority. In Anderson's words, "communication on the Internet model is unstructured by existing canons and enforcers of authority; it puts an unaccustomed measure of agency (not to mention of self-authorization) in the hands of a browser, a channel-surfer, a mobile-phone user, a desktop publisher. On the receiving end, the freedom to look implies a corresponding freedom to sample alterna-tive role models, alternative legitimation and models of authority, not just to the state but in competition with religious authorities and also the family."[37]

The most prominent and prolific chronicler of Cyber Islam is Gary R. Bunt. In the past two decades, Bunt has published dozens of essays, articles, and book reviews on the subject, in addition to three influential mono-graphs: *Virtually Islamic: Computer-Mediated Communication and Cyber Islamic Environments*; *Islam in the Digital Age: E-Jihad, Online Fatwas and Cyber Islamic Environments*; and *iMuslims: Rewiring the House of Islam*.[38] Bunt's research explores multiple dimensions of the global "digital *ummah*" in a wide array of "cyber Islamic environments"—two of the author's key neologisms.[39] His work traces the complex interconnections, tensions, and messiness of Internet Islam, offering important insights into how the Internet simultaneously facilitates and reconfigures Muslim discourse and practice. Like Anderson, Bunt spotlights the contestations over the mantle of Islamic authority in cyberspace—an alternative landscape that simultaneously facilitates novel personal interactions and reconfigures normative modes of hierarchy, power, and social interaction. "Rewiring the House of Islam has not been without its difficulties," he argues. "The Internet has reshaped the boundaries of Muslim networks, created new dialogues, and presented new transaction routes within the Islamic knowledge economy."[40] Bunt's wide-ranging scholarship explores vexing questions about audience, access, anonymity, and insider/outsider perspectives that scholars encounter while tracking Cyber Muslims. Tracing the many fault lines along the digital divide, for example, he highlights the sharp disparities of connectivity within myriad Muslim countries, emphasizing the lack of computer access among Muslim women and the consequences of pervasive government censorship.

Bunt's work is distinguished by its descriptive, encyclopedic approach. His publications provide hundreds of real-world/virtual-world examples, mapping Muslim voices online through paradigmatic case studies. Bunt's writings survey a plethora of websites, cataloguing Muslim community networking, cultural practices, and identity politics across an expansive social, political, and cultural spectrum. His analysis demonstrates how new technologies and new media spaces—podcasting, video blogs, social networking sites—access new Muslim audiences and create alternative markets for Islamic knowledge, all of which bend and stretch the boundaries of normative tradition. Bunt's eclectic case studies investigate a wide range of digital resources and interfaces, including: Qur'an recitations, translations, and interpretations[41]; *hadith* collections and debates over Islamic law[42]; *fatwas* (juridical opinions) and *fiqh* (legal interpretation)[43]; ritual performance[44]; Islamic music[45]; social networking sites[46]; mobile device applications[47]; and the Islamic blogosphere.[48]

Bunt's methodology often focuses on key exemplars, tracking how different Muslim actors employ digital technologies to communicate their own religious interpretations, ideological agendas, political goals, and discrete claims to Islamic authority. In *iMuslims*, for example, he analyzes the digital media profiles of the Qatar-based Shaykh Yusuf al-Qaradawi, Iraq's Ayatollah al-Sistani, and the Egyptian popular preacher Amr Khaled.[49] In other work,

Bunt spotlights the digital media interfaces of Sunni leaders and institutions[50]; Shi'i religious leaders[51]; Sufis[52]; Muslim governments and political dissidents[53]; and Muslim hackers, hacktivists, and government censors.[54] Most significantly, Bunt has been at the forefront of research on the use of the Internet as a critical tool in the propaganda, recruitment, and logistical operations of Muslim militants.[55] His work provides ample documentation of the multiple media forums used by tech-savvy *jihadis*, from video clips and blogs to e-magazines. Charting a variety of *jihadi* cyber-networks in multiple political contexts, Bunt highlights the "use of violent and elaborately choreographed online pronouncements and performances."[56] On the whole, Bunt's work on digital Islam spans an impressive range. Even so, his encyclopedic approach ultimately raises as many questions as it answers. By favoring breadth over depth, Bunt's analysis often lacks the kind of granular details and theoretical nuance required to fully capture how (and why) Muslim actors in local contexts deploy cyberspace.

Building on these foundations, a recent wave of scholarship offers new vistas and alternative perspectives on the variety and vibrancy of digital Islam. This new generation of scholars continues to expand the analytical frame, asking new questions about method and theory while tracking the virtual lives of Muslims in new social contexts. In *Islam Dot Com: Contemporary Islamic Discourses in Cyberspace*, for example, Mohammed el-Nawawy and Sahar Khamis examine the Arabic- and English-language discussion forums of three popular Islamic websites: www.islamonline. net, www.amrkhaled.net, and www.islamway.com.[57] Other scholars have followed suit with detailed, multidimensional case studies of particular Muslim web pages.[58] In similar fashion, recent fieldwork studies document the multimodal usage of digital media by local Muslim communities in diverse cultural settings, including Iran,[59] the Arab world,[60] and Southeast Asia.[61] Other contributions investigate the use of cyberspace by Muslim women[62]; generational divides in electronic media usage and attitudes[63]; Islamic authority and authenticity in cyberspace[64]; the Qur'an online[65]; Muslim legal scholars (*'ulama*), media preachers, and online celebrities[66]; Islamism and political Islam online[67]; *jihadi* websites[68]; the Muslim blogosphere and discussion groups[69]; Islamic dating and matchmaking sites[70]; and Islamic-themed video games.[71] The emergence of online journals and aggregating websites, such as "Digital Islam: Research of Middle East, Islam and Digital

Media" and "Cyber Orient: Online Journal of the Virtual Middle East," signal the development and growing sophistication of this important scholarly sub-field.[72]

With a few notable exceptions—studies that I draw upon in later chapters—Cyber Sufis have received relatively little scholarly attention. This is surprising (and regrettable) given that many transnational Sufi communities have a long track record as early adopters of mass media technologies for social discourse, network building, public relations, and mass marketing. Drawing on both Arab and Ottoman evidence, Muhsin Mahdi has demonstrated that aside from state governments the main patrons of print publications in Muslim metropoles during the nineteenth century—Cairo, Istanbul, Tehran, Delhi—were in fact Sufis.[73] In numerous cultural settings, Sufi leaders embraced the print revolution, publishing a wide range of texts: pamphlets, periodicals, journals, and books.[74] Print media proved to be a highly effective medium for disseminating the messages of Sufi *shaykhs* to a broader public. The widespread distribution of inexpensive texts to middle-class consumers transmitted Sufi knowledge to a vast Muslim audience—well beyond the privileged few with access to original manuscripts or the intimate, face-to-face exchanges with a living Sufi master. These publications gave select Sufi masters unprecedented fame and influence. But print media did more than advance the public reputation of individual Sufi leaders. Ultimately, it fundamentally altered the makeup of Sufi interpersonal relations and institutional life. In effect, these texts transformed Sufism from a private, esoteric community based exclusively on the interpersonal contact, oral instruction, and ritual interaction between master and disciple into a public ideology. With new confidence and determination, Sufi orders entered the public sphere to defend their own traditions and identities against the polemical attacks of European Orientalists, colonial missionaries, conservative Islamists, and secular modernists alike. Carl Ernst artfully describes this dynamic as "the publication of the secret."[75]

In the twenty-first century, Sufi publications cover an equally expansive range of genres. Vernacular translations of 'classical' Arabic and Persian Sufi texts are now commonplace throughout the Middle East, North Africa, South Asia, Central Asia, and Southeast Asia. In contemporary Pakistan, for example, Urdu translations of premodern Sufi luminaries—Sarraj, Qushayri, Suhrawardi, Ibn 'Arabi, Rumi—are readily found on the shelves of local libraries and bookstores, and in the stalls of Urdu bazaars. For bibliophiles across the Muslim world, the writings of Sufi masters are also widely available in a variety of formats—from discourses, informal lectures, essays, and biographies, to practical manuals on everything from prayer and meditation practices to the use of talismans and charms for healing purposes.

In the Internet Age, many Sufis are increasingly appropriating multiple forms of digital media to defend their own interpretation of Islamic tradition, piety, and practice. Many, but not all. At the moment, access to Sufi Cyberscapes remains the purview of the privileged. In everyday practice, the barriers of wealth, education, and access to viable computer networks mean that most Sufis around the globe still remain offline. As Ernst reminds us:

> The vast majority of participants in the Sufi tradition in Muslim countries are still from social strata that have very little access to the most modern forms of electronic communication, and many are indeed illiterate. Lower class devotees who attend the festivals of Sufi saints in Egypt and Pakistan are not represented on the Web . . . As might be expected, the authors of Sufi Web sites tend to be members of the cosmopolitan and globalizing classes: either immigrant Sufi leaders establishing new bases in America and Europe, immigrant technocrats who happen to be connected to Sufi lineages, or Euro-American converts to Sufism in one form or other.[76]

As we will see, for Cyber Sufis who do manage to overcome these pervasive structural impediments, the new virtual landscape offers unprecedented opportunities for access, social capital, and leverage in the public sphere.

CONCLUSION

The academic scholarship on the rapidly expanding field of digital religion confirms that digital media are precipitating deep structural changes to the public face of Islam around the globe. It is abundantly clear that new media technologies are quickly altering the expectations, attitudes, and practices of Muslim producers and consumers within the Islamic knowledge economy. Though constrained by the boundaries of class, gender, and the digital divide—with young, male, urban, middle-class professionals dominating the discourse—Cyber Islam is nonetheless growing at a remarkable pace. Social dynamics, both large and small, are reconstituted in the process. As Echchaibi argues, "the Internet has enabled a new cultural space for Muslims to create new networks of Islamic learning, praxis, and deliberation, causing an important shakeup in top-down approaches to religious authority and introducing new influential actors as the face of a public, visible, and global Islam. Digital media are also reconfiguring the kind of public hailed by this highly performative, engaged, and confident Islam."[77] With increasing self-reflexivity, creativity, and assertiveness, American Muslim communities (including American Sufis) are employing online multimedia to rewire social networks and reshape the contours of their own public identities.

In the very early stages of research for this book, my student research assistant emailed the webmaster of a prominent branch of the Senegalese Tijaniyya Order in the United States to inquire about the community's website and their views of digital media's unique capacities and limitations. He received a rather blunt reply: "We maintain a website to provide information to those interested in the Tariqa Tijaniyya Sufi path; however, the spiritual work required to achieve knowledge of and nearness to God is not conducted in cyberspace and, therefore, we do not accept the label 'Cyber Sufism.'"[78] In my own conversations and interactions with Sufi teachers and disciples—in Pakistan, India, Senegal, Malaysia, and the United States—I have found this to be a common refrain. When asked, Sufis are often quick to dismiss the Internet as a distraction, a trivial plaything, a sideshow. Cyberspace is, they insist, at best a faint virtual echo of the beating heart of living Sufism: the personal connection with a spiritual master and a living Sufi community, and the direct experience of embodied ritual practices. Despite such doubts and protestations, however, even a quick Google search suggests a more complicated reality. In everyday practice, most American Sufi orders do operate in the virtual realm and, in fact, spend a great deal of time, energy, and financial resources maintaining active (and often elaborate) websites and social media platforms. I find this discrepancy—the gap between what is said and what is done in regards to digital spaces—to be revealing. It points to an underlying sense of ambiguity and a pervasive anxiety about both the potentialities and disruptions of digital technologies. Is the Internet a useful tool for Sufi advertising, recruitment, and self-defense? Or is it instead a dangerous threat to the integrity and continuity of tradition? Can cyberspace be deployed to complement, extend, and expand 'real-world,' offline Sufi communities? Or is it a poison pill that ultimately undermines the efficacy of established networks, structures of authority, and standards of practice? In short: why do American Sufis bother with digital media?

In the following chapters, I draw on the scholarship on digital religion and Cyber Islam to explore these fundamental questions. In the book's final chapter, I return to these theoretical debates and methodological questions to offer an alternative road map to chart the key patterns, tropes, and trajectories—both continuities and disjunctures—in the dynamic and evolving trajectory of American Cyber Sufism. I contend that in the context of twenty-first-century liquid modernity, cyberspace now serves as a vital alternative space for Muslim self-imagining and social networking, piety and performance, politics and polemics. By adapting to this new virtual ecosystem, Cyber Sufis seek to add their own unique voices to the virtual expressions of the American Muslim experience. Analyzing the import and impact of Sufi Cyberscapes, however, presupposes a basic understanding of the Sufi tradition and its place within American Islam and the broader mosaic of religious life in today's United States—the subjects to which we now turn in chapter 2 and chapter 3.

2

(Mis)Interpreting Sufism

As the 'mystical' dimension of Islam, *tasawwuf* (the Arabic term for 'Sufism') encompasses an alternative nexus of Islamic authority, piety, and practice. Sufism is not a sect; there are Sunni Sufis and Shi'a Sufis. It is not a mysterious, exotic cult for navel-gazing, world-weary hermits. Instead, Sufism is best understood as a path to experiential knowledge (*ma'rifa*). As a distinct spiritual discipline, the Sufi path is grounded in a master–disciple teaching relationship and experienced through the discipline of bodily ritual practices. Pushing the limits of everyday experience and consciousness, Sufis strive for a direct, intimate, unmediated, and transformative encounter with God. Sufi adepts tend to emphasize the inward over the outward, intuition over intellect, spiritual contemplation over scholarly debate, and ecstatic poetry over legalistic prose. Since the twelfth century, Sufi institutional orders— discrete spiritual brotherhoods (*turuq*), each with its own spiritual family tree (*shajarah*)—have proliferated throughout the Muslim world. Sufis vary widely in their teachings and techniques. Especially in the West, some people who self-identify as Sufi are not even Muslim. Even so, in the tradition's long history the vast majority of Sufis have followed the dictates of the Qur'an and canonical law (*shari'a*), consciously modeling their ethical behavior (*adab*) on the example of the Prophet Muhammad (*sunna*).

Despite its deep roots in Islamic history, Sufism in the twenty-first century is mired in controversy and contestation. Ask any Muslim on the streets of Lahore, Cairo, Baghdad, Istanbul, Isfahan, Dakar, Kuala Lumpur, or New York City about Sufism and you are likely to elicit any number of responses: from spontaneous recitations of Sufi love poetry and anecdotes of personal experiences at Sufi shrines, to harsh invectives against the tradition and its un-Islamic innovations. Among both Muslims and non-Muslims alike there is widespread confusion about the Sufi tradition, its history, and modern manifestations. The question is *why*?

Much of this dissonance stems from the fact that such a broad range of people, places, and practices are subsumed under the umbrella rubric (and Orientalist neologism) 'Sufism.' In the United States, the tradition is most often associated with its artistic and aesthetic expressions, often entirely detached from any tangible links to Islam. Most Americans encounter traces of Sufism through the poetry of Jalal ad-Din Rumi (largely via the best-selling English renditions of American poet Coleman Barks), staged performances of the ritual dance of the Mevlevi Order's 'whirling dervishes,' and the world music industry's embrace of Sufi artists like the late Nusrat Fateh 'Ali Khan of Pakistan. In Muslim societies, by contrast, Sufism is typically equated with the veneration of saints, local healing practices, and popular worship at tomb-shrines. Across the globe, Sufi sacred spaces provide an alternative outlet for Muslim piety and pilgrimage, especially for women in societies where they are marginalized from the public, gendered space of the mosque. Muslims also engage Sufism through its texts and teachers: the legends, stories, and literary legacies of a pantheon of spiritual luminaries, as well as the piety and charisma of living Sufi masters. In capacious cultural contexts as varied as the global *umma* itself, Sufism encompasses all these expressions of Muslim piety simultaneously. So what is Sufism? In the end, the answer depends on whom you ask.

THE OUTSIDER'S VIEW: STEREOTYPING SUFIS

In the West, the legacy of academic scholarship continues to color the popular understanding of the Sufi tradition. The English term 'Sufism' is itself an invention of late-eighteenth-century European Orientalist scholarship. As part of the colonial project in Asia, Africa, and the Middle East, eminent British scholars associated with the British East India Company—men like Sir William Jones (d. 1794) and Sir John Malcolm (d. 1833)—invented a neologism (a brand new 'ism') to distinguish the poetry, music, and artistry of the 'Sooffees' they 'discovered' from what they viewed as the staid and legalistic Islam of the mosque and the *madrasa*. Influenced by the worldview and religious categories of their own Protestant Christian milieu, European Orientalist scholars tended to categorize Sufis as a unique species of Muslims. "Malcolm and Jones saw [Sufis] as freethinkers who had little to do with the stern faith of the Arabian Prophet," notes Carl Ernst. "They had much more in common, so went the argument, with true Christianity, with Greek philosophy, and with the mystical speculations of the Indian Vedanta."[1] The Orientalist portrait of Sufism as a distinct 'mystical' tradition separate from mainstream Islam left an enduring imprint. Its impact is clearly evident in much of subsequent Western scholarship, which tends to interpret Sufi thought and practice through a one-dimensional, reductive lens. In most academic studies, Sufism is typically characterized in one of three ways: as an abstract mystical philosophy inscribed in classical texts; a thinly veiled political ideology; or an ossified relic, a once-dynamic spiritual and literary tradition now devolved into popular, syncretistic 'folk' tomb cults, mired in superstition and profiteering.[2]

With their bold claims to esoteric knowledge, Sufis have often been misunderstood and maligned by other Muslims as well. Throughout Islamic history, individual Sufi masters, antinomian Sufi orders, and particular Sufi practices (saint worship and shrine pilgrimage, in particular) were at times questioned, critiqued, and even condemned.[3] Nevertheless, in the premodern era Sufism remained deeply woven into the fabric of everyday social, cultural, intellectual, and spiritual life. As Ernst argues, in Muslim societies from Morocco to Indonesia it would simply "not have been possible to formulate the statement 'Sufism has nothing to do with Islam' prior to the nineteenth century."[4]

That all changed amid the massive societal transformations of the colonial and postcolonial eras. The shattering of traditional Islamic networks of education, legal administration, social and economic power, and political patronage spurred a widespread crisis of authority. In the twentieth century, a range of new Muslim social actors emerged to fill the vacuum, prominent among them Islamist revivalists (more commonly, if controversially, known as 'fundamentalists').[5] Historically, sociologically, and politically, Islamists are far from monolithic. Shaped by local histories and social dynamics, their theological and legal interpretations, organizational strategies, and institutional structures vary widely. Some Islamists are quietist, emphasizing private piety over public politics. Others—from Sunni movements like the Muslim Brotherhood (*al-Ikhwan al-Muslimun*) in Egypt and the *Jamaat-e-Islami* in Pakistan to the ruling Shi'a theocracy in Iran—have embraced versions of 'political Islam,' forming political parties to address their grievances and advance their agendas at the ballot box. Despite their many differences, however, most contemporary Sunni Islamist movements share a common ideological universe. Influenced by Salafi and Wahhabi thought and practice, they champion a dogmatic piety, a literalist approach to scripture, law, and ritual, and a monolithic orthodoxy that allows little room for religious diversity and cultural pluralism.[6] As a general rule, Islamists tend to view Islam as a kind of prepackaged, standardized, proprietary software that simply needs to be downloaded and applied.

In the Digital Age, Sunni Islamist ideology impacts global Muslim public discourse and political life as never before. Fueled by Saudi and Arab Gulf patronage and exported around the globe, contemporary Sunni Islamists promote a conservative, essentialized, authoritarian, patriarchal, austere, puritanical, and uncompromising version of the faith. For them, history is messy and needs to be cleaned up. In the name of uniformity, homogeneity, and purity, Islamist ideologues posit a lost (and profoundly reified) golden age—the age of the 'ancestors' (*salaf*)—as the litmus test for religious authority and authenticity. In doing so, they effectively jettison a thousand years of Muslim legal scholarship and its heterodox exegetical traditions. Deviations from their own narrow definitions of Islamic orthodoxy and orthopraxy are questioned. For doctrinaire Sunni Islamists, Shi'i and Sufi communities are particularly suspect—with some hardline sectarian clerics going as far as to condemn them as heretical unbelievers (*kuffar*), idolaters (*mushrikin*), and rejecters of Sunni orthodoxy (*rawafid*).

In the twenty-first century, Sufism is often a lightning rod in contentious debates within Muslim societies over the parameters of Islamic identity, authority, and authenticity. Amid this public wrangling over 'real Islam,' Islamists remain the most outspoken critics of the Sufi tradition. Echoing the logic of European Orientalists, hard-core Islamist ideologues dismiss Sufism as an un-Islamic accretion: the hybrid byproduct of outside, 'foreign' influence (Greek, Jewish, Christian, or Hindu). They are quick to dismiss popular Sufi practices such as listening to music (*sama'*), pilgrimage to Sufi tombs (*ziyarat*), and the commemoration of the Prophet Muhammad's birthday (*mawlid*) as *bid'ah* (a corrupt 'innovation'), and belief in the intercessory power of Sufi saints as *shirk* ('associating' partners with God).

Although intra-Muslim debates over the definition of religious normativity are nothing new, the contemporary vitriol and animus against Sufi symbols, spaces, and practitioners are unprecedented in Islamic history. This new reality contradicts both demographic realities and long-standing cultural norms. As Ernst notes:

> Ironically, as a result of strategic successes by fundamentalist movements in certain key regions like Arabia, and the massive oil wealth that fell into the lap of the Saudi regime, many contemporary Muslims have been taught a story of the Islamic religious tradition from which Sufism has been rigorously excluded. It is ironic because as recently as the late eighteenth century, and for much of the previous millennium, most of the outstanding religious scholars of Mecca, Medina, and the great cities of the Muslim world were intimately engaged with what we today call Sufism. It is doubly ironic because the fundamentalist story is belied by the religious practices of more than half of today's Muslim population.[7]

Pushing the generic Islamist polemic against Sufism to its (il)logical limits, a new generation of Islamist militants have gone much further, denigrating the Sufi tradition as a cancer that must be purged from the body politic. Their critique is no longer merely rhetorical. In recent years, the Taliban and related offshoots in Afghanistan and Pakistan, Boko Haram in Nigeria and West Africa, al-Qaeda and its myriad affiliates in North Africa and the Middle East, and ISIS in Syria and Iraq have rushed to fill the vacuum precipitated by warfare, economic collapse, political instability, and the widespread disintegration of social order. These fringe groups combine political activism with technological savvy. They seek to overthrow secular, monarchial, and military governments in the Muslim world, resist Western cultural and political influence, expand their own economic and political power and, in the feverish fantasy of ISIS in Iraq in Syria, capture territory to re-establish a long-lost Islamic caliphate. Despite their diverse political visions, Islamist militants also share a basic ideological worldview: an exclusivist, apocalyptic, and hyper-muscular Sunni sectarianism. Driven by a narrow and aberrant interpretation of both Islam and *jihad*, these metastasizing militant groups sanction armed conflict and sanctify political violence as tools to 'purify' their local societies from the dual existential threats of external Western hegemony and internal Muslim heresy.[8] In their fanatical and brutal version of 'holy war,' Sufis—along with Shi'a Muslims and other ethnic and religious minorities—are at the top of the hit list.

With increasing frequency and ferocity, *jihadi* terrorists have attacked Sufi communities and their sacred spaces. In numerous Muslim-majority countries now plagued by paroxysms of violence, the bombing and bulldozing of Sufi shrines is more and more commonplace. For example, al-Qaeda affiliates desecrated numerous Sufi shrines in the ancient city of Timbuktu, Mali, in 2012. And in 2014, ISIS leveled the tomb complex of the famous Sufi saint Ahmad al-Rifa'i (d. 1182) in northern Iraq. In Pakistan, such attacks have expanded exponentially in recent years. On July 2, 2010, Taliban suicide bombers murdered forty-two Muslims and injured hundreds more at the revered shrine of the eleventh-century Sufi saint Hazrat Data Ganj Baksh in Lahore. That same year, terrorists attacked the shrine of Abdullah Shah Ghazi in Karachi, and the tomb of Baba Farid ad-Din in Pakpattan Sharif (southern Punjab). On April 3, 2011, another brutal suicide attack killed forty-one Sufi devotees during the annual *'urs* (death anniversary) pilgrimage festival at the thirteenth-century Sakhi Sarwar shrine in Pakistan's central Punjab region. And on February 16, 2017, militants claiming allegiance to ISIS bombed the famous shrine complex of Lal Shahbaz Qalandar in Sehwan Sharif (Sindh), killing eighty-eight innocent pilgrims and injuring two hundred and fifty others. In a toxic environment of widespread chaos, instability, and fear, this growing internecine violence and malicious destruction tears at the social fabric of local Muslim communities.[9]

In an attempt to counter the rising tide of *jihadi* ideology, militancy, and terrorism, numerous governments—both Western and Islamic—have in recent years publicly embraced Sufis and actively cultivated their support. Motivated both by their wanton persecution and unwavering popularity among local populations, policy pundits have tended to view Sufis as potential 'moderate Muslim' allies. In an ironic echo of a host of Orientalist tropes, this logic characterizes (and caricatures) Sufis as passive, apolitical, mystical Muslims in stark juxtaposition to the anti-Western, anti-Semitic, patriarchal, misogynist, undemocratic, and violent ideologies of disparate Salafi and Wahhabi fundamentalists. As Omid Safi argues, Muslims "are given two options in this superficial bifurcation game: to be politically destructive in the manner of terrorists or 'Islamists,' or to be politically quietist, acquiescing in the face of power. In this 'Good Sufi/Bad Muslims' dichotomy, Sufis are asked to line up in the politically quietist camp, so that they can be validated."[10] To say the least, this binary is woefully reductive, simplistic, and ahistorical. Nonetheless, it has proved to be politically efficacious.

After the attacks of September 11, 2001, numerous governments around the world actively promoted Sufism as a counterweight to militant *jihadi* movements like al-Qaeda and its many franchises in a culture war aimed largely at Muslim youth. As Hisham Aidi documents in his masterful study, *Rebel Music: Race, Empire, and the New Muslim Youth Culture*, "Music was at the heart of this 'Sufi solution,'" with various regimes—the US, Britain and Pakistan—deploying Sufi-inflected musical practices from *qawwali* to 'Muslim hip hop' to alter perceptions, calm passions, challenge Islamist narratives, and draw youth away from extremism.[11] Amid the ever-expanding global 'war on terror,' policy pundits within US think tanks and government circles frequently promoted an essentialized vision of Sufism as a bulwark against *jihadi* terrorism, at home and abroad. In 2004, for example, the Nixon Center in Washington, D.C. hosted a prominent conference: "Understanding Sufism and Its Potential Role in U.S. Policy." The gathering featured a keynote address by Bernard Lewis—the prominent Princeton historian, neo-conservative icon, adviser to the Bush administration, and a key intellectual architect of the 2003 invasion of Iraq—who extolled Sufism's "tolerance" and its potential to counter rising Salafism.[12]

In similar fashion, a 2004 RAND Corporation report by Cheryl Benard titled, "Five Pillars of Democracy: How the West Can Promote an Islamic Reformation," argued that Western governments should actively "encourage the popularity and acceptance of Sufism, a traditionalist form of Islamic mysticism that represents an open, intellectual interpretation of Islam."[13] A subsequent 2007 RAND report, "Building Moderate Muslim Networks," called for the patronage of Sufi leaders as an antidote to Islamist radicalism, at home and abroad—singling out the Turkish spiritual leader Fethullah Gülen as a model Muslim.[14] The Bush administration followed suit with substantive financial support to promote Sufi teachers, institutions, and ideas. American Muslim leaders and Sufi teachers—including Hamza Yusuf, Nuh Ha

Mim Keller, and Hisham Kabbani—were sponsored to teach and preach to Muslim audiences abroad, with a particular focus on Pakistan and the United Kingdom.[15] These ill-conceived (even if well-intentioned) counter-terrorism efforts were short-lived, however, and under the Obama administration the United States' unofficial anti-Salafi "Sufi strategy" was gradually shelved.[16]

Most Americans know next to nothing of Sufism's rich history, its diverse local manifestations, or the multiple claims to its legacy. This knowledge gap applies equally to Islamic civilization writ large. All this is no surprise. Why? Because in today's United States, the public's (mis)understanding of Islam, Muslims, and Sufism is largely shaped by the corporate media establishment. In the early decades of the twenty-first century, the chaos and entropy engulfing much of the Middle East and North Africa has dominated the world's daily news headlines. In rapid succession, a tsunami of traumatic geopolitical events has focused a bright, hot spotlight on the Muslim world: the devastating attacks in the United States on September 11, 2001; the destabilizing wars in Afghanistan, Iraq, and Libya; the torture and abuse of Muslim prisoners at Abu Ghraib, Guantanamo Bay, and CIA 'black sites' around the world; America's escalating drone strike campaigns in numerous conflict zones; Iran's intense but brief 'Green Movement'; the tidal wave of the Arab Spring uprisings and their reverberations throughout North Africa and the broader Middle East; the roiling turmoil of Israel's ongoing occupation of Palestine; the Saudi-led incursions in Bahrain and Yemen; the monstrous civil war in Syria, with waves of desperate refugees pouring into Turkey, Lebanon, Jordan, and Europe; a military coup against the democratically elected Muslim Brotherhood government in Egypt, and widespread political repression after a failed coup attempt in Turkey; the ethnic cleansing of the Muslim Rohingya community in Myanmar/Burma; political violence and terrorist attacks in Pakistan, India, and Kashmir; the rapid rise of ISIS in Syria and Iraq and its expanding global reach; the competition (and conflicts) for regional hegemony between Sunni Arab Gulf states and Shi'a Iran and its satellites; the murder of journalist Jamal Khashoggi in the Saudi Arabian consulate in Istanbul; and waves of targeted terrorist attacks by *jihadi* groups—or individuals inspired, enabled, or directed by them—in European and American cities.[17] In the United States, the mainstream media coverage of these complex (and often interconnected) events invariably paints in broad brushstrokes. It is heavy on description, shock value, and sound-bite

synopsis—and light on the details and nuances of social, political, and historical context. The cumulative result is twofold: a vast escalation of the scale of
news reporting on Islam and Muslims, coupled with a pronounced narrowing
of the scope (and quality) of actual news analysis.

Amid the ruthless competition for viewership (and therefore corporate
sponsorship), the 24/7 media machine covets the clickbait of dramatic, emotive, and sensational stories in a ceaseless stream of 'breaking news.' And in
the post-9/11 United States, nothing galvanizes the national media's attention
like the political theatre and spectacle of Islamist *jihadi* militancy. In keeping
with the old truism, 'if it bleeds, it leads,' the chaos, carnage, and paranoia
in Western streets in the aftermath of terrorist attacks dominate American
news coverage. On cable television, blogs, web pages, and newspapers, the
round-the-clock reporting of these horrific acts is almost exclusively present-
minded. Tracking the unfolding flow of events in real time, this infotainment
"disaster porn" is largely visceral and affective, with an incessant barrage of
videos transmitting the live images and sounds of atrocities around the globe.[18]
In the end, domestic media coverage of Islam tends to be overly simplistic,
reductive, sensationalist, and essentialist. It reduces Islam's global cultural
kaleidoscope to a one-dimensional caricature, reinforced by the constant
recirculation of standard tropes and stock images of Muslims: silent, invisible
women in black *abayas*, angry bearded men, shouting political slogans and
wielding guns, and smoldering cities in distant desert lands.

Inside the echo chamber of the US media industry, talking heads—journalists,
military and intelligence officers, security analysts, government officials,
think tank policy pundits and, on rare occasion, academics—proffer sound-
bite opinions and cursory analysis after every new terrorist attack. These
'experts' rarely link Islamist militant movements and *jihadi* terrorism to the
history of US foreign policy, long-standing US support of oppressive regimes
in the Middle East, North Africa, and Central Asia, or the blowback from
America's interventionist wars and military adventures abroad.[19] Moreover,
mainstream media outlets tend to amplify the incendiary rhetoric and shrill
voices of homegrown extremists and Islamophobes. National news reports
regularly spotlight Qur'an burnings, anti-mosque rallies, protests over *shari'a*
law, alarmist US congressional hearings, and incendiary political campaigns
obsessed with 'radical Islam' and Islamist terrorism.[20] With each successive
tragedy, the *ex nihilo* reporting begins all over again—and provocative stories

with headlines like "Why do they hate us?" are dusted off and redeployed. Those paired pronouns ('they'/'us') are revealing. For a woefully uninformed (and increasingly frightened) American audience, they reinforce the narrative of an inviolable civilizational divide—a timeless "clash of civilizations"—that separates the West (civilized, democratic, moral, peaceful, innocent, predominantly Christian and Caucasian) from the Muslim world (barbaric, undemocratic, immoral, violent, complicit, and comprised of mostly brown and black Muslim bodies).[21] From there, it is a small logical leap to demonize all American Muslims as Others—disloyal outsiders, a potentially dangerous fifth column, an enemy living among 'us.'

With rare exception, US media coverage also glosses over (or altogether ignores) certain incontrovertible facts: that neither Islam nor Islamists nor Muslims are monolithic; that the vast majority of the victims of exhibitionist *jihadi* violence (as well as the US-led global 'war on terror') are innocent, traumatized, and brutalized Muslim civilians; and that the overwhelming majority of the world's Muslims—including even most Salafi and Wahhabi scholars— abhor and publicly denounce terrorism as a gross violation of the teachings of the Qur'an and the legacy of the Prophet Muhammad. This silencing of Muslim voices effectively provides *jihadi* militants with free publicity and a bully pulpit. It also leaves American Muslims in a highly untenable situation. As Echchaibi argues, "Even if Muslim Americans could speak, explain their positions, or distance themselves from acts of religious radicalism in much of this narrow coverage their visibility in the media remained largely framed around a trope of the defensive Muslim who is only invited to react and whose lived experience as an American is perpetually perceived as in question."[22]

In the United States, the mass media feedback loop has, in turn, profoundly impacted attitudes and opinions about Islam and Muslims in predictable and regrettable ways.[23] As public opinion polls consistently affirm, while news coverage about Islam blankets the US media more than ever before, most American citizens remain alarmingly ignorant about the basic facts of Islamic history, the foundational beliefs and practices of the faith, and the everyday, lived realities of Muslims, both at home and across the world. Fueled by media sensationalism, overt bigotry and racism, and exacerbated by the ethno-nationalist fearmongering of nativist politicians and xenophobic demagogues, Islamophobia is on the rise.[24] In the past decade, hate crimes against Muslims and their places of worship have skyrocketed in the United States. According to a comprehensive report by the Council on American–Islamic Relations and the University of California-Berkeley's Center for Race and Gender, there were seventy-eight targeted attacks on mosques across the country in 2015 alone, a threefold increase from the previous two years.[25] A parallel FBI report documented 257 hate crimes against American Muslims in 2015—a sixty-seven percent increase from the previous year and the highest total since 2001 when more than 480 attacks occurred in the aftermath of 9/11.[26]

These disturbing trends were exacerbated by the 2016 presidential campaign and the election of Donald Trump, whose incendiary language and divisive policy proposals called for a ban on Muslim immigration, the increased surveillance of American Muslim communities, and even a registry (and possible internment) of American Muslims.[27] Predictably, this heated political rhetoric had immediate and lasting personal consequences. The Southern Poverty Law Center recorded over four hundred cases of hate-based intimidation and harassment against Muslims in just the first ten days following the November 8, 2016 election.[28] Not surprisingly, a July 2017 Pew Research Center survey documents a growing sense of anxiety and unease among American Muslims about their place in the country's social and political life. According to the authors, "Overall, Muslims in the United States perceive a lot of discrimination against their religious group, are leery of Trump and think their fellow Americans do not see Islam as part of mainstream U.S. society."[29]

To any objective observer, the symbiotic relationship between extremist Islamist ideology, *jihadi* terrorism, and the American mass media establishment is as clear today as it was to Edward Said when he published his groundbreaking book *Covering Islam* in 1981.[30] Each feeds off (and profits from) the other. Amid the hysteria of today's mass media cacophony, the Muslim terrorist boogeyman looms large, drowning out other American Muslim voices: women, Shi'a, Sufis, and the rest of the silenced majority. In the absence of an informed public, Muslim citizens of the United States are too often presumed guilty by association and left to face a backlash of stereotypes, violence, and fear. In America today, the Orientalist's fantasy is the Islamophobe's dream come true.

THE INSIDER'S PERSPECTIVE: SUFI PIETY IN PRACTICE

In the contemporary United States, Sufism is largely absent from the frenzied public media discourse and debate about Islam. On the rare occasion when journalists do turn their attention to Sufis they tend to adopt the default Good Muslim/Bad Muslim trope, portraying them as outliers: adherents of a quaint, picturesque, exotic, otherworldly sect of "kumbaya hippies" and "spiritual vagabonds," out of step with the Muslim mainstream.[31] This too is nothing new, and certainly not a uniquely American phenomenon. The full complexity and dynamism of Sufism's lived realities have consistently evaded the gaze of the corporate media, Western governments, Islamist detractors, and academic scholars alike. Yet on the ground and across the planet, Sufism survives and thrives in the twenty-first century. By studying Sufi history, by exploring Sufi piety in practice, and by seeking out the voices of Sufi practitioners, we encounter an entirely different perspective on this rich, dynamic, and deeply rooted Islamic tradition.[32]

Engaging Sufis—past and present—on their own terms reveals an alternative Islamic episteme. It also requires learning a new vocabulary. Ask a Sufi to define her own tradition and she may well respond with a well-known Arabic adage, "All of Sufism is *adab*" (*al-tasawwuf kulluhu al-adab*). In Sufi parlance, *adab* refers to prescribed rules of etiquette and ethical behavior. As a comprehensive code of moral conduct, *adab* molds individual character and shapes outward social decorum. In theory and in practice, *adab* serves as both a measure of individual propriety, civility, and sophistication and the grease that oils the machinery of social life. As Barbara Metcalf explains, "*Adab* may 'mean' correct outer behavior, but it is understood as both cause of and then, reciprocally, fruit of one's inner self. Knowing, doing, and being are inescapably one."[33] The entire scaffolding of Sufi pedagogy and the dynamics of the master–disciple relationship rests on the cardinal virtues of *adab*. Key among these ethical markers for Sufis are absolute sincerity (*ikhlas*), unwavering patience (*sabr*), thankfulness (*shukr*), God-consciousness (*taqwa*), trust in God (*tawwakul*), relentless striving (*mujahida*) and, most importantly, boundless love (*hubb* or *'ishq*). In this sense, Sufism is perhaps understood as a spiritual technology for the cultivation of virtues. To practice beautiful *adab*, Sufis assert, is to follow the example (*sunna*) and walk in the footsteps of the Prophet Muhammad.

Sufi epistemology emerges from the Qur'anic worldview. Invoking the Qur'an (57:3), Sufis understand God as "the first, the last, the outer, the inner." Sufi theorists have long distinguished between the outward (*zahir*) and inward (*batin*) dimensions of reality. A well-known Sufi formula uses a threefold rhyming structure to distinguish between the outward form of Islamic law (*shari'a*), the inner approach of the Sufi path (*tariqa*), and the ultimate reality of God (*haqiqa*). Sufi training aims at nothing less than a complete remaking of the self. Its ritual practices are designed to subdue the ego while purifying and polishing the body, mind, and heart. In this pedagogical system, spiritual growth is measured by both inner states of awareness and outer displays of pious, ethical behavior. According to a well-known tradition (*hadith*) of the Prophet Muhammad: "The *shari'a* are my words, the *tariqa* are my actions, and the *haqiqa* is my interior states."[34]

Early Sufi theoreticians translated their own spiritual experiences into a sophisticated and nuanced psychology based on a tripartite division between the *nafs* (the 'soul,' or lower 'ego-self'), *qalb* ('heart'), and *ruh* ('spirit'). This tripartite paradigm emerged with the Qur'an commentary of Ja'far al-Sadiq (d. 765) and was later appropriated by such spiritual masters as al-Muhasibi (d. 857), al-Hakim al-Tirmidhi (d. *c.*869), al-Bistami (d. 874), al-Junayd (d. 910), and al-Qushayri (d. 1073).[35] These early Sufi theorists described the arduous path to gnosis as the experience of various states (*hal*, plural *ahwal*) and stations (*maqam*, plural *maqamat*). In classical Sufi doctrine, *ahwal* are understood as sudden flashes of insight and clarity. These brief moments of illumination—like lightning bursts in the night sky—are gifts from God. They stand in contrast with *maqamat*: a series of discrete psychological and ethical qualities that the adept attains only through his/her own determined efforts and disciplined action. The Sufi spiritual journey (*suluk*) towards God is not for the faint of heart. For a select few, it culminates in the states of *fana'* (the annihilation of the ego-self) and ultimately *baqa'* (permanence in God). Because Allah is ultimately limitless, however, so too is the Sufi path. For Sufis, there is no ultimate experience of enlightenment, no final state of perfect *nirvana*—only a continual cultivation of awareness, expansion of consciousness, and deepening connection to the Divine.

The starting point for the Sufi path of purification is the source of human frailty: "the soul that commands evil" (*an-nafs al-'ammara bil-su*; Qur'an: 12:53). Through repentance, renunciation, and unwavering discipline the spiritual seeker attempts to tame the ego's base instincts and voracious appetites. With patience and determination, worldly desires are gradually replaced with an insatiable desire for God. The Sufi is aided in this quest by an activated conscience that oversees and guides his/her actions, 'the blaming soul' (*an-nafs al-luwwama*; Qur'an: 75:2). For the intrepid seeker, the ultimate reward is self-realization and a pacified soul that serves as the vehicle to salvation. In the words of the Qur'an (89: 27–30): "Soul at peace [*an-nafs al-mutma'inna*], return to your Lord, both pleased and pleasing [me]; enter among my servants, and enter my paradise!"

Sufi piety is envisioned and articulated in texts: from the Qur'an to the voluminous prose and poetry writings of well-known and oft-quoted Sufi luminaries. Even so, Sufis will insist that true knowledge about the nature of the self and its relationship to God is ultimately not to be found in abstract philosophizing or the academic parsing of legal and theological debate. Books are, at best, an invitation to practice. Spiritual progress, Sufis insist, is ultimately possible only through internal combat—a ceaseless striving against one's beastly nature through self-discipline, self-vigilance, self-sacrifice, and an aggressive pushing of personal boundaries. The word *mujahada* (spiritual 'striving') comes from the same Arabic root as *jihad*. For Sufis, *mujahada* centers on a retinue of rituals—techniques for mental concentration, combined with physical postures—that together create religious experience and communicate religious truth. In this pedagogical system, spiritual knowledge and authority are measured by the intensity of a Sufi's piety, the rigor of a Sufi's practice, and the depth of a Sufi's personal experiences. On the Sufi path, there are no shortcuts. Spiritual knowledge and wisdom must be *earned*.

Under the watchful guidance of a spiritual master (*shaykh* if a man, *shaykha* if a woman), the Sufi disciple (*murid*) voluntarily submits to intense ritual practices designed to mold the body, sharpen the mind, and purify the soul. In Sufi pedagogy, the *shaykh* serves multiple roles: he is a teacher, mentor, adviser, friend, role model, healer, and disciplinarian. As the spiritual physician, the Sufi master knows what ails each of his/her disciples and prescribes a regimen of ritual practices suited to each individual's capabilities and needs.

The transformative encounter with a spiritual mentor initiates a process of *deconstruction*. Over time, the *murid* gradually learns to reconstitute the bodily and mental practices that bind him/her to the world in pursuit of the deeper dimensions of experiential knowledge. In this process, the *shaykh* serves as the bridge between the abstraction of theoretical, book knowledge (*'ilm*) and the concrete, visceral, and transformative power of direct, experiential knowledge (*ma'rifa*). Disciples learn directly by living in the *shaykh*'s company, by listening to his words, and by observing him in action. Leading by example, the *shaykh*, in turn, gauges the state of each individual *murid*. On the basis of his intuitive knowledge and keen sensitivity to the disciple's character and temperament, he prescribes a variety of spiritual disciplines to spur higher states of consciousness. The *adab* of the master–disciple relationship mandates that the *murid* responds with humility, obedience, gratitude, and determination in the knowledge that the *shaykh* has walked the path and knows the way. In the end, it is the strength of the bond with the master that makes it possible to endure the sacrifices and burdens of the spiritual journey. Experienced through companionship and mediated via mutual love, respect, and devotion, the Sufi master–disciple relationship forms an unbreakable bond that transcends and ultimately transforms both life and death.

Ritual performance is the lifeblood of Sufism. It is through the sensorial experience of ritual practice that the Sufi adept learns to cultivate a bodily habitus in which Muslim virtue is embodied and enacted. Most Sufis view the mystical path (*tariqa*) as a natural extension and intensification of the orthodox ritual requirements incumbent on all Muslims (*'ibadat*). Sufi rituals do not replace normative piety and practice, they expand and intensify them. Like any pious Muslim, the Sufi adept begins with a strict adherence to the *arkan*. The five fundamental 'pillars' of faith are then supplemented with a host of supererogatory rituals. These prescribed ritual acts offer the Sufi adept a tangible, tactile, and immediate source of experience and knowledge. While the exact system, style, and specifications vary between different Sufi brotherhoods, typical Sufi practices include:

- A formal ritual initiation with a Sufi teacher (*bay'at*), mirroring the oath of loyalty between the Prophet Muhammad and his disciples
- Prescribed periods of fasting

- A solitary retreat (*khalwa*), typically forty days in duration
- Techniques for cultivating dreams and dream interpretation
- The "remembrance" of God via meditative chanting (*dhikr* in Arabic; *zikr* in Persian): either vocalized or silent, performed alone or among a circle of fellow Sufi disciples
- Spiritual contemplation (*muraqaba*): a meditative practice, often done in proximity to a Sufi shrine or other sacred space
- Musical assemblies that combine poetic recitation with melodies (*sama'*, the 'listening to music')
- Pilgrimage to the tombs of Sufi saints (*ziyarat*)[36]

The locus and focus of Sufi ritual techniques is the physical body. Ultimately, understanding comes only from *doing* because "what is done with the body is the ground of what is thought and said."[37] Within the Sufi teaching system, the body serves both as a medium for knowledge and the primary tool for the remolding of the self. By surrendering to the will of a spiritual master, the Sufi disciple learns to re-habituate the self through a program of rigorous and routinized ritual practice. Through the disciplining of the body, the ego is gradually transformed and ultimately transcended. In keeping with the famous prophetic *hadith,* "die before you die," the ultimate aim of the Sufi path is to reshape the acculturated, socialized, secular self into a sacralized, moral, and ethical subject. As Scott Kugle notes:

> By advocating that one die to one's own self, mystics loosen the habitual bonds that bind the self to the socially constituted body. This provides a space and freedom to re-discipline the body, to train it in a new set of stances, a new pattern of postures, a new repertoire of gestures. In short, mystics offer a method of acquiring a whole new bodily habitus, a new ground of being, driven not by selfish desires but rather by the embodiment of virtues.[38]

For Sufis, ritual performance serves as the primary vehicle for the interiorization of knowledge. Through bodily practices, combined with self-examination and ethical action, Sufis seek to break the self in order to remake the self and, in the process, draw closer to God.

CONCLUSION

Time and again, outsiders have appropriated Sufism in various ways to different ends. Pushed and pulled in different directions, Sufism has been dissected, reified, and reassembled to serve other people's agendas. European Orientalists who 'discovered' the ecstatic love poetry of such Sufi luminaries as Jalal ad-Din Rumi situated the tradition outside the parameters of mainstream, normative Islam—and they marked this difference by inventing a new 'ism' ('Sufism'). Within contemporary Muslim societies, Sufism remains a highly contested signifier in fractious public debates over the boundaries of Islamic authority and authenticity. In a profound irony of history, Muslim fundamentalists follow the standard Orientalist interpretation. Islamists too tend to view Sufism as the outgrowth of outside, foreign influences—but, in a twist of logic, critique Sufis as members of a dangerous, suspect, un-Islamic sect that needs to be expunged in order to purify the faith. With the recent paroxysm of Islamist militancy around the world, Sufism has once again been drawn into political and cultural proxy wars. In a desperate search for Muslim allies, Western governments and media have attempted to instrumentalize Sufism as a bulwark against *jihadi* ideology, characterizing (and caricaturing) Sufis as 'good Muslims' who could be recruited to serve in counter-terrorism campaigns. What is missing from all these selective and distorting accounts, of course, are the much more nuanced realities of living Sufism and the voices of actual Sufis.

If we allow Sufis to speak, an entirely different story emerges. Twenty-first-century Sufis remain connected to Islam's sacred past through genealogy, networks of knowledge, and a nexus of prescribed rituals. Sufis view these spiritual resources as the direct legacy of the first Sufi and the last Prophet: Muhammad. For them, the Sufi path is a timeless, universal teaching, as relevant today as it was in the seventh century. At the same time, Sufi practitioners understand that the tradition cannot remain static. Since Sufism does not exist in a hermetically sealed vacuum, it must respond and adapt to social change if it is to survive. In the age of liquid modernity, many Sufi communities have reformulated their identity, practices, and institutional arrangements. In this sense, Sufism is best understood as a verb rather than a noun. Sufism is not a static, homogenous 'thing' that can be studied in isolation. Rather, it is a discursive tradition and an embodied practice that is expressed and experienced in discrete temporal and cultural locations.[39] And to state the obvious, there is no Sufism without Sufis. Even when they share a common identity connected to specific genealogies of teachers, Sufi adepts are all unique individuals. Any study of Sufi piety and practice, therefore, needs to account for texts and contexts, biography and agency, continuity and change.

This book charts the intersections between American Sufi digital texts online and the offline social contexts that shape them. Before diving into the realm of digital Sufism, however, we need a better understanding of the tradition's place within both American Islam and the broader religious ecosystem of today's United States. These topics are the focus of chapter 3.

3

Sufism in the American Religious Landscape

Diversity, heterogeneity, and hybridity are embedded in the DNA of the United States of America. This societal mélange is a product of the country's multilayered history: the flight of European exiles, the subjugation of indigenous peoples, slaves stolen from Africa, and successive waves of immigrants from across the globe—all mixed together and fermented in a complex cultural soup. To say the least, America's complex demography stretches the limits of the term 'multicultural.' In Bruce Lawrence's apt phrasing, the United States in the twenty-first century is nothing less than a "kaleidoculture," a "piebald, pluralist profusion of different accents, profiles, outlooks and, yes, religions."[1] As the Pew Research Center's 2015 study "America's Changing Religious Landscape" illustrates, tectonic social changes continue to transform the nation's religious terrain.[2] Today, new generational dynamics are altering religious life—beliefs, practices, institutions—in America yet again, across all regions of the country and among most demographic groups. To be sure, the US remains a predominantly Christian country, with roughly seventy percent of the population self-identifying as Christian (forty-seven percent Protestant and twenty-one percent Catholic). Even so, the trend lines show a clear pattern: Christian affiliation is in a slow but steady decline, replaced by corresponding growth among the religiously unaffiliated (the so-called 'nones') and other non-Christian religious groups (especially Hindus and Muslims).

As the American experiment continues to evolve, the nation's "spiritual marketplace" will no doubt become increasingly complex.[3] These shifting cultural dynamics raise a host of questions that increasingly dominate domestic political discourse. How will the citizens of the United States respond to these changing demographic realities? In what ways will established religious institutions and leaders adjust to accommodate these deep cultural shifts? Just how expansive and inclusive is the American notion of "we the people"? As Robert Wuthnow reminds us, "The United States is a diverse society religiously, ethnically, and culturally. There is no question about the reality of this diversity or about the fact that it is increasing. But diversity and pluralism are not the same. We can be diverse without being truly pluralistic. Pluralism is our response to diversity—how we think about it, how we respond to it in our attitudes and lifestyles, and whether we choose to embrace it, ignore it, or merely cope with it."[4] Amid the chaos, confusion, and divisiveness of the post-9/11 era, nothing unsettles the enduring myth of white, Christian America at the heart of xenophobic nativism—or challenges the nation's commitment to the fundamental values of religious freedom and pluralism—more than the presence (and growing prominence) of American Muslims. As a springboard for our analysis of Cyber Sufism in practice, this chapter contextualizes the place of Sufis amid the mosaic of American Islam and within the United States' morphing religious landscape.

LOCATING MUSLIMS IN AMERICA'S RELIGIOUS KALEIDOCULTURE

The living legacy of Islam's storied history in the United States was on full public display during the funeral of perhaps the most famous American Muslim of all time: boxing legend, social activist, and global icon, Muhammad Ali. In the last years of his life, Ali himself carefully designed his own interfaith funeral as a public 'teaching moment.' On June 9, 2016, Imam Zaid Shakir—a co-founder of Zaytuna College in Berkeley, California—led the traditional Muslim funeral prayers (*janazah*) before a large audience in Ali's hometown of Louisville, Kentucky. Broadcast live on American television networks and streamed online around the world, this remarkable event provided an unprecedented global platform for the American Muslim community. As Sherman Jackson, a prominent African-American scholar of Islam, told the assembled crowd of mourners: "Ali did more to normalize Islam in this country than perhaps any other Muslim in the history of the United States.

[Ali] put the question of whether a person can be a Muslim and an American to rest. Indeed, he KO'd that question. With his passing, let us hope that that question will now be interred with his precious remains."[5] The outpouring of grief and sympathy for Muhammad Ali—and the rare positive media spotlight on American Muslims—was eclipsed just three days later by one of the deadliest mass-shootings in US history at a gay nightclub in Orlando, Florida. The stark juxtaposition of Ali's Islamic funeral and this horrific attack by an American Muslim terrorist who claimed allegiance to ISIS was jarring. For Muslim communities across the United States, it also served as yet another sobering reminder of their increasing vulnerability and marginalization amid the social convulsions, heated politics, and glaring media coverage that shape public opinion in the era of President Donald Trump.[6]

Beyond the heated rhetoric, what is the reality of Islam in America today? With an assorted mix of global immigrants, African Americans, and indigenous converts, the American Muslim community is a microcosm of the worldwide *umma*: multi-ethnic, multiracial, multilingual, and multicultural to the core. The multiple vectors and trajectories of American Islam blend the local with the global. "The claim to an American Islam as a construct, a project, and a reality should not overlook the fact that American Muslim communities are simultaneously indigenous and a product of migratory movements," argue Juliane Hammer and Omid Safi. "Consequently, any topic in regard to the study of American Muslims needs to take into account the interplay between domestic and localized dynamics and transnational ties, connections, and exchanges."[7] This remarkable complexity is the inheritance of the long history of Islam in the United States. Indeed, Muslims have been a part of the American story since before the founding of the nation. The first significant population to arrive on America's shores were West African slaves: victims of a "larger transnational context in the Black Atlantic world of enslaved African Muslims in the Caribbean, Latin America, and Brazil since the 1500s."[8] During the late nineteenth and early twentieth centuries, subsequent waves of immigrant Muslims from Europe, the Middle East, and Asia added new dimensions—different languages, cultures, religious practices, social networks, local histories, and identity politics—to the tapestry of American Islam.[9]

The size and scope of the American Muslim community skyrocketed following the passage of the Immigration and Naturalization Act of 1965.

This groundbreaking legislation significantly altered the country's cultural makeup, spurring the arrival of as many as 1.1 million new Muslims to the US by the end of the twentieth century. While expanding the numbers of Arab and South Asian Americans, new Muslim immigrants from sub-Saharan Africa, Iran, Southeast Asia, southeastern Europe, and Latin America dramatically transformed the religious fabric of American life.[10] With significant numbers of educated professionals (academics, physicians, lawyers, business entrepreneurs and executives, and engineers) among their ranks, these new American citizens soon began to challenge the older generation of assimilated immigrant leaders, creating an array of new national Muslim organizations. As Edward Curtis notes, "In the 1960s, 1970s, and 1980s, they often presented themselves as the voice of authentic Islam, and for the most part, the media, academics and the intelligence services, otherwise ignorant of the diversity among Muslims abroad, took their word for it."[11]

Today's American Muslims are the heirs to this complex kaleidocultural history. How many Muslims are there in the United States today? This simple question is surprisingly difficult to answer. Because the US Census Bureau does not collect data on religious identification, exact numbers are impossible to pin down with any degree of certainty. In the absence of objective and consistent scientific polling data, we are left with a perplexing array of conflicting (and often contradictory) demographic estimates—from educated guesses to politically charged, hyperinflated assertions. According to the Pew Research Center, the 2017 American Muslim population was approximately 3.35 million, meaning that Muslims make up roughly one percent of the total US population.[12] By contrast, multiple American Muslim organizations insist the number is much larger (closer to ten million), while many scholars who study Islam in America peg the population at between six and eight million.[13] Whatever the actual numbers, the growth curve is certainly trending upwards. Due to high fertility rates, strong retention rates, conversions, and immigration patterns, American Muslims are projected to comprise 2.1% of the US population by 2050. If current projections hold, Muslims will surpass Jews as the second largest religious group in the United States by mid-century.[14]

While precise, granular demographic data remains elusive, the racial, ethnic, and cultural diversity of today's American Muslim community is undeniable. The 2017 Pew survey documents that three quarters of US Muslims are either first-generation immigrants (fifty-eight percent) or the children of immigrants (eighteen percent).[15] The remaining twenty-four percent are from families who have been in the US for three generations or longer. A statistical breakdown of the total Muslim population estimates that forty-two percent were born in the United States, twenty percent in South Asia, fourteen percent in the Middle East and North Africa, thirteen percent in other parts of Asia (including Iran), five percent in sub-Saharan Africa, two percent in Europe, and two percent in the Americas (outside the US). The vast majority of Muslims now living in the United States (eighty-two percent) are officially American citizens.

The American Muslim community is also incredibly racially and ethnically diverse. According to the 2017 Pew survey, a plurality (forty-one percent) self-identify as white, twenty-eight percent as Asian, twenty percent as black, eight percent as Hispanic, and three percent as another race (or multiple races).[16] Approximately a third of native-born Muslims are black, and more than half of all Muslims whose families have been in the US for at least three generations are black. In religious terms, fifty-five percent of American Muslims describe themselves as Sunni and sixteen percent as Shi'a; a significant number (fourteen percent) report no specific affiliation, describing themselves, for example, as "just a Muslim." Overall, the American Muslim community is relatively young, well educated, middle-class, socially assimilated, and politically mainstream. In the wake of 9/11, and faced with significant social and political pressures amid the endless 'war on terror'— racial profiling, the surveillance of American mosques, a surge in hate crimes, organized Islamophobia—the overwhelming majority of American Muslims remain patriotic citizens and utterly reject *jihadi* militancy and political violence in all its forms.[17]

The remarkable diversity of the American Muslim community is its defining characteristic and perhaps its greatest strength. With family genealogies, interpersonal networks, and social memories linked to long-departed homelands across the world, diasporic Muslims contribute multiple strands to the rich fabric of American religious culture. At the same time, for many immigrants a sense of displacement and dislocation persists. As Zareena Grewal notes, "Lost homelands and lost glories have dominated the religious imaginations of Muslim Americans for at least a century, reflecting an enduring sense of being out-of-place in the US."[18] Even Muslims who enthusiastically embrace their US citizenship often preserve distinct cultural traditions by carrying on inherited practices of diet, dress, language, gender relations, marriage customs, religious beliefs, and ritual practices.

In significant ways, this pervasive diversity also challenges the cohesive unity of American Islam. Amid the hyper-hybridity of US culture, individual Muslims must negotiate multiple identities simultaneously. How, for example, does a recently arrived Sindhi Shi'i woman from Karachi, Pakistan understand, articulate, and perform her new American identity? How does she describe herself? Does she privilege one marker of her personal identity over another? At a broader level, how does the American Muslim community as a whole define itself? As Grewal asks, "what might an authentic, American Islam look like in the context of a mobile, heterogeneous, transnational community of believers?"[19] Who has the authority to speak for Islam? What Islam, interpreted how, and defined by whom? Even if there is strength in numbers, is it possible (or desirable) to represent so many disparate Muslim voices as a single, coherent whole? What is lost if differences are erased in the name of uniformity and unity? These are difficult questions. "The ethnic and religious diversity of American Muslims also means there is no single source of Muslim authority or authenticity, no group to which all others can claim allegiance in matters of religion or public affairs," argues Zain Abdullah. "Who then has defined faith, religious practices, and their interpretations for Muslims in America? Can there be one American Islam? The answer to these questions are many and few, and this has made questions about Islamic authenticity so unsettling."[20]

For scholars who study Islam in America these questions are equally vexing. The challenge is to chart the multiple, overlapping vectors of the American Muslim experience without getting lost in the echo chamber of identity politics, arbitrating debates over 'real Islam,' or reifying both 'Islam' and 'America' as fixed categories. In the past, as Kambiz GhaneaBassiri illustrates, "scholarly burrowing into American Muslim articulations of their religious identity has dimmed the significance of the larger American and Islamic socio-historical context on which American Muslims have been acting for nearly four centuries."[21] In response to this erasure of history, a new generation of scholars has begun to question and critique old models and entrenched assumptions. These scholars aim to document the polymorphous and polyvalent nature of Islam in America in changing times and places. As Curtis notes:

One of the important methodological moves in this new scholarship was to ground Muslim Americans in U.S. history, showing how larger political and social forces shaped and even constrained their behavior and how Muslim American protest and dissent (as much as Muslim American patriotism and consent) adopted American cultural forms. In addition, these works stressed how Muslim Americans could identify as U.S. nationals in both a legal and an ideological sense while also celebrating their ethnic loyalties and diasporic consciousness. Such multiple identifications were seen as Americanization, not alienation.[22]

Challenging standard narratives of 'Islam versus America,' this revisionist scholarship aims to shed new light on the manifold experiences of American Muslims through nuanced accounts of the shifting contours and myriad manifestations of Islam in America.

SUFISM: RED, WHITE, AND BLUE

Sufism is one facet of the vast kaleidoculture of American Islam. Surprisingly, to date there has been relatively little scholarship on Sufism in the United States, and far less on its cyberspace iterations. To say the least, academic studies have certainly not kept pace with the dramatic demographic shifts and cultural mixing among new generations of American immigrant Sufis and assorted spiritual seekers drawn to the tradition's teachings, practices, and artistic expressions.[23] One important exception is William Rory Dickson's 2015 monograph, *Living Sufism in North America: Between Tradition and Transformation.* Combining religious history with interviews of prominent Sufi teachers and disciples, Dickson's account offers a sweeping overview of the transmission of Sufism into North America and the diverse leadership styles of American Sufi *shaykhs*. His book is an important intervention—and hopefully a prelude to a new wave of scholarship that will document the local histories, personal stories, and unique experiences of new generations of Sufi teachers and their communities in the West.[24]

Just how many Sufis are there in the United States? In a 1996 article, Marcia Hermansen estimated that "at most a total of 25,000 persons have been involved in all Sufi movements combined over the past two decades. Perhaps

10,000, at most, are still involved."[25] Even for the time, these estimates seem low and are certainly in need of updating. Unfortunately, here again a lack of reliable statistical data makes the demographics impossible to verify. Even if a Sufi order does maintain accurate and up-to-date records of its followers, it is often not inclined to share that information with random pollsters (or nosy academics). Whatever their actual numbers, Sufis remain a minority within the small but growing American Muslim community and an outlier in the continuum of American religion writ large. One thing is for certain, however: despite their double-minority status, American Sufis constitute a vocal and dynamic group with a popularity, presence, and influence that transcends their demography.

Contemporary American Sufi communities—like American Muslims and global Muslims in general—are remarkably diverse and defy easy categorization. There are dozens of independent Sufi orders in the United States, each with its own particular blend of institutional history, spiritual genealogy, and ritual practices. Over time, many of these Sufi communities have split into various genealogical branches and sub-branches. In addition, there is a dizzying array of self-styled Sufi masters and eclectic religious groups (both Muslim and non-Muslim) who lay claim to the Sufi legacy in some fashion. Even so, by painting with a broad brush it is possible to identify several historical watersheds, prominent features, and resonant themes of contemporary American Sufism amid this abundant variety.

In the long history of Islam in America, Sufis are relative latecomers. Gisela Webb delineates three historical phases in the tradition's historical interface with American society over the last century.[26] "First Wave Sufism" emerged in the first decades of the twentieth century. Shaped by the legacy of nineteenth-century European colonialism and Orientalist scholarship, this formative period was characterized by a pervasive interest in 'Oriental wisdom,' 'Eastern spirituality,' and 'comparative mysticism' among elite circles of European and American spiritual seekers, artists, writers, and intellectuals. Popular English translations of the poetry of Sufi luminaries like Hafiz, Sa'di, Rumi, and Omar Khayyam, for example, had a major impact on American Transcendentalist literary figures such as Ralph Waldo Emerson and Walt Whitman.[27] In similar fashion, the founding of the Theosophical Society in New York City in 1875 by Madame Helena Petrovna Blavatsky (1831–1891) and Colonel Henry Steel Olcott (1832–1907), and the impact of the inaugural 1893 World's Parliament of Religion in Chicago, spurred the public obsession with East–West cross-cultural pollination.[28] In the wake of the traumatic horrors of the First World War, these intellectual currents and institutions laid the groundwork for the transmission of Sufi teachings in North America by early-twentieth-century "First Wave" Sufi masters like Hazrat Inayat Khan (1882–1927)—the eponymous founder of the Inayati Order which we will discuss in the following chapters.

Building on these firm foundations, Webb argues, the countercultural movements of the 1960s initiated American Sufism's "Second Wave." In a period of cultural fermentation and political upheaval—the civil rights movement, the feminist movement, the anti-war movement—the 'baby boomer' generation challenged traditional political institutions and social mores. A growing emphasis on religious experimentation created widespread popular interest in New Age mysticism and 'Eastern religions' (especially Buddhism and Hinduism), along with the concomitant growth in comparative religion departments on US university campuses.[29] Following the Immigration and Naturalization Act of 1965, numerous immigrant Sufi teachers and diasporic Sufi orders were transplanted into the American milieu from various parts of the Islamic world. This dynamic gave rise, Webb asserts, to "Third Wave Sufism" during the 1970s: the latest evolutionary phase, marked by an increase in the hybridity, fluidity, and complexity of American Sufism. These trends accelerated during the mid-1990s, as new Sufi immigrants—and new generations of devotees within established American Sufi movements—responded to the profound challenges and accelerating changes of global modernity in various ways.

The terrorist attacks of September 11, 2001 marked a significant watershed in Sufism's public profile in the United States. The revelation of the Saudi origin of fifteen of the nineteen 9/11 hijackers immediately turned a bright spotlight on the origins and ideology of Wahhabism. In multiple venues, American politicians, intelligence agencies, and media outlets scrutinized Saudi charities and religious organizations. As we have seen, numerous policy experts responded by championing Sufism as an antidote to Salafi ideology and Islamist militancy. Among American Muslims too, 9/11 provoked deep introspection. In many ways, it led to a palpable change in perspective: a new willingness to rethink tradition, as well as the status quo of Muslim leadership and established institutions. After 9/11, GhaneaBassiri observes, "American Muslim organizations came to represent a wider spectrum of Muslims' diversity, in terms of theology, politics, and gender, in the American public sphere."[30] This included a re-evaluation of Sufism as well. In response to internal and external critiques, prominent scholars and Sufi masters mounted a powerful public defense of the Sufi tradition, its Islamic credentials, and its potential as a wellspring for American Muslim identity. As Dickson documents, "Sufi claims to a traditional, orthodox, balanced, spiritual and open-minded Islam suddenly gained increasing appeal among many Muslims in the West . . . Sufism went from being a bad word, often unspeakable in public Muslim forums, to being more frequently affirmed as an integral part of a tolerant, orthodox Sunni Islam."[31] Today, Sufi literature, ideas, and perspectives are openly discussed in numerous Islamic forums, including the annual convention of the conservative Islamic Society of North America (ISNA). According to Syed Zain al-Abedin, founder of the Sufi-inspired Islamic Studies and Research Association (ISRA), three hundred Sufi retreats and public events were held in the United States in 2015 alone.[32] Through myriad publications, lectures, workshops, musical and poetry performances, and digital media platforms, Sufi teachers and Sufi ritual practices are now more publicly visible and accessible than ever before. Whether these momentous changes signify a new phase in American Sufism's "Third Wave" or the genesis of an entirely new 'Fourth Wave' era remains to be seen.

Against the backdrop of America's transfigured cultural landscape, how do we delineate and differentiate between American Sufi communities? In pondering this question, Marcia Hermansen's groundbreaking scholarship is required reading.[33] In an influential 1996 article, Hermansen outlines a taxonomy of three predominant types of Sufi movements: hybrids, perennials, and transplants.[34] According to this botanical metaphor, "hybrids" mark American Sufi communities that closely identify with Islamic sources and content, typically founded and led by immigrant Sufi masters who were born and raised in Muslim societies. "Perennials" designate Sufi groups that de-emphasize Islamic identification and content in favor of a 'perennialist,' 'universalist,' or 'traditionalist' outlook. Adherents of this sub-tradition—influenced by such prominent thinkers as René Guenon, Frithjof Schuon, and Seyyed Hossein Nasr—often claim an ultimate, universal truth underlying all wisdom traditions and spiritual paths.[35] "Transplants," by contrast, refer to more traditional Sufi movements among small circles of insular immigrant communities that are less concerned with adaptation to the American context. As the case studies in this book illustrate, while Hermansen's model is useful as a general classification system, in actual practice there is a great deal of overlap and blurring of boundaries within and between contemporary American Sufi orders. As American Sufi communities continue to evolve over time, therefore, this typology will need to be nuanced and updated.

Amid all the diversity in the verdant 'garden' of American Sufism, certain pervasive themes are apparent. Markus Dressler identifies five key features of Sufism in the West, all of which hold true in the American context. These interdependent markers include:

1) *The legitimacy of Sufism vis-à-vis the state.* Unlike the situation in many contemporary Muslim countries, American Sufis "do not need to defend their legitimacy against an authoritarian state that fears their potential to create and/or organize opposition; neither do they have to prove themselves against a state-endorsed definition of Islam that criminalizes Sufi practice."[36] Liberated from outright government persecution, American Sufis are relatively free to interpret Islam, define the parameters of their own tradition, interact with others, and assert the authority to speak in public discursive spaces (offline and online).

2) *The possibility of advertisement and outreach activities.* As religious groups protected by US law and constitutional rights, American Sufis face no official legal barriers to religious organizing, public gathering, or free speech. Through institutional organization and mass media advertising (from print publications to Internet outreach), Sufis are free to actively spread their message and compete in the United States' lively spiritual marketplace.

3) *The commodification of Sufism.* The capitalist rebranding of Sufism in the United States has spurred new formulations and new forms of marketing. As Dressler argues, this happens "largely independent of contemporary Sufi movements, especially when it comes to the commodification of Sufi poetry and music. But some Sufi circles try to get their own—if mostly small—share of the Sufi market. Doing so they can capitalize on their authority as authentic transmitters

of Sufi knowledge, and thusly use the esoteric market as a means for both *dawa* [missionary work] and business."[37] Many American Sufi websites, for example, sell books, DVDs, music CDs, as well as a wide variety of religious paraphernalia including calendars, artwork, clothing, perfume, incense, and prayer beads.

4) *Sufi traveling and intra-Sufi competition.* For many spiritual seekers 'shopping' for a Sufi teacher, engagement with (and movement between) multiple Sufi orders is a common practice. Hermansen calls this dynamic "*baraka*-surfing." The relative openness of individual Sufi orders in the contemporary United States, however, is often matched by underlying tensions, divisions, and competition within and between Sufi circles.[38]

5) *The regularity of multiple affiliations and intra-Sufi networking.* When compared to other local contexts around the Muslim world, the barriers and boundaries between most American Sufi orders are relatively low and permeable. As a result, affiliations with multiple orders is not uncommon among individual Sufi adepts. Over time, Sufi groups in the United States have also developed overlapping, interdependent networks, forging bonds and promoting intra-Sufi dialogue through shared conferences, symposia, and initiatives.

In the remaining chapters, I track and test all these taxonomies and trajectories through an extended case study of a contemporary American Sufi order—and comparative portraits of seven other prominent American *turuq*—in both the online and offline worlds. Throughout, my analysis views Sufism as both protean and paradigmatic. Like Americans of other religious backgrounds and faiths, Sufis in the United States have been forced to respond to the many disruptions and dislocations of liquid modernity. Whether they are third-generation American citizens ensconced in a comfortable middle-class existence, or newly arrived immigrants struggling to gain a foothold in an alien culture, American Sufis have had to learn to adapt to the 'new normal' of twenty-first-century life. After all, there is simply no escape from the forces of globalization and the social hybridity, heterogeneity, and complexity it engenders. Yet despite the many challenges, all the Sufi communities I examine in this book have proved to be incredibly resilient. Their savvy ability to accommodate change is all the more remarkable given the ambiguity, anxiety, and outright hostility that all American Muslims have experienced in the post-9/11 era.

As we will see, American Sufi communities have responded to the key questions of Islamic authority, cultural assimilation, and public outreach in markedly different ways. Over time, discrete Sufi orders developed their own distinct approaches to mainstream American culture and their own unique strategies for navigating its evolving religious ecosystem. To put it succinctly: there is no single model for American Sufism. The ability to adapt (or, in some cases, the conscious refusal to do so) is driven by multiple factors. One prominent variable is the impact of generational shifts in attitudes, interests, and orientations. Although it is difficult to document, for example, there are tangible signs of a growing interest in Sufi devotionalism among young American Muslims. As Carl Ernst illustrates:

> Muslims who came to the United States after the liberalization of immigration laws in 1965 have tended to be middle-class technical and medical specialists who gravitated towards reformist and fundamental-ist forms of Islam. Their children, who are reaching college age today, have been unexpectedly enchanted by the world music phenomenon, and large numbers of them are discovering Sufism through the power-ful music of Nusrat Fateh 'Ali Khan and others.[39]

Here we see evidence of a new (or renewed) interest in Sufism, driven to a large extent by the instruments and trajectories of global modernity itself. Young American Muslims encountering established practices like Sufi poetry and music for the first time—traditions their parents and grandparents experienced first-hand growing up in their pre-immigration homelands—are themselves an outgrowth of America's hybrid and now hyperlinked religious landscape. These trends will be interesting to follow and important to document in the years to come, especially as new generations of Muslims in the US encounter Sufism through ever more accessible and ubiquitous multimedia platforms.

Perhaps the most important determining factor in a Sufi order's ability to accommodate the American cultural context is the continuity of tradition. Institutional Sufism is by nature 'conservative' in the sense that authority and authenticity are always measured against past precedents, previous moral exemplars, and established routines. Within each Sufi order, collective memories, a shared nostalgia for departed homelands, and common cultural practices cement loyalty, cohesion, and solidarity—even in the midst of transformative societal change. In a similar fashion, mainstream Sufi orders are singularly obsessed with historical genealogy. The living teacher (*shaykh/ shaykha*) wields power and commands loyalty because he/she is recognized as the latest link in an unbroken spiritual family tree that extends back to the Prophet Muhammad. If that living connection is broken or cannot be historically established, it must be finessed; if tradition cannot be invoked, it must be invented.

For institutional brotherhoods with long histories and deep cultural roots, as well as for newly constituted, distinctly American Sufi orders, tradition (however defined and constituted) shapes the present. In Nile Green's assessment:

> For all the epistemic ruptures of modernity and the fashionable fusions of the global religious marketplace, in their emphasis on the authority of the past masters and the teachings they have handed down through the ages, many of the Sufis in the world today constitute genuine bearers of the tradition that was created from the memory and legacy of the early Sufis of Baghdad. Other more 'entrepreneurial' or 'fusion' Sufis offer more clearly invented or appropriated forms of tradition, while still nonetheless drawing on the logic of tradition to connect themselves to the sayings and practices of the Sufi past masters.[40]

It is this sense of the *persistence* of tradition—whether real or imagined—that provides a bridge between today's American Sufi practitioners and their spiritual ancestors.

Although we can trace similar styles of leadership, organizational structure, beliefs, and ritual practices across divergent Sufi orders, the precise contours of tradition vary greatly from group to group. In the end, all Sufism is local. Each American Sufi order has its own story to tell about the past. Each *tariqa* has its own unique allegiances, ritual requirements, sacred geography, gender dynamics, identity politics, and modes of expression. Given this inherent multiplicity, we should not be surprised to see different Sufi groups responding to the complex interplay of global and local forces in divergent ways as well.[41] After all, religious traditions are never static. If it is to survive across the generations—and learn to swim in new cultural waters—a Sufi order must change with the times.

CONCLUSION

Throughout Islamic history, Sufi communities have found ways to constantly evolve and adapt to changing circumstances. Sufism's inherent dynamism is readily apparent in its interface with twenty-first-century American kaleido-culture. The emergence of a new generation of tech-savvy Sufi teachers, the expansion of new social networks (local and global, digital and analog), and the ubiquity and seamless integration of new digital media technologies—all these factors profoundly influence the experience and expression of Sufism within the social matrix of today's United States. The challenge for students and scholars is to document these massive changes while not losing sight of the underlying structures, foundational beliefs, and embodied ritual performances that continue to bind today's Sufi adepts to their premodern predecessors and historical antecedents.

In an effort to unravel this complex new reality, the next three chapters provide an extended case study of American Cyber Sufism in practice. My analysis spotlights a unique transnational Sufi community headquartered in the United States at a moment of transformational change: the Inayati Order under the leadership of its current spiritual master, Pir Zia Inayat Khan. In my view, the Inayati community's ambitious digital media campaign makes it an especially compelling (and revealing) example. Through a detailed, thematic analysis of its reconstructed website and rapidly expanding social media, I aim to identify and explain how American Sufi identity, piety, and practice are rewired in the Internet Age. In an effort to provide some sense of the visual dimensions of these virtual spaces, these case-study chapters combine text and images—with multiple screenshots drawn from the refurbished Inayati website. In chapter 4, we turn our attention to Inayati identity, examining how this distinct Sufi *tariqa* defines the boundaries of 'tradition' and 'community' through its digital media productions.

4

Narrating Identity in Cyberspace:
Inayati Tradition and Community

On January 1, 2016, Pir Zia Inayat Khan, the spiritual leader of the oldest Sufi order in the United States, posted a video message to the community's official website. The live recording was filmed at the Abode, a spiritual retreat and at that time the order's North American headquarters in New Lebanon, New York.[1] Seated before the camera, Pir Zia appears with a full black beard, dressed in a long, dark-brown robe and wearing a light-brown pointed cap. Around his neck hangs a chain bearing a large pendant with the symbol of his Sufi lineage: a pair of wings surrounding a heart that contains a five-pointed star, resting above a crescent moon. On the uploaded video, next to the title, "Our New Name," a small, circular black-and-white photograph of Pir Zia's paternal grandfather, Hazrat Pir-o Murshid Inayat Khan, is clearly visible.

Holding prayer beads in his hands, Pir Zia begins his address with a solemn recitation of "The Invocation"—a supplication composed by his grandfather that serves as the community's signature prayer:

Toward the One
The Perfection of Love, Harmony, and Beauty
The Only Being,
United with all the Illuminated Souls
Who form the Embodiment of the Master, the Spirit of Guidance.[2]

Acknowledging the gathering of disciples—a live audience that is heard but not seen in the video—Pir Zia offers New Year's greetings and salutations.

Pir Zia's New Year's 2016 video announcement (http://inayatiorder.org/our-new-name/)

"On this occasion," he says, "I would like to share with you some important news, news that is of great importance for our community and our organization. This news, this decision, which I will be announcing, is the result of a process of reflection, guidance, and reasoning. And I believe that the decision will do much to clarify the work that is ours to do in this world."

From this day forward, Pir Zia proclaims, the Sufi Order International—originally established by his grandfather as the 'Sufi Order' in London in 1918—will be known by a new name. And in concert with this rebranding, he declares to the laughter of his devotees, the order's North American branch has launched a refurbished website "after many years of wishing for one." After outlining the community's storied history, Pir Zia explains the rationale for this momentous change:

> It isn't the custom of founders of [Sufi] orders to name the order after themselves. That is to be done by succeeding generations, that is to be done later, in retrospect . . . It is very proper and now most necessary that we ourselves do so. In doing so, we honor his [Inayat Khan's] memory, and we make it clear that we are confirming our allegiance to the Sufi message that he brought. So, in consideration of these facts and with the feeling, the deep feeling, that the time has come, I am

very happy to announce that as of today this order will be known as the Inayati Order and, as a fuller designation, as The Inayati Order: A Sufi Path of Spiritual Liberty.

He goes on to explain the importance of the term 'Inayati,' a word that both honors his grandfather's legacy and defines a key ethical virtue that the Sufi path aims to cultivate. In Pir Zia's words:

And finally, in this regard let me remind us all of the meaning of the word *inayat*. It means 'loving kindness.' This meaning is important in our adoption of this name for the order because this is a name that refers to the founder but it also refers to a quality that we all seek to realize and manifest in our life, an ideal. The ideal of living a life of consideration, and friendship, and respect and kindness and good will and beneficence toward all. May we live in this spirit and, in this way, serve God and humanity. Ameen.

The video address concludes with a performance of Sufi *zikr* ('remembrance,' a form of meditative chanting). "All that impedes the heart's natural joy, sweep it out," Pir Zia says, before leading the assembly in the recitation of *la ilaha* ('there is no god') thirty-three times. "We open our minds, open our hearts, open our souls to receive the rays of light that are streaming through the cosmos, upwelling from the light of lights, and cascading through the plains. All of this abundance of spiritual nourishment, we open ourselves to partake of it, saying, *illa'llah hu* ['except for Allah, Him']." Following Pir Zia's lead, the disciples echo this phrase aloud in a slow, rhythmic cadence thirty-three times. With the ritual completed, the video comes to an end, ushering in a new stage in the historical evolution of American Sufism.

With this choreographed video as a backdrop, this chapter (together with the two chapters that follow) explores the digital media profile of the Inayati Order—the twenty-first-century iteration of one of the largest and most prominent Sufi communities in the West. Shaped by the enduring legacy of Hazrat Inayat Khan, this hybrid Sufi *tariqa* has from its inception embraced a universal mysticism. In keeping with the eponymous founder's teachings, the Inayati Order insists on the fundamental unity of all religions and remains open to all people, regardless of background. Its disciples are not required to follow a particular creed, nor are they forced to adhere to the formal teachings, rules, dogma, or rituals of a specific religious path. Under the current leadership of Pir Zia Inayat Khan, however, Inayati digital media amplify an Islamic and South Asian inflection in a distinctly American idiom. Through its interweaving of language, symbols, and imagery, the order's sophisticated, multilayered website and related social media accounts demonstrate the community's deep linkages to Islamic identity, the Indian subcontinent, and the Chishti Sufi *tariqa* from which this eclectic tradition emerged. With attention to both continuity and change, we begin by exploring how Inayati digital media articulate the order's distinct version of Sufi identity, tradition, and community in a time of profound internal and external transformation.

BACKGROUND AND BIOGRAPHIES

The Inayati Order is a hereditary Sufi order. "Our Lineage," a link on the home page of the community's new flagship website (https://inayatiorder. org), highlights the four key members in this familial chain (*silsila*) of spiritual authority: the eponymous founder, Inayat Khan (1882–1927)[3]; his daughter, Noor-un-Nisa Inayat Khan (1914–1944)[4]; his eldest son, Vilayat Inayat Khan (1916–2004)[5]; and his grandson, Zia Inayat Khan (b. 1971).[6] Separate web pages provide photographs and biographical overviews of each of these paradigmatic Inayati figures. While a full account of the history of the Inayati Order—and its many competing branches and offshoots—is well beyond the scope and scale of this book, a basic appreciation of the lives and legacies of these central personalities will help us better interpret how contemporary digital media reflect and refract the community's complex institutional memory.

HAZRAT PIR-O MURSHID INAYAT KHAN[7]

Inayat Khan was born in 1882 in the city of Baroda (now Vadodara) in Gujarat, western India. He was raised in a religiously pluralistic and culturally cosmopolitan environment. His grandfather was a renowned musician in the court of the local Hindu *maharaja*. Following in the family tradition, the young Inayat trained as a musician and quickly became an accomplished composer and performer in his own right. At the age of twenty-one he accepted a prestigious appointment in the court of the Nizam of Hyderabad, the Muslim ruler of another independent princely state in the central Deccan region. It was there that Inayat Khan met and studied with a spiritual master, Sayyid Abu Hashim Madani (d. 1907), who formally initiated him into the Chishti Order. Although Inayat Khan received initiations into multiple Sufi *turuq*, this primary Chishti affiliation had the most enduring impact on his own personal identity, hybrid teachings, and spiritual career.

In South Asia—the vast geographic and cultural zone encompassing the contemporary nation-states of India, Pakistan, and Bangladesh—the Chishtiyya has been the most prominent Sufi brotherhood (*tariqa*) since the twelfth century.[8] With its doctrine of social equality, tolerance, and spiritual discipline, the order spread rapidly eastward from its roots in the remote town of Chisht in central Afghanistan. Under the guidance of charismatic spiritual leaders (*shaykhs* or *pirs*) who embodied Islamic doctrine through their piety, Sufism helped translate Islam for the indigenous (and predominantly Hindu) population. Versed in local customs and proficient in vernacular languages, Chishti *shaykhs* established centers of learning and hospices (*khanqahs*) that offered food and shelter for the wayfarers and mendicants who survived on their charity, solace for the pilgrims who visited them for spiritual blessings (*baraka*), and intensive spiritual training for their select disciples. The posthumous reputation of many Chishti *shaykhs* often led to the development of elaborate shrine complexes (*dargahs*) that attracted multitudes of devotees in search of spiritual power to alleviate their worldly troubles. As loci of sacred geography and fonts for public social welfare, these regional shrines continue to thrive as pilgrimage sites and symbols of local Indo-Muslim culture and identity. Inayat Khan's spiritual inheritance from his own mentor, Sayyid Abu Hashim Madani, rooted him in Chishti history, identity, and piety—a legacy that continues to shape the twenty-first-century Sufi community that bears his name.

According to the hagiography, on his deathbed Shaykh Madani encouraged his young protégé to "harmonize the East and the West" through his music.[9] Accompanied by his brother and cousin, Inayat Khan toured

widely throughout Europe and North America from 1910 to 1926, offering performances of classical Hindustani music, as well as public talks
on Sufism. Cultivating a reputation as an Indian mystic and Sufi spiritual
master, Inayat Khan encountered a welcoming environment everywhere
he traveled. In the context of the anti-Muslim feelings that still dominated
Western (and predominantly Christian) societies in the late colonial era,
however, he gradually modified his message. Over time, he downplayed
overtly Islamic language in order to frame Sufism as a universal, perennial
mysticism beyond any particular religion or creed. Even so, the Chishti
foundations of Inayat Khan's teachings remained. As Mark Sedgwick has
aptly observed:

> The teachings on Inayat Khan's 'Sufi Order' were superficially quite
> distinct from those of Sufis as found in the Muslim world, present-
> ing Sufism as something older than and separate from Islam as 'the
> essence of all religions and philosophies.' Khan's early works are more
> likely to quote the Bible than the Quran. The *content* of his teachings,
> however, is far closer to Sufism as found in the Muslim world than is
> the *form* of his teachings. In a sense, Khan took Sufism and dressed it
> up as something other than Sufism in order to make it more palatable
> to modern Westerners.[10]

Inayat Khan's arrival in Manhattan in 1910 marks the beginning of "First Wave"
Sufism in the United States. In 1911 he lectured to receptive audiences at the
Hindu Vedanta Society in San Francisco, and it was there that he initiated his
first Sufi disciple: Rabia Martin (born Ada Ginsberg), a Jewish member of
the Martinist Order. Returning to New York, Inayat Khan made numerous
contacts in Theosophical and Spiritualist circles, including Ora Ray Baker
(cousin of Mary Baker Eddy, the founder of the Christian Science Church)
who in 1912 became his wife (known in the community as Pirani Ameena
Begum).[11] During subsequent travels in Europe, moving back and forth
between England, France, and Russia, Inayat Khan wrote his first book, *A
Sufi Message of Spiritual Liberty*, published in London by the Theosophical
Publishing House in 1914. As his reputation and following continued to
expand—facilitated, in particular, by the patronage of a number of prominent
female British disciples—Inayat Khan formally established 'the Sufi Order' in

London in 1918. In the aftermath of World War I, he moved with his family to Suresnes, France (on the outskirts of Paris), establishing residence in a house known as Fazal Manzil ('House of Blessing') in 1920. His growing movement subsequently moved its headquarters to Geneva and was formally incorporated as 'the Sufi Movement' in 1923. In 1927, at the height of his fame and influence, Inayat Khan suddenly and unexpectedly died at the age of forty-four during a trip home to India. He is buried within a beautiful tomb complex located in a walled oasis a short walk from the bustling main gate of the massive shrine (*dargah*) of the famous thirteenth-century Chishti Sufi saint Nizam ad-Din Awliya' in south New Delhi.[12]

HAZRAT PIRZADI NOOR-UN-NISA INAYAT KHAN[13]

Amid his incessant travels, Inayat Khan was also a family man and the father of four children (two girls and two boys). His eldest child, Noor-un-Nisa Inayat Khan, was born in Moscow in 1914. After her father's tragic death, Noor was left to care for her grieving mother, Pirani Ameena Begum, and her three younger siblings in France. In keeping with the family tradition, she studied music at the Ecole Normale de Musique de Paris as a young woman before enrolling at Sorbonne University in 1932, where she studied child psychology and launched a career as a writer of children's stories. With the rise of Nazism, Noor and her brother Vilayat Inayat Khan moved to London and joined the war effort. As a member of the Women's Auxiliary Air Force, Noor was trained in wireless operations. With her fluency in English and French, she was integrated into the Special Operations Executive and, under the code name 'Madeline,' was sent to work as a covert radio operator for the French Resistance in Nazi-occupied France. Captured by the Gestapo, she was interrogated and tortured before being sent to the Dachau concentration camp, where she was executed on September 13, 1944.

Celebrated for her immense bravery and selfless service, Noor Inayat Khan was honored by the British government with the unveiling of a commemorative statue by Princess Anne in Gordon Square, London, in 2012. Within today's Inayati Order, she is remembered and honored as the daughter of Inayat Khan (*Pirzadi*), a martyr (*Shahida*), and a Sufi master (*Shaykha*) in her own right. In a public statement issued on February 5, 2018—and an accompanying video uploaded to the community's Facebook page on March 4, 2018—Pir Zia declared that his aunt would henceforth be included in the Inayati Order's official spiritual genealogy (*silsila*).[14] On September 13, 2018, the Inayati community marked the anniversary of her death ('*urs*) with the installation of a portrait of Noor Inayat Khan in the meditation room of the new headquarters in Richmond, Virginia.

HAZRAT PIR VILAYAT INAYAT KHAN[15]

Inayat Khan's eldest son, Vilayat Inayat Khan, was born in London in 1916. Like his elder sister, he immersed himself in music at Ecole Normale de Musique in Paris as a young man, going on to study philosophy and psychology in Paris and Oxford. With the outbreak of World War II, Vilayat joined the Royal Air Force and then the Royal Navy, serving as an officer in minesweeping operations in the coastal waters off France, Belgium, Holland, and Norway. He briefly pursued careers in diplomacy (working at the India High Commissioner's Office in London and later at the Pakistani Embassy) and in journalism (reporting on the Algerian independence movement for the Karachi-based newspaper *Dawn*). Throughout this time, however, he remained drawn to the spiritual path. Leaving his professional life behind, Vilayat traveled widely and studied with a variety of Christian, Hindu, and Muslim teachers in Europe, the Middle East, and South Asia. This included guidance from Sayyid Fakhr ad-Din Jili Kalimi in Hyderabad, who formally appointed him as a teaching *shaykh* in the Chishti Sufi lineage. This recognition "reinforced both his personal sense of initiatic authority and his alignment with the Chishti tradition as the source of that authority."[16]

In the decades following Inayat Khan's death in 1927, his movement fractured into a number of discrete (and occasionally divisive) organizations in Europe and North America that each laid claim to the mantle of his spiritual authority. Asserting his position as his father's chosen successor, Vilayat began to accept disciples of his own in 1951 and formally broke from the Sufi Movement in 1956. In order to distinguish his own lineage and circle of *murids*, he revived the name 'the Sufi Order' in 1968 (later reconstituted as 'the Sufi Order International').[17] Like his father before him, Vilayat took up the life of a peripatetic and prolific spiritual teacher. Fluent in French, Dutch, German, and English, he traveled constantly, lectured around the world, published numerous books, and cultivated thousands of devotees. While living and teaching mostly in Europe, he also spent time in the United States, establishing a Sufi community at the Abode of the Message in upstate New York in 1975.

Vilayat mentored students via personal interviews (which he called *darshan*, a Hindu term for the 'seeing' of the Divine), encouraging them to practice daily concentration, contemplation, and mediation and to attend one intensive retreat each year, either individually or in a group.[18] His teachings were remarkably eclectic, blending Sufi rituals (*wazifa* and *zikr*), Buddhist meditation practices, Hindu tantric exercises based on *chakra* visualization, Christian and alchemical symbolism, holistic healing, and Western psychology.[19] Yet even as his hybrid pedagogy drew on a bricolage of traditions, Vilayat was careful to ground his authority and legitimacy in his father's Chishti lineage. As Dickson notes:

> Beginning in the 1960s, Vilayat Inayat Khan began to reemphasize the Chishti lineage of the Sufi Order, against the tendency of some branches of Inayat Khan's movement to focus on 'the Message' as a unique, universal spiritual development unconnected with the Indian Sufi traditions. Pir Vilayat studied with Chishti teachers in India and further understood Inayat Khan's message in light of classical Sufi masters like Ibn 'Arabi and Suhrawardi. He presciently recognized the Sufi Order's legitimacy as a Sufi tradition would be easily challenged if it eschewed the traditional sources of spiritual legitimacy: its Indian Sufi lineage, primarily from the Chishti order, and its substantial basis in the classical Islamic tradition.[20]

Pir Vilayat died on June 17, 2004 at the family home, Fazal Manzil, in Suresnes, France. He was subsequently buried in a tomb in a busy alley "just a few steps away" from his father's *dargah* and the neighborhood Hope Project which Vilayat founded in south New Delhi.[21] Significantly, this location is illustrative of fractious divisions at the time. The final site of Pir Vilayat's tomb was the result of internal disputes among several competing Inayati branches, some of whom actively resisted his burial inside the precincts of his father's nearby shrine complex.

PIR ZIA INAYAT KHAN[22]

Zia Inayat Khan—affectionately known as Sarafil Bawa—was born in Novato, California, in 1971, the first son of Pir Vilayat Inayat Khan and his American wife, Taj Inayat. Raised in the United States, he spent extensive time in India (especially in Baroda, Ahmedabad, and Hyderabad) as a young man, learning Urdu and Persian and studying the sources of the Chishti Sufi tradition. His immersion in Chishti ritual practices included extensive training with his father, a period of seclusion at the Chishti *khanqah* in Ahmedabad, and personal guidance from the Chishti master Sayyid Muhammad Rashid al-Hasan Jili Kalimi (d. 2013) in Hyderabad.[23] Deepening his personal ties to South Asia, Pir Zia married an Indian woman from his extended circle of Gujarati relatives, Pirani Sartaj. A serious scholar and prolific writer, he studied Persian literature at the University of London and then completed a doctoral degree in Islamic Studies at Duke University under the guidance of Professors Bruce Lawrence and Carl Ernst, scholars with expertise in South Asian Sufism and Indo-Muslim culture. His dissertation, completed in 2006, documents his grandfather's life and offers a historical survey of the numerous organizations that carried on his legacy.

In 2000, Zia Inayat Khan was publicly confirmed as his father's spiritual successor; he assumed the mantle of leadership upon Pir Vilayat's death in 2004. Reconstituting the community as the Inayati Order in 2016, he now holds multiple offices:

- *Pir-o Murshid* and President of the Inayati Order (head teaching *shaykh* of the global Inayati *tariqa*)
- President of the Six Activities (Esoteric School, Universal Worship, Kinship, Healing Order, Knighthood of Purity, and Ziraat)
- *Sajadda-Nishin* of the *dargah* of Hazrat Inayat Khan, New Delhi (head custodian of his grandfather's tomb-shrine)
- Chairman of the Board of the Hope Project, New Delhi
- President of the Suluk Academy[24]

A constant traveler, Pir Zia works from two primary Sufi lodges: Fazal Manzil, the ancestral home in Suresnes, France, and the Astana, the Inayati Order's new North American headquarters in Richmond, Virginia, where he resides with his wife and two children, Rasulan and Ravanbakhsh.

With these biographical sketches as a backdrop, the following pages trace how the contemporary Inayati Order under the direction of Pir Zia utilizes digital media to preserve the Indo-Muslim heritage of its founder, Hazrat Inayat Khan, while at the same time responding to the shifting currents of liquid modernity and twenty-first-century American culture.

THE CONTINUITY OF TRADITION

In myriad ways, the Inayati Order's new website emphasizes the *continuity* of tradition, asserting a linear, organic connection between the eponymous founder and the current generation of devotees. Hazrat Inayat Khan's presence—his image, his charismatic personality, his words—reverberates throughout this complex, interconnected digital document. The link, "The Inayati Order," features a striking photograph of Inayat Khan as a young musician, with a full beard and dressed in a flowing white robe, seated on a carpet and holding a *veena* (a classical Indian stringed instrument). An accompanying quote provides a synopsis of the Inayati Order's mission: "The objectives: to realize and spread the knowledge of unity, the religion of love and wisdom, so that . . . the human heart may overflow with love, and all hatred caused by distinctions and differences may be rooted out." Below this quotation is a succinct description of the community's institutional identity: "The Inayati Order, formerly known as the Sufi Order International, is an international organization dedicated to spreading the Sufi Message of Hazrat Inayat Khan, who first introduced Sufism to the Western world in 1910. The Sufi Message proclaims the knowledge of divine unity—of all peoples, all religions, and all existence—and the religion of the heart awakened to the beauty in all creation."[25] As this statement affirms, Hazrat Inayat Khan's perennialist and universalist philosophy remains the bedrock of the reformulated Inayati Order. Linking past to present, today's community maintains that all religions and revelations illuminate the universal and ongoing disclosure of the Divine.

The centrality of Inayat Khan's teachings is amplified via numerous hyperlinks found under the rubric "Teachings." "Ten Sufi Thoughts," for example, offers a distillation of the order's foundational beliefs which, the text asserts, "comprise all the important subjects with which the inner life is concerned." On the web page, these doctrinal principles are summarized in a bullet point list:

1) There is One God, the Eternal, the Only Being; none exists save God.

2) There is One Master, the Guiding Spirit of all Souls, Who constantly leads followers towards the light.

3) There is One Holy Book, the sacred manuscript of nature, which truly enlightens the reader.

4) There is One Religion, the unswerving progress in the right direction towards the ideal, which fulfils the life's purpose of every soul.

5) There is One Law, the law of reciprocity, which can be observed by a selfless conscience together with a sense of awakened justice.

6) There is One Brotherhood and Sisterhood, the human brotherhood and sisterhood, which unites the children of earth indiscriminately in the Parenthood of God.

7) There is One Moral, the love which springs forth from self-denial, and blooms in deeds of beneficence.

8) There is One Object of Praise, the beauty which uplifts the heart of its worshippers through all aspects from the seen to the unseen.

9) There is One Truth, the true knowledge of our being, within and without, which is the essence of all wisdom.

10) There is One Path, the annihilation of the false ego in the real, which raises the mortal to immortality, and in which resides all perfection.[26]

The emphasis on unity and harmony in this passage is immediately striking. As a theological affirmation of monotheism and a testament to hyper-ecumenicalism, these core Inayati doctrines erase the boundaries of religious difference to assert a single, uniform wellspring of spiritual wisdom that animates all of the world's mystical traditions. By clicking on an accompanying link, curious cyber surfers can download Inayat Khan's own detailed commentary on each of these core teachings.[27]

In the Inayati system, 'Sufism' serves as a catch-all term for a timeless, universal path of spiritual transformation that transcends the particularities of history and culture. The link "What is Sufism?" summarizes this worldview with another quote from Inayat Khan: "If anybody asks you, 'What is Sufism?' you may answer: 'Sufism is the religion of the heart, the religion in which the most important thing is to seek God in the heart of humanity.'" This is followed by a synopsis of the community's distinct approach to spiritual life. The ultimate goal of Sufi pedagogy, the web page claims, is "to develop the capacity of the heart—the capacity to hold all the complexities of life in a matrix of love—and to discover the divinity inherent in all of creation." Sufism, therefore, "is not a religion in the sense of being a system of beliefs, separable from other religions, but a school of experience focused on the cultivation of the heart and the deepening of awareness through the practice of prayer, meditation and spiritual inquiry." While recognizing that there are many Sufi lineages, the website asserts that Inayati Sufism "is universalist in its acceptance of all people and paths leading to the unfoldment of the light and power latent in the human being." And while each individual's spiritual journey is "an endless path, pursued over a lifetime," the digital text assures the reader that "the simple pointers you will find here—to information, books, audio, video, as well as classes and retreats—we hope will bring you closer to that which you seek."[28]

This passage synthesizes the Inayati Order's distinct approach to Sufi piety and pedagogy, emphasizing the universality of religious truth; the innate human capacity for love; a theology of divine immanence; the transformative potential of experiential learning; and the absence of barriers to spiritual discipleship. On a more instrumental level, it also positions the new website as both a public archive (a digital repository that preserves institutional memory) and a springboard to private practice (a stepping stone to direct, personal engagement with the 'real world' Inayati community offline).

In the Inayati Order's formulation, Sufism is a universal path of individual spiritual transformation most effectively encountered and experienced in community. Above all, Inayat Khan viewed his role as a bridge-builder between cultures—an ideal that continues to shape his contemporary heirs. Another link, "Objects of the Order," articulates the organization's missionary aim: "To help bring the world's two opposite poles, East and West, close together by the interchange of thoughts and ideals, that the universal brotherhood-sisterhood may form of itself, and people may meet beyond the narrow national and racial boundaries."[29] Following past precedent, today's Inayati Order has no barriers to access, no litmus test for participation. As in the time of his grandfather, Pir Zia leads a *tariqa* comprised largely of American and European devotees who self-identify as Sufi but most of whom do not practice the five pillars of Islam, follow the *shari'a*, or even consider themselves to be Muslims.[30] In their daily lives, Inayati disciples tend to adopt few distinctive symbols of Islamic identity, such as names and dress codes. The order's ritual spaces and teaching forums, both public and private, eliminate gender boundaries, with men, women, and children mixing freely. And although the community is not homogenous, monolithic, or monochrome, the majority of its members are white and of Christian or Jewish background.[31]

Visual cues throughout the new website's myriad links reflect these demographic realities. This includes various images of Pir Zia leading integrated groups of men and women in prayer and conversation[32]; female devotees in typical American clothing with uncovered hair[33]; and a montage that includes a group of disciples with raised hands, smiling for the camera.[34] At the same time, the website narrative emphasizes Inayat Khan's enduring vision of inclusivity. In an online letter posted to the website on November 18, 2015, the order's Executive Director, Jennifer Alia Wittman, affirmed the order's commitment to broadening diversity in an era of widespread societal change. "Today, the Inayati Order is an organization on the cusp of making a new and more significant impact on the world's spiritual community, but it is also an organization in need of greater unity among its diverse membership," she exclaims. "We all wish to continue to emerge as a relevant, cohesive, all-inclusive spiritual school, welcoming people of all ages, all cultures and backgrounds, under a clear Message of Spiritual Liberty."[35] As the primary public relations platform, the revitalized website embraces Inayat Khan's original vision of an open, hospitable Sufi community open to spiritual seekers of any background—but now dressed (both literally and figuratively) in a distinctly American idiom and style.

LINKING THE INDO-MUSLIM PAST TO THE AMERICAN PRESENT

One of the most striking features of the new website is its bright spotlight on the Inayati Order's Indo-Muslim roots. While this is neither a rejection nor a reinvention of institutional history, I argue that it does signal an important shift in emphasis. By highlighting the living connection to Inayat Khan's own life story, the website ties Pir Zia's leadership style and public persona to South Asian Islam and, in particular, Chishti Sufi identity.

This is especially evident in the link "Our Lineage."[36] At the top of the page is a fascinating photograph taken at the tomb of the thirteenth-century Chishti Sufi luminary, Nizam ad-Din Awliya' (1238–1325 CE). Since the fourteenth century, this saint's shrine (*dargah*), located in an important Muslim area of south New Delhi, has been a prominent site of pilgrimage and a resonant symbol of South Asian Muslim identity.[37] Given its popular association with spiritual power and divine blessing (*baraka*), many important historical figures are buried within the shrine's precincts and throughout the surrounding neighborhood that also bears the saint's name (Nizam ad-Din *basti*). Every year, groups of Inayati devotees from around the world travel to New Delhi for pilgrimage (*ziyarat*) to memorialize the death anniversaries (*'urs*) of both Hazrat Inayat Khan (February 5, known as Visalat Day) and Vilayat Inayat Khan (June 17).[38] While honoring the lives and legacies of their own spiritual teachers, these pilgrims encounter the sacred history, sacred space, and lived realities of the Chishti *tariqa* in India.

The website photograph was taken on Visalat Day 2012, during Hazrat Inayat Khan's annual *'urs* ceremony.[39] In the image, Pir Zia is seated near the threshold of Nizam ad-Din's tomb, playing a flute. He is flanked on his right side by Sayyid Ahmad Shah Chishti Maududi (d. 2018), the international leader of the Chishti order based in Herat and Chisht Sharif, Afghanistan, and other prominent male Sufi teachers and disciples. To his left are several women and children family members. In the background, a large group of devotees are seated in the courtyard, observing the proceedings. This includes both Indians and Americans, all dressed in clothing appropriate for pious Muslim pilgrims, with the men in skullcaps and the women with their hair covered by a simple headscarf (*dupatta*).

About   Calendar   Programs   News   Teachings   Multimedia   Donate

Our Lineage

"A mystic order...was inaugurated by the Prophet, and afterwards was carried on by [his] successors, who were called Pir-o-Murshid, Shaikh, etc., one after another, duly connected as links in a chain (silsila)."

— Hazrat Inayat Khan

Sufism is said to have existed among the prophets of all peoples and cultures from the earliest times. From the prophets, the wisdom of Sufism was imparted to the saints and masters of all traditions. However, a historical tradition of Sufism can be clearly dated to the 7/8th-century C.E. in the Near East, from which stem numerous unbroken lineages passed from master-to-disciple down to our own day.

In the chain of transmission of the Inayati Order, the teachings and lineages of four great Sufi orders—the Chishti, Suhrawardi, Qadiri, and Naqshbandi—are united in its founder, Hazrat Inayat Khan. Today, there are numerous lineages and organizations tracing their origins to him. The Inayati Order represents the lineage passed directly to his eldest son, Pir Vilayat Inayat Khan, and currently led by his grandson, Pir Zia Inayat-Khan.

The Silsila

Hazrat Inayat Khan

Noor-un-nisa Inayat Khan

Pir Vilayat Inayat Khan

Pir Zia Inayat-Khan

Pir Zia with Inayati Disciples at the Nizam ad-Din dargah, February 2012
(https://inayatiorder.org/about/our-lineage/)

For a Sufi audience, this visual tableau immediately communicates a great deal of vital information and affective power. The photo places Pir Zia at the epicenter of a ritual ceremony in one of the most sacred spaces of Sufi piety in South Asia and one of the most important sites of Muslim pilgrimage on the planet. In doing so, it affirms a direct and intimate relationship between the paragon of Muslim virtue (the Prophet Muhammad), the revered medieval South Asian saint whose *baraka* blesses this place (Nizam ad-Din Awliya'), a renowned Chishti Sufi master from the order's homeland (Sayyid Ahmad Shah), the eponymous founder of the Inayati Order and his son/successor buried nearby (Inayat Khan and Vilayat Inayat Khan), and the current heir to this unbroken lineage of spiritual wisdom (Pir Zia). Without the need for words, this evocative image confirms—and for the Sufi faithful, *sanctifies*—a living connection between the Inayati Order's Indo-Muslim past and its American present.

The importance of the Inayati Order's trans-historical and cross-cultural networks is made explicit in the accompanying text and hyperlinks. Below the photograph is another quote from Inayat Khan: "A mystic order . . . was inaugurated by the Prophet, and afterwards was carried on by [his] successors, who were called Pir-o-Murshid, Shaikh, etc., one after another, duly connected as links in a chain (*silsila*)." This sentence firmly grounds Inayat Khan's teachings within the Islamic tradition and the supreme authority of the Prophet Muhammad. Subsequent paragraphs provide greater clarification:

> Sufism is said to have existed among the prophets of all peoples and cultures from the earliest times. From the prophets, the wisdom of Sufism was imparted to the saints and masters of all traditions. However, a historical tradition of Sufism can be clearly dated to the 7/8th-century CE in the Near East, from which stem numerous unbroken lineages passed from master-to-disciple down to our own day.
>
> In the chain of transmission of the Inayati Order, the teachings and lineages of four great Sufi orders—the Chishti, Suhrawardi, Qadiri, and Naqshbandi—are united in its founder, Hazrat Inayat Khan. Today, there are numerous lineages and organizations tracing their origins to him. The Inayati Order represents the lineage passed directly to his eldest son, Pir Vilayat Inayat Khan, and currently led by his grandson, Pir Zia Inayat-Khan.[40]

This statement offers a salient distillation of the contemporary Inayati Order's view of its own institutional history and identity. It reaffirms Inayat Khan's perennialist and universalist teachings while simultaneously locating the Inayati tradition within Islamic sacred history and established Sufi lineages. A hyperlink, "The Silsila" (the 'chain' of authority), provides a detailed spiritual family tree (*shajara*) for each of the "four Sufi schools" that Inayat Khan was initiated into by his own spiritual master, Sayyid Muhammad Abu Hashim Madani. These genealogical charts all begin with the Prophet Muhammad and end with Pir Zia. In between are the names of thirty-eight Sufi masters in the Chishti Order, forty-one Sufi masters in the Suhrawardi Order, forty-three Sufi masters in the Qadiri Order, and thirty-four Sufi masters in the Naqshbandi Order.[41] Together, these interlaced webs of Sufi lineages chart a continuous, interdependent spiritual network spanning 1,400 years of Islamicate history.

These digital materials narrate an unambiguous message: that as a twenty-first-century Sufi teacher in the United States, Pir Zia is the scion of a hereditary Indo-Muslim tradition whose history, teachings, and practices are legitimized via multiple chains of authority directly linked to the Prophet Muhammad. The website also confirms that the Inayati Order is a family affair, primarily rooted in the Chishti-Nizami Sufi *tariqa*, but deepened by its association with other global Sufi *turuq* with long histories and renowned reputations.[42] At the same time, the passage above signals that today's Inayati Order recognizes the legitimacy of other claims to Inayat Khan's lineage and legacy. This ethic of inclusion is echoed in Pir Zia's 2016 New Year's video address. In describing the rationale for the order's name change he states:

> In adopting this name, we make no claim of exclusivity in representing the spiritual legacy of Hazrat Inayat Khan. And we indeed express our deep solidarity and respect for our friends and fellow travelers who derive their work likewise from Hazrat Inayat Khan through other channels, other branches and communities and organizations. We are united with all who serve and practice the Sufi message of Hazrat Inayat Khan which itself reaches out in solidarity and friendship with all spiritual paths traced back to the messengers, the messengers of all faiths.[43]

This message of inclusivity is amplified in a separate web page, "Related Organizations," which contains a list of global Inayati centers—as well as hyperlinks to the home web pages of other active Sufi communities that also claim the legacy of Inayat Khan.[44] These include the Federation of the Sufi Message[45]; the International Sufi Movement[46]; Sufi Ruhaniyat International[47]; the Sufi Way[48]; and Sufi Contact.[49] As evidenced in the contestation over Pir Vilayat Inayat Khan's burial site, the divisions among and between these competing groups have, at times, been contentious and schismatic. The website narrative, therefore, shows the Inayati Order walking a tightrope. In an attempt to heal old wounds and build new bridges, the digital text promotes a sense of communal unity and shared identity while also recognizing the diversity and differences among the multiple Sufi groups that claim legitimacy and authority through their own historical links with Inayat Khan. Even so, the renamed and reconstituted order under the leadership of Pir Zia strongly asserts the singular importance of the Inayati family bloodline. The website marks a clear and significant distinction between "Inayati lineages" (all groups that claim Inayat Khan's legacy) and the "Inayati Order" (the community based on—and legitimized by—an exclusive hereditary line of transmission, from Inayat Khan to his daughter, son and grandson).[50]

Pir Zia unambiguously invokes this Indo-Muslim past and these deep institutional links to global Sufi orders to frame his own personal identity. This is apparent in his public demeanor, his dress, his language, and his own descriptions of twenty-first-century Sufism in the United States. Throughout the website, Pir Zia's personal grounding in Islam is amplified via digital texts and images. Like his grandfather and father before him, his clothing and personal style reflects the appearance of a traditional Chishti Sufi master: a full beard, long flowing robes, a skullcap or turban, and prayer beads.[51] In similar fashion, his public persona and overall comportment reflect cus-tomary, time-honored Sufi expressions of personal etiquette and 'beautiful behavior' (*adab*).

Both online and offline, Pir Zia's language is also often Islamized: steeped in references to the Qur'an, Islamic history, Indo-Muslim idioms, and a distinctly Chishti Sufi worldview. Echoing his grandfather's philosophy, he describes Sufism as a malleable mystical path that interfaced with different religious traditions over time and across cultures. Even so, he rejects the suggestion that the Inayati Order is therefore un-Islamic or simply a reduc-tive, fuzzy form of 'universalism Sufism.' Pir Zia's views are encapsulated in an interview with William Rory Dickson that is worth quoting at length:

At inter religious discussions here at the Abode, I always like to ask the question, "What meaningful perspective does your tradition have to contribute to those who do not belong to it?" When it comes to Islam, my answer would be, at least in part, the *universalism* of Islam, the acknowledgment of the existence of a *nabi* [prophet] in every era up until the *khatm an-nabiyin* ['Seal of the Prophets,' the Prophet Muhammad], in all lands. The Qur'anic statement [3:84], "We make no distinctions between them," compels recognition of all prophets, across the world. Wherever you go, one has to assume that that culture has had its prophet, and one has to accept that prophet as being on par with one's own prophet, and the prophets of the whole world. If that can be a starting point, then one can conceive of the planetary lineage of prophecy. Ultimately, one can see the message of these prophets as the heritage, the birthright of all of us. As a Muslim, I can still have an authentic spiritual relationship with the Buddha, or the Christ, or mother Mary.

Ibn al-'Arabi speaks about this specifically. He speaks about his experience undergoing the tutelage of several prophets successively, and how this did not alter his Islamic commitment, but was an initiatic process where something of the uniqueness of each prophetic personality was dispensed to him . . . This is the template for a universal spirituality that doesn't flatten out the plurality of faiths. It doesn't mean one has to renounce one's Judaism or Christianity or Islam or Buddhism. One can remain within a faith tradition, but have access to the planetary lineage of grace, which includes all of the prophets, and one can receive the guidance of a series of them in the course of one's life.[52]

As a Muslim and a Sufi teacher, Pir Zia asserts that it is no threat to anyone's faith to draw upon the prophetic wisdom of other spiritual traditions. In private conversations with his disciples, as well as in published writings and public talks, he affirms the compatibility and complementarity between his grandfather's perennialist message and Islamic identity by pointing to the inherent universalism in the Qur'an, the example (*sunna*) of the Prophet Muhammad, and the teachings of luminaries like the famous Andalusian poet, scholar and Sufi master, Ibn 'Arabi (1165–1240 CE).

While drawing attention to the Islamic foundations of the Inayati lineage, Pir Zia also looks to the Chishti Sufi tradition as a blueprint for identity formation, community building, and decision-making. He argues, for example, that the Inayati Order's acceptance of non-Muslims is based on the teachings of the famous Chishti-Nizami revivalist of the late Mughal era, Shah Kalim Allah Jahanabadi (1650–1729). "There are other cases, especially in India," Pir Zia notes, "where to this day there are many Sufi *murshids* [guides] whose followers, whose *mureeds* [sic], are in part—or in some cases the majority—are non-Muslims, Hindus. Within our order the policy was officialized in the time of Shah Kalim Allah Jahanabadi in the seventeenth/eighteenth century, to grant *bay'at*, initiation, to non-Muslims. That policy was intentionally propounded. So it has been our tradition since that time. For us, that question has already been answered."[53]

As each of these examples demonstrates, the digital reframing of Inayati identity, tradition, and community is, above all, a *historical project*. Pir Zia clearly views the past as a bountiful resource for inspiration and guidance—and he shapes his own identity and the contours of his contemporary Sufi community by referencing Islam's canonical texts (the Qur'an and *hadith*) and moral exemplars (prophets and saints). As a result, I argue, there is now a self-conscious and purposeful Islamic inflection to the Inayati Order's public profile—both online and offline—under his leadership.

THE MATRIX SHIFT

Although the past is present throughout the Inayati website and social media, the organization's redesigned Cyberscapes narrate a story that is primarily about *change*. In both content and style, the community's digital media communicate a purposeful rebooting of tradition—with a particular accent on the singular personality, charisma, piety, and authority of its current spiritual leader, Pir Zia Inayat Khan. Since 2013, a separate website, www.pirzia.org, has served as the main online source for information on Pir Zia's personal history, teachings, travels, and activities. Although this site remains active, its materials and message are now largely mirrored on the flagship website. Pir Zia now posts important updates, personal reflections, summaries of past events, and descriptions of forthcoming programs via a monthly digital newsletter, The Zephyr, that is accessible on the new website's "News" link.[54] In a clear demonstration of the order's protean adaptability, inayatiorder.org embraces the legacy of Inayat Khan while modulating its message for a twenty-first-century American audience.

Pir Zia's influence and impact are perhaps most apparent in the reconfiguration of the Inayati Order's institutional architecture. In a systematic overhaul described as a "matrix shift" and the "Great Repositioning," the Inayati website documents the ongoing transformation of the organization's administrative apparatus and public profile.[55] As the designated successor, leader, and teaching *shaykh*, Pir Zia stands at the apex of a highly organized corporate structure. He is assisted in his duties by a Board of Trustees and an Advisory Board comprised of influential members from across North America, all of whom have an extensive personal history as disciples and teachers in the Inayati tradition. In 2018, the Inayati Board consisted of eight members: four women and four men, with Pir Zia serving as President; the seven-member Advisory Board included four prominent women, one of them Pir Zia's mother, Taj Inayat. A website link, "Inayati Order Board," provides photographs and detailed biographies of each member of the Inayati leadership team.[56] Significantly, in their professional lives these individuals represent an eclectic range of backgrounds: commercial interior designer, airline pilot and psychotherapist, immigration lawyer, geologist, physician, executive coach, judge and hearings officer, business consultant, real estate developer, school teacher and principal, and ordained Unitarian Universalist minister. This range of technical, bureaucratic, and business expertise clearly informs the Board's approach to the Inayati Order's organization, long-term planning, marketing, and messaging. A parallel organization, the Message Council, oversees the community's multidimensional religious activities and guides its overall direction. Pir Zia serves as the Council's President and his mother, Taj Inayat, as its Vice President. They are assisted by a group of ten high-ranking spiritual guides and teachers who form sub-committees organized around the Five Activities created by Inayat Khan during his lifetime (the Esoteric School, Universal Worship, Kinship, the Sufi Healing Order, and Ziraat)—all of which are discussed in greater detail in the next two chapters. While most of these senior leaders are based in the United States, the Message Council also reflects the order's global reach, with additional representatives from the UK, Austria, and Pakistan.[57]

Another link on the new website, "Organization Blog," provides frequent updates on the community's internal operations—documenting decisions and plans regarding programming, finances, technology, and communications, as well as detailed summaries of committee meetings and Board deliberations.[58] Remarkably, this digital document is accessible to both Inayati disciples and the general public. The Inayati Order's complex bureaucratic organization is perfectly encapsulated in the "2015 North American Annual Report." [59] This fifteen-page text outlines the many moving parts of the organization's administrative machinery. Complete with colorful photographs and graphics, financial pie charts, and graphs of statistical data, the report describes the order's myriad gatherings, training programs, and spiritual retreats. It also details Pir Zia's global travels and describes the community's expanding communication networks, current leadership teams, financial expenditures, internal debates, and overarching vision for the future. Although the Inayati Order's corporate structure is hierarchical—with Pir Zia as the driving force, spiritual authority, and public face of the institution—its organization and operation reflect a degree of bureaucratic sophistication, accountability, and transparency rarely seen in institutional Sufi orders, past or present.

The Inayati community's public rebranding efforts are equally striking. The most obvious sign of this transformation is the renaming of the order itself—with "The Inayati Order: A Sufi Path of Spiritual Liberty" now emblazoned on all institutional documents and public messages. The Inayati logo, the 'heart and wings' symbol created by Inayat Khan, has also been updated for the Digital Age, redesigned by a professional "graphic and web designer specializing in publications and editorial design and production." In an online letter addressed to the global Inayati community, the International Coordinator, Gulrukh Patel, explains that this logo will be incorporated "into all of our print and digital media," and that a "style guide" will be distributed to the order's branches throughout the US and across the world. This document, Patel explains, will outline "how to use the logo, specially created for Inayati Order Centers and related organizations. Our centers and organization will also receive copies of the logo in *.tif* and *.pdf*, in color and black and white. Also, if an Inayati Center, there will also be a version of the logo that allows you to insert the location and/or name of your center."[60] As marketing tools, the new name and updated logo identify the Inayati Order as a distinct, autonomous, and transnational corporate franchise, formatted for the Digital Age.

The most salient expression of the Inayati Order's reanimated identity is the refurbished website itself. Its launch on January 1, 2016 in concert with Pir Zia's video announcement was clearly designed to signal a key hinge moment in the organization's history. As a vast digital warehouse, the new website serves as the primary vehicle for broadcasting the order's unique vision of Sufi identity, community, and tradition to the world. By design, it preserves the past even as it aims to solidify and expand the boundaries of community in the United States and beyond. In the words of Executive

Director Jennifer Alia Wittman, "Through inayatiorder.org (and its related social media platforms), we are envisioning new means of deepening our practice and friendship together, growing and strengthening our worldwide community of 'Wayfarers on the Endless Path.'"[61] In outlining the aspirations for the order's digital future, Wittman asserts "this is just a first step" and that the digital communications team "will be gradually refining the image and voice of the site, as well as rolling out new features." Going further, she provides granular details about the community's ambitious long-term vision for the World Wide Web. New website features, paired with other digital interfaces, will eventually include:

- A growing collection of new teachings and resources for the public;
- A special section of resources specifically for students within The Inayati Order;
- New video and audio resources of Inayati Order teachers-for free, for rent and for purchase;
- A growing social media presence on Facebook and Twitter (adding other social media sites over time);
- A comprehensive events calendar for The Inayati Order (including select senior teachers in addition to Pir Zia);
- An ever-improving map and listing of Inayati Order centers worldwide;
- A list of Inayati Order Spiritual Guides by state and region;
- As well as other improvements and updates (reasonable for our small staff and volunteers) to be implemented over time.[62]

While implementing these additional elements into a seamless, interlinked virtual matrix will take time, the order has quickly and resolutely pushed this process forward. As the 2015 Annual Report illustrates, there is a concerted effort to upgrade the organization's online capabilities, with a particular emphasis on live-streaming video productions. In 2015 alone, $10,000 was invested in equipment and a "top-notch team of audio and video experts, mostly volunteers, [were] trained in how to run the technology behind online courses." In the first year of experimentation, Pir Zia led an eight-part teaching series entitled, "Unfolding the Message." Over a two-month period, successive lectures were filmed before a live audience and streamed online, drawing a real-time virtual audience of more than 1,200 individuals. Almost twenty thousand more people watched the recorded webcast within a month of the live events, and 2,600 subsequently purchased individual classes or the full series via Vimeo.[63] On the refurbished website a link, "Digital Media," provides access to live events, as well as a host of archived audio and video programs, lectures, workshops, and leadership training sessions for purchase.[64] This link—previously entitled "Multimedia"—is organized into three separate rubrics: "Vimeo Livestream", "Audio and Video", and "YouTube."

In similar fashion, the Inayati Order is also targeting social media. A community Facebook page ("The Inayati Order") is up and running and, to date, has attracted more than two thousand followers. Regular postings include reminders of upcoming events, excerpts from the teachings of Inayat Khan, and personal messages from Pir Zia. The order's website also provides links to Twitter and YouTube accounts. In addition, Pir Zia maintains his own active Facebook page ("Zia Inayat-Khan") and Twitter account (@birdlanguage). In my view, these early, tentative experiments with social networking tools are potentially transformative—an important trend to follow in the coming years. Working in unison, Inayati digital media narrate a story of a twenty-first-century Sufi community that is firmly rooted in tradition but, at the same time, adaptive to new circumstances and responsive to change.

CONCLUSION

As numerous scholars of digital religion have documented, cyberspace is altering the dynamics of religious identity and community. "The Internet's ability to facilitate and mediate social relations," Heidi Campbell notes, "has shifted many people's notions of friendship, relationship, and community in an age of networked, digital technologies."[65] Liberated from the monopoly of established religious institutions and authorities, individuals are discovering new virtual pathways to meet, form new alliances and relationships, and rethink the definitions and boundaries of religious life. In the words of Pauline Hope Cheong and Charles Ess:

> In the digital age, adherents, audiences, listeners, communities of shared practice and shared memory, and various 'publics' are now

active in the production, circulation, imbrication, selection, and re-making of 'the religious' and 'the spiritual.' It's not just that authority faces competition from new sources, it's that the whole mode of practice that defines cultural participation today operates on logics that put authority in a different place than in the past. The inventory of resources and practices through which religion and spirituality are known and done today is an increasingly 'horizontal' inventory, where the traditional sources exist alongside a range of other ones. But, more importantly, those who turn to that inventory are increasingly finding themselves empowered to both contribute to it in new ways and to think critically about who is responsible for each of those resources.[66]

As this quote suggests, the "horizontal inventory" facilitated by digital religion is rewiring the offline networks of contemporary religious life.

This is not to say, however, that old, established networks and authorities are no longer relevant. In the midst of the centrifugal forces of change, traditional religious institutions and their gatekeepers are also reasserting themselves in cyberspace. Both the Vatican and the Dalai Lama, to take just two prominent examples, maintain elaborate and multidimensional digital media footprints.[67] As Cheong argues, scholars of digital religion remain attuned to the parallel trend of the persistence of tradition:

In sum, a growing body of research points to the recurrent logic of continuity and complementarity of religious authority, situated in the contemporary zeitgeist surrounding Internet use as incrementally and routinely incorporated within individual, collective, and institutional norms, practices, and orderings. As the literature demonstrates, while religious leaders are recognized as being increasingly dependent on online resources, overall, they are increasingly portrayed as adaptive and as exercising significant control by, for instance, curtailing the negative impact of false and inflammatory interpretations and reclaiming their audience's respect and trust. Furthermore, religious leaders have also been portrayed as assuming expanded competencies as strategic arbitrators of online-offline religious information, to restore relational bonds and credibility important to the development of convergent multimedia and corporate promotional strategies.[68]

Faced with the sea change of the digital revolution, the leaders of mainstream religious institutions have quickly learned to swim—pushing back against the erosion of their authority by deploying digital technologies to defend tradition and assert control.

This chapter has demonstrated how today's Inayati Order skillfully utilizes new multimedia technologies to plot a path to the future without abandoning the past. As we have seen, digital media offer a powerful vehicle for storytelling. As tools for both internal meaning-making and external public relations, they blend words, sounds, and images to express how a community defines itself and, more importantly, how it wants to be perceived by outsiders. A well-crafted website is descriptive, offering a public account of what a community was (its past) and is (its present). It can also be aspirational: a creative imagining of what a group hopes to become (its wished-for future). Weaving together a narrative of both continuity and change, the Inayati Order's refurbished website—intertwined with its flourishing social media outlets—combine both these elements. They communicate a story of twenty-first-century Inayati identity that honors Inayat Khan's perennialist and universalist teachings, preserves the community's historical connection to a South Asian Sufi past, and embraces the contemporary American cultural milieu. An exegesis of these digital documents reveals a great deal about the contemporary Inayati Order's articulation of its own history, its understanding of Sufi identity and authority, and the trajectory of its evolving and expanding institutional structure. In combination with its new name and revitalized administrative structure, Inayati digital media provide a useful barometer of the organization's overarching rebranding efforts. With these themes as a backdrop, chapter 5 explores another key dimension of Inayati digital media: ritual practices and teaching networks.

5

Virtual Practice: Inayati Rituals
and Teaching Networks

Sufis, like all religious seekers, are spiritually impatient. Amid the distractions of everyday life, they pursue a deeper awareness of their own true selves and a more direct and immediate relationship with God. Sufi disciples learn by listening, observing, conversing, questioning, and reading. But ultimately, words and books only go so far. In the end, Sufis insist, spiritual awareness, insight, and wisdom must be cultivated and earned through discipline, sacrifice, and hard work. Going beyond the boundaries of discursive learning and the limits of rational knowledge (*'ilm*), Sufis lay claim to an alternative episteme. As a coherent, practical system for achieving experiential knowledge (*ma'rifa*), the Sufi path (*tariqa*) is mediated through the intimate relationship between a spiritual master and his/her devotees and experienced through ritual performances. In the twenty-first century, however, the new virtual spaces of digital Sufism alter the logic and logistics of these traditional pedagogical dynamics, prompting an unprecedented question: can (or should) Sufi rituals be replicated online? Tracking the symbiosis between online and offline experience, this chapter examines how the Inayati Order leverages digital media to augment ritual practices, bolster its teaching networks, and supplement the spiritual training of its devotees.

CYBER RITUALS

The centrality of ritual practice is clearly reflected throughout the Inayati Order's new website. And here again, the founder's lasting imprint is palpable. As with its foundational teachings, Inayati rituals are hybrid in nature—drawing on the rich vein of Islamic piety and South Asian Sufi traditions, but couched in Inayat Khan's perennialist philosophy, universalist language, and cross-cultural, cross-creedal message. To put it another way, while the content of Inayati doctrine and the form of its practices are unique, much of the underlying source code is Islamic and Sufi (and, in particular, Chishti).

Although Pir Zia publicly self-identifies as Muslim, the community he leads is comprised mostly of non-Muslims. In keeping with the precedent established by his grandfather, prescribed Islamic rituals such as the five daily prayers (*salat*) and fasting during the month of Ramadan (*sawm*) are not a central part of the Inayati Order's spiritual curriculum. Even so, the contemporary community maintains many of the central doctrines and ritual features of a traditional Islamic Sufi order: the master–disciple relationship, a spiritual genealogy rooted in Indo-Muslim history, and a host of distinctly Sufi spiritual exercises. In particular, the Inayati ritual repertoire foregrounds the Chishti practices of meditative *zikr* (the 'remembrance' of God), the formulaic recitation of *wazifas* (prescribed 'mantras' such as the Ninety-Nine Names of God), pilgrimage to the tombs of Sufi saints (*ziyarat*), and musical assemblies featuring Sufi poetry (*sama*).[1]

Universal Worship—one of the original Five Activities initiated by Inayat Khan, originally known as the 'Church of the All'—is the community's most distinctive ritual innovation. As its name suggests, this core Inayati practice is quintessentially universalist. According to the Inayati website, Universal Worship is the order's foundational "inter-religious activity," a universalist "church" designed to promote "harmony between the world's major religious traditions. In this service, ordained facilitators (*cherags*) light candles symbolically representing the world's religious traditions and read from their sacred texts, often introducing participants to an experience of the teachings, music, or chants of these traditions."[2] A link directs the reader to a separate web page with numerous resources that detail the history, meaning, and logistics of the performance. "The Universal Worship," the site explains, "exists to gather together followers of different religions in the understanding of the one truth behind them, so that they may hold in respect all the teachers of humanity who have given their lives in the service of truth."[3] In an accompanying forty-five-minute YouTube video—broadcast live on February 3, 2013 during the celebration of World Interfaith Harmony Week—Shahabuddin David Less, a prominent Inayati teacher and the First Vice President for Universal Worship, explains the symbolism of the altar and the deeper meanings behind this hybrid, interfaith ritual before leading the assembled congregation through the entire ecumenical service. A separate link provides text and audio files for each of the four cycles of prayers that form the central liturgy of Universal Worship.[4]

By watching this video while reciting the prayers, web surfers anywhere in the world can participate in this ritual experience online. Intriguingly, however, the Inayati website says nothing about the efficacy of such virtual ritual performance. Are spiritual blessings (*baraka*) digitized and transmitted to someone watching, listening, and participating via a computer in the privacy of their own home? Or is such second-hand experience nothing more than passive distance learning or cyber voyeurism? The website does not say. There are no online discussions of these questions, no disclaimers, and no flashing 'don't try this at home' warnings to be found. Even so, I would suggest that an answer can be found by reading between the lines.

A link, "The Activities of the Universal Worship," for example, asserts that each Inayati *cherag* ('lamp') is an "ordained minister" with years of formal training and hands-on experience. Authorized and empowered by these credentials, a *cherag* "holds religious services, performs marriages, officiates at funerals, gives spiritual assistance to those in need, performs charitable and social service work, holds programs of spiritual education and training, provides spiritual direction and guidance, and upholds the principles and ideals of the Universal Worship."[5] Another link, "Code of Conduct," outlines the "moral, ethical and legal standards of behavior" for Inayati *cherags*, emphasizing that "in providing spiritual direction or guidance, Cherags must recognize the limits of their competence and practice and refer individuals to other professionals when appropriate."[6] For the curious reader, there is also a search engine, "Find a *Cherag* Near You," which identifies the nearest teacher according to address, zip code, or country.[7] Together, these digital resources reaffirm the institutional power and authority of the Inayati Order. In doing so, they also imply that in the absence of a direct connection with a qualified teacher—and outside

the circle of the living offline community—any solitary online ritual will
be insufficient at best.

Inayat Khan's enduring legacy is also evident in several links located on
the website's main page under the rubric "Teachings." "Prayers," for example, outlines the cycles of litanies composed by Inayat Khan that form the
backbone of daily ritual life. While these combinations of morning, midday,
and evening prayers echo the logic and mechanics of Islamic worship, they
replace the formal Qur'anic language and prescribed bodily postures of
formal Muslim prayers (*salat*) with words and techniques rooted in Inayat
Khan's universalist philosophy.[8] The website includes additional prayers
for healing, meal times, peace, and protection. An accompanying glossary
provides translations for a number of key terms, including several words that
are firmly rooted in Islamic and Sufi epistemology: *hazrat* ('noble presence'),
murshid ('teacher' or 'guide'), *pir* ('an elder spiritual guide'), *nabi* ('prophet')
and *rasul* ('messenger').

In effect, these digital materials serve as a springboard to practice, with
brief descriptions designed to help guide online participation. According
to the website:

> These prayers can be said silently or aloud, but are considered more
> effective when said aloud, as the sound-vibration of the prayers pen-
> etrates the energy centers of the body and reaches the inner planes of
> our being. Although all the prayers are honored and recited by Inayati
> Sufis, *Saum* [a morning prayer] and *Salat* [a midday prayer] are given
> special emphasis. It is said that it is more important to recite these
> two prayers daily than any of the others. Likewise, these two prayers
> can be recited with accompanying movements suggested by Hazrat
> Inayat Khan.[9]

The language here—both what is said and left unsaid—is significant. Reflecting
Inayat Khan's own training in the Chishti Order, the description of "sound-
vibration" and "energy centers of the body" echoes traditional Chishti
teachings on *zikr* and *lata'if* (the 'subtle centers' of the spiritual body).[10]
Significantly, however, the "accompanying movements" for prayer taught
by Inayat Khan are invoked but never explained on the website. The digital
text provides no accompanying photographs or videos to show the reader

the requisite gestures and proper bodily postures for Inayati prayer. Without having to say so, therefore, the website reinforces the need for personal, face-to-face instruction with a living teacher.

In similar fashion, "Purification" provides a brief overview and a cursory 'how-to' guide for Inayati meditation practices.[11] Once again, the psychophysical techniques of traditional Chishti *zikr* are colored and coded with Inayat Khan's universalism. The web page describes a series of specific breathing exercises designed to deepen awareness. According to the digital text, "As essential as Prayer is Purification. In fact, the word Sufism *(tasawwuf)* means 'purification.' If you are new to the Sufi path, these two practices are a good place to begin. Each morning, before meditation, we recommend washing your hands and face, saying the Morning Prayers, and then doing the following breath practice as an act of purification." The online instructions encourage the reader to perform the following exercises every morning, preferably outdoors or in front of an open window:

> Stand upright in a comfortable position, feet slightly apart, hands at your side, palms forward.
>
> **Earth Breath:** In the nose, out the nose (5x), visualizing the color gold.
>
> **Water Breath:** In the nose, out the mouth (5x), visualizing the color green.
>
> **Fire Breath:** In the mouth, out the nose (5x), visualizing the color red.
>
> **Air Breath:** In the mouth, out the mouth (5x), visualizing the color blue.
>
> **Ether Breath:** In the nose, out the nose, very refined (5x), visualizing the color grey, or imaging transparency.
>
> If you wish to add another dimension to the practice, you may silently say *Ya Shafee* (the Healer) on the in-breath, and *Ya Kafee* (the Remedy) on the out-breath.

This language is revealing. The suggested Arabic 'mantras' (*Ya Shafee, Ya Kafee*) point to the Islamic roots of Inayat Khan's techniques, and the pairing of concentrated, breathing meditation with the visualization of particular colors mirrors established Chishti meditation practices. Significantly, the text concludes with an important qualification that emphasizes the limits of individual, 'at home' practice, reminding the reader that "additional instruction, if desired, can be given by one of the Spiritual Guides within the Inayati Order."[12]

All these examples illustrate both the possibilities and limitations of Inayati ritual practice in cyberspace. Throughout the new website, select rituals are described but never fully explained. The absence of interactive features such as instructional videos, live-streaming performances, open chat rooms, or 'help lines' ultimately leaves the curious cyber seeker with more questions than answers regarding the explicit details of ritual etiquette and propriety. I would argue that this is no accident. Although the website offers a 'taste' (in Sufi parlance, *dhawq*) of key ceremonies and rites, it never reveals the full panoply of Inayati rituals. It is apparent that for today's Inayati Order there is no virtual equivalent for the intimacy and intensity of the master–disciple relationship, the face-to-face interactions with the living Sufi community, and the sensorial, embodied experience of ritual performance. There are tantalizing signs, however, that this too may soon change.

In January 2014, the Hurkalya Sufi Center in San Rafael, California launched an innovative teaching program called New Rain. Led by Pir Zia's mother, Taj Inayat, and a well-known and experienced Inayati teacher, Gayan Macher, New Rain offers an array of digital resources and a series of annual on-site retreats open to initiates from any of the lineages linked to Hazrat Inayat Khan. Most intriguingly, in October 2017 the group introduced a series of webinars and a digital subscription expressly focused on ritual practice. For a monthly fee, participants gain entry to New Rain Online: a virtual community that offers a live class one Saturday every month; weekly emails with inspirational and instructive "practice tips"; the option of forming "Practice Partner groups" with other participants; the ability to pose personal questions to Inayati teachers; and access to a private Facebook group, as well as archived recordings. According to the program's website:

> Even if you meet regularly with a guide, the spiritual path can be a lonely pursuit. New Rain Online fills the spaces between disparate spiritual events. It's a place where you can freely explore everyday doubts and difficulties that arise in your individual practice. And you'll find companions here, too: in addition to the support of Taj

and Gayan, two highly experienced guides, you'll also join a dedicated group of seekers. Within this safe and supportive community, you can share new insights, ask questions, and receive continual inspiration for your spiritual practice.[13]

If this groundbreaking experiment in personalized, virtual ritual training proves effective, it is possible that the Inayati Order will be tempted to follow suit by refining and expanding the ritual dimensions of its own digital media productions. At the present moment, however, Inayati ritual practice remains carefully circumscribed in cyberspace. In this sense, the order's official website is best understood as a signpost, a window, and an *invitation to practice*. Ultimately, a cyber surfer drawn to the Inayati path must circle back to the community's 'real world,' analog networks to fully engage the sensual, affective, and transformative power of Sufi rituals—and the visceral, tactile, three-dimensional experience of sacred space. To this end, the Inayati website provides multiple avenues that strategically redirect cyber surfers back to the living Sufi *tariqa* offline.

TEACHING NETWORKS

For more than forty years, Inayati ritual practices and teaching networks in the United States centered on the Abode of the Message. Located on an idyllic 400-acre forested property in the Berkshire-Taconic mountains near New Lebanon, New York, the Abode did double duty as both a residential Sufi community and an administrative center. Originally established by Pir Vilayat Inayat Khan in 1975, from 2003 it served as the headquarters of the Inayati Order's North American Secretariat, the main campus of Suluk Academy, and the location of the Sufi Retreat Center which hosted a wide variety of annual programs. Formerly part of the Mount Lebanon Shaker Village, the property maintains many of the original mid-eighteenth-century buildings, along with a large organic farm, expansive gardens, hermitage huts, campgrounds, hiking trails, and a pond.[14] In 2016, twenty-four adults and six children lived full-time at the Abode—though the community's numbers expanded with temporary staff and students during annual retreats, especially during the busy summer months. Pir Zia, his wife, and two children resided on the site for many years in a house known as Inayati Manzil (now referred to as the Pir Vilayat Center). In significant ways, the Abode mirrored the dynamics of a traditional Chishti Sufi lodge (*khanqah*), providing living quarters for a Sufi master and select devotees, a gathering place for the broader community, and a space for ritual practices. In a message posted to the order's website on September 20, 2015, Pir Zia voiced his immense affection for this spiritual oasis, saying, "I am a founding member of the Abode of the Message. I was four years old when the Abode was founded and I grew up here as a child. When I married and had my own family, with my father's encouragement I returned to the Abode. We have lived here for the last fifteen years. I cannot put into words the reverence I have for this land or the warm feeling I have for the many friends who have lived in, or passed through, this enchanted garden."[15]

Yet here again change is the order of the day. On September 30, 2016, Executive Director Jennifer Alia Wittman posted an announcement to the order's new website, declaring that after years of careful research and planning, the official North American headquarters of the Inayati Order would be moving to Richmond, Virginia, in the summer of 2017. "We looked at many cities—Boston, Philadelphia, Washington, D.C., Baltimore, Atlanta, Charlotte, Nashville, Louisville, Chicago and Austin," Wittman explained. "Along the way, we learned and decided that we'd rather be in a smaller, mid-sized city than a metropolis, that culture and diversity are important to us, as is cost-of-living. We also wanted to find a city with a sense of *cultural emergence* and *possibility*, on the brink of becoming something greater. We believe Richmond is this city."[16]

Despite its deeply troubled racial history—Richmond was a major hub in the Atlantic slave trade and the capital of the Confederacy during the Civil War—the Inayati leadership senses a new spirit in the city's changing landscape. With its larger and more diverse population, growing cosmopolitan culture, and close proximity to Washington, D.C. and other nearby urban centers, Richmond provides a more expansive platform for the order's myriad activities and a more suitable environment for its own institutional revitalization. According to the Organization Blog, the new headquarters will serve as a "hub for organizing webcasts, programs, print and digital media; supporting students, teachers, guides and center leaders; as well as managing Pir Zia's teaching and writing schedule."[17] In time, the work of the Six Activities will be fully integrated into the new headquarters' responsibilities as well.[18] Since the completion of the move, the Inayati Order no longer directly manages or maintains offices at the Abode of the Message. Even so, the New Lebanon site continues to serve as both an "Eco-Sufi" spiritual community dedicated to the teachings of Inayat Khan and a retreat center for some of the order's programs. Over the Labor Day weekend in 2018, for example, Pir Zia hosted a three-day immersive workshop at the Abode entitled "The Alchemy of Happiness."[19]

On May 11, 2017, dual postings on the Inayati website and its Facebook page announced the purchase of a Richmond property. Renamed the Astana ('Threshold'), this historic three-story brick building and carriage house—originally built in 1856—is located near the campus of Virginia Commonwealth University and the city's lively downtown area. The sprawling site includes a reception area, an archive and library, a meeting and meditation space, an audio and video studio, executive offices, a full kitchen, two kitchenettes, bathrooms, laundry facilities, and an outdoor patio. In a message posted to the website Pir Zia explained his vision for the new site: "Our intention is that it [the Astana] be the beating heart of our order; a magnetic and energetic center; its outer physicality reflecting our inner quest for harmony. Our hope is to fill it with an atmosphere of hospitality, with music, visiting scholars, a shared commitment to matters of the heart, and abiding *adab* [etiquette]."[20] To keep pace with these ambitious plans, the order has expanded the Richmond staff to include five full-time, salaried positions: Executive Director, Executive Assistant and Operations Manager, Administrative Assistant, Musical Director, and Digital Media Manager.[21]

On July 6, 2017, Pir Zia posted a Facebook message to announce his family's arrival in Richmond. "I would like to invite you all to come and visit in the autumn, or some time thereafter," he exclaimed. "When all is ready, a regular meeting schedule will be posted. A new chapter is beginning, and the writing of it is for all of us together, by the grace of God—at the Abode, in Richmond, and wherever we gather to study, pray, meditate, remember, and serve in the path of Love, Harmony, and Beauty. I hope to see you soon."[22] Although he now lives with his family in a nearby private residence, Pir Zia teaches a weekly class (on Sunday afternoons), leads a weekly meditation and *zikr* session (on Wednesday evenings), and hosts frequent events at the Astana when his busy travel schedule allows.

A new website link provides an updated Google calendar for all the Astana's myriad activities, as well as logistical advice for visitors.[23] By design, the location of the new Richmond hub provides close proximity to domestic and international travel, allowing Pir Zia easier access to the Inayati Order's expanding global networks. In a website post he outlined his long-term strategic thinking about the order's future:

> I believe that we are now on the threshold of a new phase in the work of the Sufi Order . . . In this next decade of my service to the Sufi Message, in order for me to be more present to the bustling, diverse world of interaction between people of many walks of life . . . it is my determination that I should, with my family, move to a metropolitan environment and establish the headquarters [of the order] in that new setting, joined by all who wish to live and serve in such a setting. I envision a flourishing metropolitan center serving as a clear focal point from which the Sufi Order can effectively radiate its work throughout North America and the world.[24]

In concert with the order's new name, refurbished website, and expanding social media profile, this spatial reorientation represents the final piece of a carefully crafted and coordinated campaign to propel the Inayati Order into the twenty-first century under Pir Zia's leadership.

The contemporary Inayati Order is a "global movement" that claims a membership of fourteen thousand devotees in thirty-six countries.[25] In order to serve this transnational and cross-cultural community, an expansive network of worldwide teaching centers radiates outward from the new central headquarters in Richmond. The flagship website now includes a link, "Inayati Order Centers World Map," with a Google satellite map that tags with a red icon each of the teaching centers in the United States, Canada, Europe, Turkey, Pakistan, Australia, and New Zealand.[26] Reminiscent of restaurant apps or hotel-chain advertisements, the site allows readers to zoom in and out, creating an elastic visual image of the Inayati Order's territorial reach and global aspirations. As Hermansen notes, such interactive features are increasingly common in American Sufi orders with "more elaborate and professionally designed web pages" that "tend to have stronger commercial interests and objectives."[27] A separate link, "Local Centers," provides an alphabetized list of seventy-three active Inayati teaching centers in North

America—in twenty-nine US states plus the District of Columbia, as well as five Canadian cities—along with the names of local contacts, email addresses and, in several cases, separate web pages.[28]

As we have seen, over the years a wide spectrum of individuals and groups across the globe have claimed the mantle of Inayat Khan's legacy. These centrifugal forces have resulted in a vacuum—and, at times, openly contentious disputes—that the Inayati Order seems determined to repair under Pir Zia's leadership. As part of its comprehensive institutional restructuring, the community is moving to centralize and formalize its teaching networks. According to the 2015 report, "Over the years, as an organization, we have proliferated into many parts—Centers, Regions, Nations, and Activities—for the most part working separately to encourage the study, practice, and realization of Hazrat Inayat Khan's teaching in the world. We are now actively and deliberately working to unify all of these parts, initiating and participating in many conversations exploring how to co-create a clearly unified, coordinated, and navigable organization."[29] In the interest of unity, the Inayati Order aims to formalize a series of concentric circles of authority that extend outward from the singular presence of Pir Zia—a matrix of global teaching networks, augmented by technological innovations designed to connect the growing ranks of Inayati devotees.

At present, most of the Inayati Order's teaching centers operate out of the home of individual teachers and vary widely in the scope and scale of their activities. As the 2015 report illustrates, this loose, informal organizational structure is now being rethought and reconstituted:

> Over the next year, together with Center Leaders, we hope to develop a plan to refine the Center model, creating a unified public face with consistent and high-quality offerings from Boston to Tucson, and from Vancouver to Richmond! Of course, we recognize that many people do not belong to a Center, either by choice or because there is no local group nearby. Recognizing this, we are developing a plan for meeting people where they are, through more regional events and a greater emphasis on online programming and video-based guidance through Skype, Zoom or other video-conferencing technologies.[30]

This statement reveals a conscious attempt to create a seamless, symbiotic integration between the order's offline and online worlds. In accommodating to the changes and challenges of the Internet Age, today's Inayati Order strategically deploys digital media to shrink the barriers of geographic and cultural distance, draw new audiences into its orbit, and bridge the gaps in its administrative and institutional infrastructure.

While every Sufi order requires gathering places for its ritual activities and physical spaces for the experience and expression of its communal identity, Sufi pedagogy ultimately centers on the presence of a living teacher. A sick patient does not diagnose her own disease, prescribe her own medicine, or operate on herself; in the interest of her own health, she goes to a hospital and follows the advice of a trained, knowledgeable doctor. In the same way, each Sufi novice requires the hands-on advice, care, and spiritual insight of an expert 'physician of the heart': the Sufi master. For today's Inayati community, Pir Zia serves as the order's designated teaching *shaykh*, its principle ritual specialist, and the living embodiment of its Sufi heritage. Wherever he is located (at the Astana or on the road, at home, or abroad) his physical presence and personal example (his words, gestures, actions) provide a touchstone for historical continuity, ethical behavior (*adab*), and spiritual piety. While Inayati authority begins with Pir Zia, however, it does not end with him. In everyday practice, an expansive, interconnected pedagogical network assists him in carrying out the demanding duties of spiritual mentorship. With Pir Zia as the hub of the wheel, Inayati leadership comprises a worldwide circle of Sufi teachers and guides, assisted by administrative staff who supervise regional centers and coordinate local events.

A website link, "Teachers and Guides," provides a clear summary of the order's teaching philosophy and pedagogical system. It is an important statement that merits careful attention:

> Initiates of the Inayati Order are asked to find a guide within the Order to work with them as they explore the Sufi path. A guide in the Inayati Order is a person with deep experience and grounding in the Universalist Sufism taught by Hazrat Inayat Khan.
>
> The goal of training in Sufism is to become fully human, not to transcend one's humanity. Thus, a guide in the Inayati Order is not conceived of as an enlightened or perfected being, but simply as a more experienced spiritual friend and companion on the path, providing inspiration and guidance. The guide does not give directives or

attempt to substitute their own will and conscience for those of the seeker, but instead helps the seeker to gain confidence and develop their own will and conscience. In this, Inayati Order teachers are bound by clear ethical standards and guidelines.

Inayati Order Spiritual Guides and Teachers may be found through-out North America and beyond. Some are teachers who regularly travel to various locations, while others head local Inayati Order centers or lead personal retreats. Almost all meet regularly with the people they guide, whether in person or through the use of a common technological medium (Skype, Facetime, etc.). Finding a guide to suit your needs is a personal matter around which one should both seek advice and consult one's own heart.

It should be noted that not all Inayati Order teachers function as guides for *mureeds*, nor do all guides consider themselves teachers.[31]

As this passage confirms, Sufi knowledge is ultimately mediated only through direct experience. The Inayati spiritual 'journey' (*suluk*) demands immense dedication, discipline, sacrifice, and personal responsibility on the part of each individual seeker. Even so, nobody travels the path alone. Companionship and community are essential. Reflecting on the evolution of religious move-ments in the United States, Pir Zia points to the emergence of an array of high-profile spiritual teachers during the 1960s and 1970s. Since that time, he asserts, "the prominence of the *gurus* or spiritual masters is lessened in the sense that there is a greater emphasis on personal responsibility and the collective creation of a culture. I think that is a very healthy development."[32] In the Inayati system, the spiritual guide (*murshid* or *murshida*) does not carry the disciple up the mountain. Instead, as a "friend and companion on the path," the appointed mentor draws on his/her own wellspring of experience in order to orient, encourage, and inspire each disciple along the path towards self-realization. There is no single model for Inayati pedagogy. Different seek-ers have unique personalities, proclivities, and needs, and spiritual mentors too possess diverse skill sets, techniques, experiences, and teaching styles. By design, the Inayati master–disciple relationship is cultivated through inti-mate, direct, face-to-face interactions—now augmented through the use of digital technologies (Skype, Facetime) and the community's internal digital networks (websites, Facebook, YouTube).

Pir Zia with Aziza Scott (https://inayatiorder.org/about/teachers-guides/)

A photograph on the link "Teachers and Guides" displays Pir Zia seated in front of a microphone, leading a prayer. To his right is Aziza Scott, one of the order's most prominent American teachers, who has worked closely with both Pir Vilayat Inayat Khan and Pir Zia for more than thirty years as a spiritual guide, retreat leader, and trainer for Inayati teachers.[33] This resonant image affirms the vital importance of personal spiritual guidance in Inayati pedagogy. By pairing Pir Zia with a female counterpart, it also signals the central importance of women in Inayati history, teachings, and everyday practice. "Among the universalist Sufi movements, female participation and leadership began early and reaches high levels," Hermansen notes in a study of South Asian Sufi movements in America. "In these groups restrictions on women in matters such as dress codes are often seen as cultural and outmoded. What does remain is a sense of the 'feminine' as a distinct category that needs to be appreciated and, to an extent, nurtured and protected in an extroverted Western culture that is by nature dismissive of it."[34] Within today's Inayati community, numerous women serve in key public roles as disciples, administrators, teachers, and authorized guides (*murshidas*). Their presence and status are reflected in images throughout the revamped website.

Significantly, Pir Zia views the vital role of women within the Inayati community as the inheritance of his grandfather's legacy. In his words,

"Yes women can be [teachers] and they are. It goes back to the time when my grandfather, Murshid [Inayat Khan], coming from India to the Western world, recognized the emergence of women in public roles and saw the great promise of this emergence. He said, 'I see as clearly as daylight that the day is coming when women will lead humanity to its further evolution.'"[35] This attitude continues to shape contemporary Inayati teachings and practices. In December 2017, for example, several disciples debated the status of women in the Inayati community on the organization's Facebook page. In a remarkable moment, Pir Zia added his own thoughts to this online conversation:

> Since its founding in 1917 the Inayati Order has maintained a policy whereby gender is not a consideration with respect to appointment in any role. In Murshid's [Inayat Khan's] lifetime, the four senior-most teachers and initiators working alongside the founder were women. When Murshid told Khwaja Hasan Nizami in India that he had appointed four women *khalifas* [spiritual successors], the latter was at first surprised, and then decided himself to follow suit. Noor-un-Nisa is named "the first saint of the Order" in *Toward the One*. While I happen to be a man, my position as Pir of the Order is by no means restricted to men. Historical sacred traditions are of course embedded in the social forms of their time, and new social environments and possibilities create opportunities for traditions to evolve in their ways of working. In my view, our Order's egalitarian policies represent just such a step, a very important step. Though as a man I cannot know all that women experience, I believe in the vital importance of gender justice, and am committed to working to ensure that it is present in our community.[36]

In this important message, Pir Zia describes his own firm commitment to gender inclusion as the outgrowth of historical precedent. Inayat Khan's attitudes and actions towards women, he asserts, represented a conscious (and controversial) break with the dictates of Indo-Muslim culture and Chishti Sufi tradition, both of which proscribed public roles for women's authority. His grandfather's bold innovations, Pir Zia notes, were subsequently adopted (and thereby authenticated) by the towering figure of Khwaja Hasan Nizami (1878–1955), a renowned twentieth-century Chishti-Nizami reformer.[37]

And his father, Vilayat Inayat Khan, went a step further to name his sister, Noor-un-Nisa Inayat Khan, as a saint in her own right in his book, *Toward the One*—a status now confirmed in the order's official genealogy. Given this history, Pir Zia proclaims, the prominence of women is a distinguishing feature of the Inayati Order that will continue to shape its future trajectory.[38]

Yet even as it celebrates its progressive legacy, the contemporary Inayati Order openly acknowledges that equality and diversity remain an unfinished project. The website outlines concrete plans to diversify its membership through an overhaul of its leadership training, working groups, and public programming. A separate web page, "Diversity Statement," makes this intent explicit:

> We commit to developing diversity of participation in our activities and work among all people, recognizing that the wide variety of personal experiences, values, and worldviews that arise from differences of culture and circumstance make us stronger as an organization and more reflective of humanity as a whole. Such differences include, but are not limited to: differences in ethnicity, gender and gender identity, age, national origin, disability, sexual orientation, education, socio-economic status and religion; cognitive diversity; and cultural diversity. We seek to develop an inclusive approach in all the activities and work of the Inayati Order through active outreach, communication and understanding.
>
> To accomplish this, we recognize the necessity of increasing awareness of and working to remove barriers that exist on individual, group and societal levels, and which have historically led to marginalization and exclusion. We commit to the growth of understanding and awareness, so that we may know, understand and serve the whole of humanity better, rising above distinctions and differences which divide us and offering harmony, understanding, inspiration and healing to all who wish to receive it.[39]

With its long-standing tradition of gender inclusion as a guidepost, today's Inayati community pledges to continue working to promote a broader range of ethnic, racial, and class diversity among both its leadership and followers. Under Pir Zia's guidance, homogeneity is seen as a contradiction of Inayat

Khan's universalist vision and an impediment to the order's twenty-first-century global aspirations.

Amid its overarching push towards centralization and standardization, the Inayati Order is establishing new criteria for the next generation of spiritual mentors. "As we lay our infrastructure across the United States and Canada, we will need to increase our overall Inayati leadership capacity," exclaimed Executive Director Jennifer Alia Wittman in a web post. "Region by region, we will need to access and better highlight our strengths, and also look for ways to deepen and grow our offerings, developing new guides and teachers, and increasing our regional public profile."[40] At present, Inayati leadership training is provided under the direct supervision of a senior representative of the order. This happens through a combination of individual instruction, group retreats, and annual programs that explore specific themes. An expansive new website, "Leadership Training," provides voluminous information for advanced Inayati disciples who wish to transition into formal leadership roles.[41]

In the spring of 2017, a series of Inayati leadership retreats took place at the Abode of the Message. From March 28 to March 30, the Jamiat Khas—a select group of the order's most experienced spiritual teachers and advanced guides—held its annual spring gathering. This was followed by a three-day program aimed at a broader audience: Inayati Leadership Training. Azar Baksh Weiner, the head of the Inayati Esoteric Training Committee, explained the itinerary in an invitation on the website. In his words:

> Please join us for these inspiring sessions with Sarafil Bawa [Pir Zia] and other senior teachers in our Order. There is a great power created by our being together, doing practices and meditating together. During this leaders' training, Bawa will present all three mornings on practices specifically drawn from the new representatives training forms. This will include sharing many practices together, particularly those that may not be familiar to many representatives.

> Some of the topics covered in the afternoons will explore the growth and the evolution of the Order, such as the two types of initiation and six aspects of the Order, outreach and diversity, center development, the Message Council, emerging leaders, senior teachers, Inayati Order board, relocation of Inayati Order Headquarters, and the future. The

afternoons of the training will also have an emphasis on the guide/mureed relationship, training, and spiritual guidance.

The Inayati Order Leadership Spring Training is open to all leaders of the 'Six Activities,' including Coordinators (and those in training), Representatives, Retreat Guides, Cherag/Cheragas, Healing Conductors, Ziraat Farmers, and leaders within the Knighthood and Kinship concentrations.[42]

This digital message illuminates the Inayati Order's sophisticated administrative architecture. Its pyramidal, hierarchical authority structure and myriad interlinked programs are reflected in the various leadership positions and their relative titles. The online registration, fees for tuition, room and board, and logistical complexity demonstrate a high level of organizational acumen. The curriculum itself looks backward and forward simultaneously. Combining practical discussions and administrative updates with fellowship and ritual practices, the training program is designed to cement the continuity of Inayati identity while, at the same time, empowering a new generation of leaders to respond to the realities of changing times in new contexts. Most remarkably, the entire 2017 spring retreat was recorded, and for many months after the event an audio file of the proceedings was available for purchase by current Inayati leaders on the website's "Digital Media" link. In March 2018, the annual Jamiat Khas and Inayati Leadership Training retreats were held for the first time at the Astana headquarters in Richmond.[43]

Over the past several years, a Leadership Training Committee was tasked with revising the system for leadership development. To this end, the committee created a series of "training modules" focusing on key dimensions of Inayati spiritual practice, including Spiritual Guidance, Breath, Concentration, Contemplation, and Meditation. In February 2018, the order launched a pair of two-day courses focused on several themes. Each of these classes was available both "in person and online." According to the website: "Modules run all day for two days and are taught via Skype or Zoom . . . You may attend alone or share a computer with a registered friend. Open to all Inayati Order Leaders and leaders-in-training, all Inayati Order Concentrations' Leadership, Retreat Guides, and advanced *mureeds* with their guide's permission. The Federation of the Sufi Message Inayati branches' leadership or those in training are also welcome. Each weekend is full with teachings, practices, meditations, and includes dyads, sobhet [*sic*] [conversations with the teacher], questions and answers."[44] Beginning in June 2018, the community augmented these experimental digital forums with a new, two-year training course, The Inayati Order Emergent Leaders Program, that combines biannual in-person retreats with three online sessions with core faculty.[45] As each of these innovations illustrates, by aligning its online and offline teaching networks around a common curriculum and standardized operational model, the Inayati Order is moving to streamline its pedagogy while broadening its outreach and appeal.

TRAINING DISCIPLES

In the Inayati pedagogical system, the individualized instruction disciples receive from their own local spiritual mentors is augmented by participation in the community's public retreats and workshops. In effect, today's Inayati Order has replaced the logic and practice of the traditional Chishti Sufi lodge (*khanqah*)—a permanent, static space where a Sufi master lived, surrounded by disciples—with an annual cycle of revolving programs. I think of this matrix of spiritual retreats as 'serial *khanqahs*.' For these forums, disciples leave their homes and travel to a particular site, living together with other *murids* for short but intense periods of spiritual immersion under the guidance of a spiritual mentor (who is often assisted by a larger group of teachers). Because most Inayati programs require travel and charge tuition fees (for instruction, room, and board), they demand a significant investment of time, energy, and money. This system also insures that Pir Zia and other Inayati instructors are frequently on the road, constantly traveling between cities across the United States (and around the world) to meet with disciples and local audiences. This peripatetic serial *khanqah* model is in fact prevalent among many other American Sufi orders—a practical and logical response to the American cultural milieu where summer camps, corporate retreats, and 'self-improvement' workshops are now commonplace.

For Inayati disciples, the Esoteric School is the primary vehicle for spiritual education and Sufi training. One of the original Five Activities, its teachings and practices are firmly grounded in the Chishti Sufi piety that Inayat Khan originally encountered in India. Centered on the paradigmatic master–disciple relationship, the Esoteric School offers multiple platforms for the acquisition of esoteric knowledge (*ma'rifa*) through a combination of rigorous academic study and intensive ritual practice. A separate, multilayered website, "The Esoteric School," outlines its core principles, the developmental stages of the Inayati path, and the school's diverse programs. As the digital text explains:

> The classes of the Esoteric School offer profound insights of mystical masters which are to be absorbed in a meditative atmosphere. Although much written material is available for study, the primary teaching is offered heart to heart by a spiritual guide. The relationship between guide and student is a sacred bond in which trust in oneself and in one's insight and inner guidance can grow. Guides offer transformative practices that work with breath, prayer, and sacred sound to bring out the latent qualities the guide sees in the student. From time to time, the student can withdraw from life responsibilities to engage in an intensive retreat. A retreat is an opportunity to dive deep into practices that lead to transformation. While the goal of the school is to catalyze awakening in the individual, it is assumed that this outcome will lead to a life of service toward humanity and the wondrous gift of the manifested world.[46]

The Season of the Rose Summer School is a mainstay of the Esoteric School. This annual five-day summer spiritual retreat, led by Pir Zia and other core teaching faculty, offers a thematic introduction to Inayat Khan's teachings along with hands-on training in Inayati ritual practices. In the summer of 2017, it was held at the Abode of the Message as a final send-off for Pir Zia and his family before their move to Richmond. The Season of the Rose combines daily *suhbat* ('conversation') with Pir Zia, break-out sessions with other Inayati teachers, thematic meetings on the Six Activities, and a host of communal ritual performances: morning silent meditation, afternoon yoga practice, and evening *zikr* and music sessions. A parallel Kids' Camp provides a range of activities for children of ages five to twelve, including "nature connection teachings, games, Sufi practices with the elements, teaching of love, harmony and beauty, Universal Worship, medicine wheel, creative arts and crafts, storytelling, singing, dancing, drama and lots of laughter and fun."[47] All participants pay registration fees—ranging from $125 for Kids' Camp to nearly $900 for a private room package—that cover a range of housing options, along with daily vegetarian meals, tea, and snacks.

The primary training ground of the Esoteric School is the Suluk Academy. Since its establishment by Pir Zia in 2003, 420 students across the world have completed this two-year immersive program.[48] *Suluk*, meaning 'journey,' is an important, multivalent concept in classical Sufism. In theory and practice, *suluk* functions as both a noun and a verb. In a general sense, the term describes the Sufi adept's spiritual journey towards God. At the same time, *suluk* defines the process and manner of traveling, invoking the embodied rituals and rules of etiquette (*adab*) required of every 'traveler' (*salik/salika*) on the Sufi path. Since its inception, Suluk Academy has been taught in multiple locations, both in the United States and France. Until recently, a separate web page (www.sulukacademy.org/en) provided expansive details on the program's curriculum, including numerous video clips from past retreats spotlighting ritual performances, lectures, and testimonials from Inayati students and teachers. An accompanying photograph on this website's main page showed Pir Zia leading a group of disciples in meditation, signaling the Suluk Academy's emphasis on "personal transformation and a deepening of heart-centered relationships with others."[49]

In essence, Suluk Academy combines the theoretical training of a university with the experiential learning of a monastery. Echoing the logic of the traditional Sufi spiritual retreat (*khalwa* or *chilla*), the program involves forty days of on-site, face-to-face interactions over a two-year period. In the past, Suluk Academy was open only to initiates in the Inayati Order and other recognized "Hazrati Orders," and participation was vetted through a formal application process.[50] As originally envisioned, the Core Training's academic curriculum focused on the writings of Inayat Khan, as well as "the prose and poetry of the Masters, Saints, and Prophets throughout the ages and across traditions."[51] As they progressed through the formalized training, advanced initiates also received access to a series of esoteric papers on the intricacies of Sufi piety and practice composed by Inayat Khan between 1925 and 1926 and entitled (in Sanskrit) the *Gathas* (verses), *Gitas* (songs), *Sangathas* (recitals), and *Sangitas* (choruses). As part of its ongoing efforts to update, expand, and standardize these teaching materials, the Inayati Order now plans to makes these once-secret texts available to initiates in both print and digital formats.[52]

Pir Zia with Disciples at the Suluk Academy (http://www.sulukacademy.org/en)

Suluk Academy, past and present, combines lectures, conversation, and focused study with daily ritual practices. During the residential retreats, Inayati disciples—newly minted initiates, experienced practitioners, and future teachers alike—live, eat, study, and practice together in an intense and intimate environment of spiritual immersion. In between, they work on assignments (including readings, journal writing, and formal essays), engage in individual or group rituals (meditation, *zikr*, yoga), or rest. Evening programs—including communal *zikr*, *sama'* concerts, and sessions with special visiting faculty—are offered regularly throughout each retreat. Disciples also have regular opportunities for private interviews with Pir Zia and other teachers. In the past, graduation from Suluk Academy required one final step: an individual three-day Suluk Retreat. During this mini-*chilla*, the disciple remained in isolation in a location of their own choice, punctuated with occasional interactions with a designated spiritual guide. For those who completed the Core Training, the Suluk Graduate Studies program extended and deepened a *murid*'s knowledge and experience. Previous courses for advanced practitioners focused on a range of themes, including Sufism and Buddhism, the life and legacy of Inayat Khan, the teachings of Pir Vilayat Khan, the Chishtiyya Lineage, and the Wisdom of the Prophets.[53]

Over the years, Suluk Academy programs took place in three different locations: Suluk at the Abode, in New Lebanon, New York; Suluk in the West, in San Rafael, California; and Suluk Europe, in Épernon, France. For the 2018–2020 class, however, the Inayati Order initiated a new cycle of eight five-day retreats (four each year, in September, December, March, and June) at the Astana in Richmond. During each retreat, Pir Zia serves as the sole teacher, assisted by other established Inayati mentors and administrative staff. In keeping with tradition, this revised format maintains a focus on intensive study and ritual training centered on four themes. According to the updated Inayati website:

> Over the course of two years, students, called *Salik(a)*s, deeply explore the fundamentals of Hazrat Inayat Khan's school of Sufism under the rubric of Concentration, Contemplation, Meditation, and Realization. Among the topics of study are the purification of body and mind, prayer, breath, the elements, light, the inner senses, the Chivalric Rules, the God Ideal, the Divine Names, the subtle centers [*lata'if*], and the Spirit of Guidance. A direct transmission is shared through a mix of practice, lecture, *suhbat*, and *zikr*, held within a container of spiritual companionship.[54]

In this new iteration of Suluk Academy, each day typically begins with a morning group meditation session. This is followed by ninety minutes of lectures and discussion led by Pir Zia. After a shared lunch, participants break out into discrete "Mentor Groups" and "Pods" to engage in further study and devotions. According to the new website, "Mentor Groups are small groups of 10–12 people, led by a mentor, that Salik(a)s belong to throughout the course of the program. These groups are meant to provide a home base as one processes and assimilates the teachings. Pods are smaller, self-guided groups, involving 5–6 people from each Mentor Group. Pod mates support one another as spiritual friends throughout the program."[55] In the evening, disciples share a communal dinner, followed by a range of activities. Mixing tradition with new digital innovations, "there is homework between sessions including reading and writing assignments, possible Zoom calls with one's mentor group, and also a requirement to participate in a three-day, individual Suluk Retreat."[56]

Tuition for the 2018–2020 Suluk Academy is $5,400. This fee includes all teachings, mentoring during and between sessions, five community meals and refreshments throughout each session, and the logistical support necessary to run the program. In addition, *salik(a)s* are responsible for their own travel, housing, and select meals—along with extra costs for the required three-day retreat and the assigned books. Partial scholarships are available for those with financial needs. In a noticeable break from past precedent, the 2018–2020 Suluk Academy is now open "to all sincere seekers taking the steps necessary to enter and participate in a given program."[57] According to the website, Suluk Europe will offer a new two-year course beginning in 2020. Despite these modifications in format, the logic and aim of this revised program remains unchanged. As a laboratory for hands-on Sufi training, Suluk Academy translates Sufi theory into practice for a new generation of Inayati devotees.

DIGITAL EXPERIMENTS

For Inayati disciples, the annual sequence of workshops, retreats, and pro-grams—coupled with more frequent, routine interactions with a personal spiritual guide—inculcate spiritual wisdom, cultivate ritual discipline, and infuse the living present with the sacred past. Digital media now play an increasingly important support role at every level of this pedagogical process. The Inayati Order's website and social media outlets are aimed at multiple audiences, both internal and external. At the moment, however, these are *not* flat, boundary-free spaces that facilitate open dialogue and uninhibited social networking. Instead, the traffic flow on these digital spaces is largely unidirectional, with Inayati gatekeepers coordinating content and maintaining careful control over access. The order's website contains a separate "Log In" page, for example, where Inayati disciples and teachers can enter an official username and password to access 'insiders-only' materials not available to the general public.[58] Similarly, the order's public Facebook page—its most active social media account—allows only "moderator-approved posts," ensuring that the space is limited to sanctioned conversations "directly related to Inayat Khan's teaching and Inayati Order offerings."[59] Although the community has yet to unlock the full potential of digital media, there are tangible signs of a shift in attitude and approach—a slow but perceptible loosening of the institutional grip.

As we have seen, in the past several years the Inayati leadership has revi-talized its technological infrastructure, with significant investments in audio and video productions, live-streaming events, online marketing and sales, virtual classes and programs, digital archives, and social media outreach (via Facebook, Twitter, and YouTube). In a late-2016 web post, Executive Director Jennifer Alia Wittman outlined a host of ambitious plans for the order's media outlets and public relations campaigns. "The world feels—at least to me, and maybe to you—like new, unexplored territory," she exclaimed with palpable excitement. "Like you, we also want to see Murshid's [Inayat Khan's] teach-ing represented in media throughout North America. This means hiring a public relations firm to help place Pir Zia and other Inayati spokespeople in national publications, radio and television interviews, digital media, and as speakers at relevant, large-scale events. It also means ramping-up our presence online through articles, podcasts and video, and more active representation through social media."[60]

This new attitude towards innovation is equally apparent on an interper-sonal level. Inayati teachers and disciples now regularly send and receive messages on Skype, Facetime, or Facebook to facilitate conversations and deepen connections. Taking a cue from the Inayati leadership, *murids* are also discovering new pathways to interact with (and learn from) each other. In Facebook posts, for example, disciples solicit advice on both doctrine and practice. On October 22, 2016, a male *murid* posted, "I pray, meditate and do *wazifa* practice [*zikr* recitation] three times a day. I have been doing *Ya-Mumin*—The Inspirer of Faith. I can find nowhere in the 99 Beautiful Names for God [a name] that has anything to do with Love. Can anyone help me? Must I stay with the 99? Can anyone suggest something with the subject of Love?"[61] In a subsequent Facebook message, a female disciple shared some personal insights, complete with Arabic calligraphy, from her cellphone. "Pir Zia has given the *wazifa* of 'Amaan,' repeated 501 times, for those who feel called," she wrote. "Here it is in Arabic script; this will print nicely on a 4x6 photo sheet, if you feel so-inclined."[62] Another male disciple's post asked, "By intuition I do *dhikr* aloud while the moon waxes and silently in the waning days. Anyone else? Thoughts? Reflections?"—an inquiry that prompted several suggestions and words of encouragement from fellow Inayati practitioners.[63] In my view, this horizontal pedagogy—with *murids* sharing knowledge and experience with each other—adds a vital, symbiotic dimension to the Inayati system of learning that complements and extends the hierarchical, vertical pedagogy of the central master–disciple relationship.[64]

Another salient example of this growing culture of experimentation is "The Gayan: Notes From the Unstruck Music": a digital application developed by Inayati disciples that is available for free download on Apple and Android devices. On May 23, 2017, a spokesman for the group posted an announcement on the order's Facebook page: "Hello everyone, we have just finished the Gayan app finally. It is a volunteer effort by a few mureeds. Please visit www.gayanapp.org to download for iPhone or Android. All proceeds go to further app improvements. We would love to have your feedback on whether you find the app helpful, and how we can make it better for you. Thank you!"[65] The Gayan app provides full translations of *Gayan*, *Vadan*, and *Nirtan*: collections of the sayings, poems, and prayers composed by Hazrat Inayat Khan. By asking a question and pushing the orange button on the home page, the reader is taken to a random passage from the texts which provides an answer. As the corresponding website explains, "Based on the ancient art of bibliomancy, the Gayan app works by setting aside linear thinking and searching for inspiration, clues and signs and by randomly opening a page from a sacred book."[66] In my mind, this creative digital application signals intriguing possibilities for the Inayati Order's digital future.

All of these examples, I suggest, point to an emerging pattern. With each passing month, the Inayati Order's technological infrastructure morphs and grows. Combining their collective talents, ingenuity, and creativity, Inayati administrators, teachers, and disciples are experimenting with alternative digital media outlets in an organic process of trial and error, pushing the technological boundaries to discover new modes of expression and experience. Although these efforts remain embryonic and uncoordinated at the moment, I predict that it will be impossible to put this genie back in the proverbial bottle. By creating symbiotic spaces for dialogue, interaction, and feedback (as well as pushback), the seamless integration of immersive and interactive digital media interfaces has the potential to turbocharge the Inayati community's ability to communicate and connect, to advertise and collaborate, to cement internal networks and reach out to new audiences. In the end, the benefits of cyber technologies will likely trump any lingering anxiety and doubts about their permissibility or utility.

CONCLUSION

For all the sweeping changes and sheer novelty of cyberspace, digital religion remains firmly grounded in the lived realities of everyday life—a virtual reflection of the material, terrestrial world of flesh-and-blood human beings. To what extent can religious rituals—so firmly rooted in the physical body, the senses, and emotions—be replicated online? While answers to that question vary, recent scholarship proves that many religious groups are in fact actively experimenting with numerous cyber venues for ritual performance. "Online ritual is not representative of some form of extraordinary activity—rather it shows 'ordinary' religious engagement in an extraordinary environment," argues Christopher Helland. "This challenges us to explore new forms of online religious engagement, patchwork forms of religious participation, and patchwork ritual structure as very authentic and very real forms of religious activity in our wired world."[67]

Ritual is the lifeblood of Sufism. Sufis learn to tame the desiring ego (*nafs*) and cultivate a moral, ethical self through the daily discipline of embodied ritual practices. Following the example (*sunna*) of the Prophet Muhammad, Sufi pedagogy is mediated via the intimate, face-to-face interactions with a teaching *shaykh*. This 'vertical relationship' is deepened and extended through the 'horizontal relationships' within a Sufi community, with disciples learning from the experience and wisdom of their peers. As this chapter has demonstrated, digital media increasingly play a vital role in the Inayati Order's pedagogical networks. Erasing the barriers of physical distance, the organization's flagship website and social media outlets provide a conduit between Inayati teachers and disciples. For Inayati leaders, cyberspace provides an inexpensive and instantaneous way to communicate with their followers around the globe. For the current generation of tech-savvy Sufis, digital media serve as a message board, a reference library, a virtual calendar of events, and a supplementary teaching tool. Even so, Inayati online rituals remain carefully circumscribed. This is in fact quite common among American Sufi *turuq*—evidence, I suggest, of a pervasive anxiety about the loss of control and concerns about short-circuiting the logic and practice of the traditional master–disciple relationship. Recent experiments with Inayati social media, however, indicate a willingness to test the digital waters and push further into the virtual frontier. As a tangible example of the changing tide of digital religion in practice, this will be a fascinating development to track in the years ahead.

In chapter 6, we shift our attention from the internal dynamics of Inayati pedagogy to the community's outward, public face, exploring its external networks, interfaith outreach, and expanding global reach. Today's Inayati Order forms an expansive, transnational, cross-cultural, and cross-creedal web that radiates outward around the world from its new headquarters in Richmond, Virginia. An analysis of the order's public programs and social engagement will illustrate how the Web now serves as an important bridge between the local Inayati community and the broader public sphere.

6

Bridging the Digital and Analog Worlds: Inayati Social Engagement

The primary mission of any Sufi order is the moral, ethical, and spiritual training of disciples. To that end, the lion's share of its energy, time, and resources is focused inward. Even so, no Sufi *tariqa* exists in a vacuum. In keeping with the *sunna* of the Prophet Muhammad, the Sufi path to God goes straight through the world. Even as they practice private piety, American Sufis remain enmeshed in the minutiae of everyday public life: they live in local neighborhoods, go to school or to work, raise families, pay bills, vote in elections, consume mass media, and interface with popular culture. As double-minority communities within America's vast spiritual marketplace, Sufi orders pay a price for insularity and isolation. This is especially true in the current political climate, where they are further marginalized and assailed by the dual forces of xenophobia and Islamophobia. In the interest of good relations with their neighbors, and in pursuit of potential allies and converts, many American Sufi communities have chosen to follow a different path: entering the public sphere, opening their doors to outsiders, and actively pursuing interfaith outreach.

This is certainly true of the contemporary Inayati Order. Balancing *din* (religion) and *dunya* (the world), today's Inayati community simultaneously promotes both individual spiritual development and external social engagement. As part of its ongoing institutional overhaul, the organization harnesses the power of digital media to amplify all its social outreach efforts—accessing new audiences, cultivating the next generation of followers, and building bridges with other religious groups in the United States (and beyond) via its public Activities, multidimensional publications, and myriad public programs.

THE PUBLIC ACTIVITIES

As a comprehensive system of knowledge and practice, Sufism engages both inward (*batin*) and outward (*zahir*) dimensions of reality: the spiritual realm and the material world; the soul, mind, and body; the individual and society; religion and politics. In the Inayati pedagogical system, ritual practice leads to self-discipline, self-awareness, and the taming of the desiring, concupiscent ego (*nafs*). Having learned to master the self, the Sufi adept then demonstrates inner wisdom through outward beautiful behavior (*adab*) and selfless action. It is no accident that four of the order's Six Activities—Kinship, the Knighthood of Purity, the Healing Order, and Ziraat—aim to inculcate an ethic of social consciousness, altruism, and activism. Each of these public Activities applies Inayat Khan's teachings to address real-world problems. And significantly, they are all open to the general public; one need not be formally initiated as an Inayati *murid* or an active member of the Esoteric School to participate in these forums.

Kinship—originally known as 'Universal Brotherhood'—was initiated by Inayat Khan to promote kindness, love, empathy, and human connection through philanthropic work. According to the official web page:

> The Kinship Activity is one of six concentrations within the Inayati Sufi Order. This concentration is a form of community service open to all. Kinship cultivates the natural connection from one heart to another, fostering harmony, goodwill, and caring action. Kinship nurtures the flowering of the individual and carries it outward through friendship, collaboration and service. Kinship inspires people to work together to help those in need, to protect and restore the web of life on Earth, and to create a more beautiful world. Kinship awakens the conscience, and builds the spiritual maturity needed to address the planetary crises we face. Kinship aims to serve as a nucleus of understanding, sympathy and dedication to help unite humankind in the spirit of universal loving kinship.[1]

As this quote suggests, this key Inayati Activity centers on a series of core values: inclusiveness, respect for life, compassion, friendship, and service. Putting these virtues into practice, Kinship Circles around the United States sponsor a range of fundraising campaigns to bolster the Inayati community, spread the Inayati message, and support a host of local social welfare projects. In the past, this has included a five-kilometer running race in Austin, Texas (raising funds for Just Vision, a group working to promote peace between Israelis and Palestinians); a bike ride, Spirit Rides the Wind (with proceeds going to the distribution of a DVD chronicling the life and legacy of Inayat Khan); a barn raising at the Abode (with volunteers helping to refurbish old buildings); a Mureeds Emergency Relief Fund (providing financial assistance to ten Inayati disciples per year); a Kindness Drive (enlisting people across the country to commit to doing one act of kindness daily for forty days); and a Prison Book Project (to raise funds to donate books to prisoners).[2] Both the Kinship web page and a related Facebook group ("Sufi Kinship") provide regular updates and information for Inayati disciples and outsiders interested in participating.

The main platform for Kinship is the Hope Project. Founded by Pir Vilayat Inayat Khan in 1980, this remarkable institution provides a range of social services for impoverished Muslim families living in the Nizam ad-Din *basti*: the neighborhoods surrounding Inayat Khan's and Pir Vilayat's tombs in south New Delhi. Another multidimensional website, www.hopeprojectindia.org, outlines the Hope Project's myriad programs, which include a community health center, a nursery, a school, vocational training courses, a thrift and credit system, and a women's micro-enterprise initiative.[3] With a staff of seventy members, mostly drawn from the local community, the Hope Project is funded by private donations and the support of numerous donor agencies. The proceeds from the sale of a variety of locally produced goods and services (greeting cards, a cookbook, bakery and catering services, textiles, jewelry, and an on-site walking tour) provide additional financial support to help fund the program's various activities.[4]

The website brings all these efforts to vibrant life, with annual reports and newsletters, colorful photographs, biographical profiles of local residents, and links for online donations. Here we see evidence of a clear circular symmetry. For Inayati disciples in the United States, the Astana in Richmond now serves as the central node in an expansive matrix of teachers with Pir Zia

Home page of Hope Project India (http://www.hopeprojectindia.org/)

at its center. By accessing the Hope Project's website and donating money, American disciples are symbolically linked to the order's Indo-Muslim roots as well. And going one step further, by volunteering time at the Hope Project or by visiting the Nizam ad-Din *basti* for pilgrimage, the abstractions of Inayati genealogy and history are made real via a direct, personal encounter with Chishti sacred space and the living Sufi community in India.

The Knighthood of Purity—now distinguished as a separate (sixth) Activity in addition to the original Five Activities initiated during Inayat Khan's lifetime—is another distinctly Inayati institution that weds Sufi piety with social service. Inspired by Inayat Khan's teachings on "chivalric virtues" and mirroring the framework of a medieval guild or monastic order, this society is open to anyone who wants to "study and practice his [Inayat Khan's] philosophy and art of life, irrespective of initiatic affiliation or lack thereof."[5] Participants in the Knighthood of Purity commit to model their lives on "the Chivalric Rules": a prescribed code of moral virtues. According to the order's website:

> Hazrat Inayat Khan composed four sets of rules to cultivate a morally attuned culture and instill awareness in our inter-relationship with all beings. These belong to the tradition of spiritual chivalry (*futuwwa*), an essential part of the Sufi path. At first, the rules may seem self-evident and obvious, but if you work diligently with them, you will find that each rule opens up onto a vast field of inquiry and awareness. For this reason, some take on the rules as a disciplined practice. Starting with the first one, you say a rule out loud every day for forty days and seek to apply it in your life. Then you do the same for the next rule, until all are finished. The rules come in four sets of ten rules, forty in all, called the Iron Rules, the Copper Rules, the Silver Rules, and the Golden Rules.[6]

As a form of daily devotional practice, each rule is recited once every morning during a forty-day period. If no days are missed, the completion of all four sets of rules takes 1,600 days (four years and 140 days). Beyond memorization, however, the aim is to inculcate individual moral virtue which, over time, translates into public acts of empathy and compassion for others. A separate website provides a link to the complete set of rules—in multiple languages—as well as a detailed commentary by Pir Zia. "We are here on earth to be tested because virtues are not so real in heaven," writes Pir Zia. "It is all too easy there. Virtues become real when tested and tried, when we are challenged. And so here we are on earth that we may face limitation, opposition, and all of the trials and tribulations of this world, and uphold what is true and good and beautiful so that it may be made real. We must hold ourselves to the highest standard of accountability and to see the challenges as God's given opportunity. 'Make God a reality, and God will make you the truth.'"[7] Modeled on the spiritual teachings of the Prophet Muhammad and the central Sufi concept of beautiful behavior (*adab*), the Knighthood of Purity promotes a system of practical, everyday ethics designed to cultivate individual moral responsibility, self-sacrifice, and altruistic service.

The two other public Activities, the Healing Order and Ziraat, are also both designed to bridge the spiritual and material realms. Originally established by

Inayat Khan in 1910, the Sufi Healing Order North America offers a holistic program for human health and well-being. Under the guidance of Pir Zia, Devi Tide (the institution's *Kefayat*, or 'Head'), and a host of ordained Healing Conductors and *Shafayats* (advanced instructors), its programs provide education and training in the techniques of spiritual healing taught by Inayat Khan. For those suffering from afflictions of the body, mind, and soul, the Healing Service provides "distance healing through prayer and concentration."[8] An annual cycle of seminars, workshops, classes, and retreats offer more personalized instruction. A sophisticated, multimedia website outlines the Healing Order's core mission and diverse programs:

> The Healing Order is a network of people worldwide who are inspired to help transform illness and suffering into wholeness and greater unity–for individuals, groups and the planet. We work through prayer, circles of prayer and energy healing, and sharing how the simple beauty of healing is a gift that everyone can offer in various ways in all aspects of daily and sacred life–the spark of divine healing is in every being. The Healing Order is part of the Sufi vision of love, harmony and beauty brought by Hazrat Inayat Khan: an inclusive path, honoring all sacred traditions, and open to everyone. There are local groups and we run courses and retreats. Many activities are available remotely online and through Zoom conferencing. We join with all healers in unveiling the capacity for healing that is in the heart of humanity.

The website also provides access to a litany of prayers for healing, a digital library, a range of e-classes, and an online store selling books and manuals on Inayati healing practices. A parallel Facebook page ("Sufi Healing Order") offers a wealth of additional resources: photos, videos, an events calendar, a message board, and regular posts about the Healing Order's monthly activities. For individuals who wish to become Inayati healers themselves, a formal initiation ceremony followed by an immersive training program is required.

Ziraat, meaning 'agriculture,' applies a similar logic to the healing of the natural world. Inaugurated by Inayat Khan in 1926, this school draws on his expansive and eclectic teachings on spiritual alchemy and ecology. Putting the philosophy of 'Green Hermeticism' into action, Ziraat combines Sufi pedagogy with environmental stewardship, using "the symbols and processes of agriculture to promote an understanding of the earth's sacredness, and to describe and facilitate growth in the inner life, bridging both the material and spiritual worlds."[10] A separate website, www.ziraat.org, explains Ziraat's mystical symbology, with links to its annual retreats and workshops, suggested readings, and contact information for local chapters throughout North America. According to the digital text, "Ziraat is an initiatic school, open to all who feel a commitment to spiritual awakening and to the protection of this sacred world. It is an activity of the Inayati Order, but one need not be a member of the Inayati Order to join. Initiation in Ziraat confirms a pledge to affirm and cultivate the divine seed within our being, and thereby to help in the preservation and restoration of our world."[11] Like all the public Activities, Ziraat bridges the gap between inward piety and outward action.

For Inayati disciples, these experiential learning forums are a proving ground for faith. By practicing what they preach, *murids* cultivate empathy and compassion through public acts of altruistic service. For outsiders, participation in these Activities offers a hands-on introduction to the Inayati path—and, potentially, a pathway for deeper engagement with the order's ethical teachings, ritual practices, and community life.

PUBLIC OUTREACH AND INTERFAITH PROGRAMS

Beyond the formal Activities, the Inayati Order cultivates avenues for public outreach and social engagement in numerous other spaces and places. On the home page of the order's refurbished website a prominent link, "Events," provides an archive of past events and an evolving, updated calendar that lists upcoming Inayati programs. The page also offers access to detailed daily and monthly calendars for events at the Astana in Richmond, as well as a panoply of other programs in North America and across the world.[12] The vast majority of Inayati public programs have no barriers to access and are designed for a variety of audiences: from curious novices with no previous knowledge of Sufism or the Inayati tradition to more experienced and advanced *murids*. To spread the order's message and broaden its appeal, Pir Zia and other senior Inayati teachers are frequently on the road, traveling between venues across the United States and around the globe. In order to cover costs, many of these programs charge tuition and fees, typically on a sliding scale with various roam and board options for multi-day events, and discounts for young adults and online participants. As the primary conduit for public interface and social engagement, these diverse forums—both offline and online—aim to educate, edify, and inspire, drawing spiritual seekers, potential allies, and future devotees into the Inayati orbit.

The Inayati Order hosts an annual international summer camp for anyone interested in personal development and spiritual growth: the Zenith Institute. Initiated by Pir Vilayat Inayat Khan in the late 1950s, the program has been held in various locations in the Austrian, Swiss, and French Alps over the years. In summer 2018 (July 23 – August 18), it took place in a temporary encampment in a remote alpine meadow near the town of Olivone in the mountainous Ticino region of southern Switzerland. The 2018 program was entitled "Music for the Soul." Over four successive weeks, Pir Zia and numerous other teachers and speakers from diverse religious backgrounds led participants through an immersive crash course on the Inayati path. According to the multidimensional and multilingual (English, French, and German) website, www.zenithinstitute.com:

> Everyone who attends Camp contributes to its creation, so there are many ways you can participate. Before the seminar and workshops begin, we collectively build the sacred space where we practice by assembling the buildings and infrastructure. After camp ends, we take them apart, leaving the meadow as we found it. During camp, you may chose to take part in group seminars, group retreats, or a guided individual retreat. There is a camp within the camp for children and workshops for teenagers and young adults. You can participate for one week or all four weeks.[13]

At the 2018 summer camp, individual and group workshops emphasized contemplative silence, coupled with a daily diet of Inayati spiritual exercises: breathing meditation, silent walks, *wazaif*, and *zikr*. In the second week of camp, Pir Zia himself led a silent community retreat for all participants. During other weeks, participants were free to choose from a menu of options: an array of lectures, seminars, and workshops that explored a wide range of topics, along with group classes that incorporated music, dance, healing practices, dream work, yoga, Sufi alchemy, storytelling, and the comparative study of world religions. The website notes that although the Zenith Camp is "a part of the Inayati Order and many of the people that come are students of this path," everyone is welcome to attend and "there will be no attempt to convert you. In fact, on this path we do not proselytize."[14] Throughout the month of spiritual exploration, campers live together as a community—with nightly accommodations in either tents or a nearby dormitory—immersed in nature against the backdrop of the idyllic mountain setting.

In the United States, Inayati public outreach is mediated primarily through an array of live events, all constructed to appeal to diverse audiences from different backgrounds (Sufis and non-Sufis, Muslims and non-Muslims). In an important sign of changing times, many of these programs are now also digitally documented, forming a growing virtual archive which preserves 'real-world,' 'real-time' experiences for posterity. To take one salient example, "The Way of Illumination: An Introduction to the Sufi Path" was an Inayati workshop specially designed for participants with no previous background in Sufism or the teachings of Inayat Khan. Developed by Pir Zia, it was offered every other year for several cycles. A final iteration took place at the Abode of the Message on May 7, 2015. Over three consecutive days, Pir Zia led participants through a detailed exploration of Inayati beliefs and rituals organized around a cluster of themes. In an important moment for the order's digital media productions, the entire event was streamed live. A lengthy video recording of the lectures and discussions remains accessible through YouTube and has since drawn over sixteen thousand online viewers.[15] With this initial experiment as a springboard, Pir Zia has since offered an expanding variety of live workshops and seminars in rapid succession. In conjunction with the order's comprehensive administrative restructuring, these programs signal a new institutional model for public outreach—combining live, face-to-face interactions with print and digital media publications.

In a clear indication of careful coordination, many Inayati public events are thematically linked to the order's own book publications. Suluk Press, an imprint of Omega Publications, is the Inayati Order's in-house publishing operation based in New Lebanon, New York. The importance of the printed word is affirmed on the home page of the order's flagship website, which spotlights colorful images of the covers of its latest books, along with a link that leads to an expansive online bookstore offering forty-one separate titles for purchase via a digital shopping cart.[16] In effect, these texts—available

Suluk Press, the Inayati Order's publishing house (https://inayatiorder.org/suluk-press/)

in print and, in multiple cases, e-book formats—define the literary canon of Inayati tradition. This includes dozens of books by Inayat Khan (mostly drawn from his voluminous oral discourses), Vilayat Inayat Khan, Noor Inayat Khan, and Pir Zia, as well as several memoirs about the family written by prominent disciples. In addition, the bookstore includes multiple English translations of classical Arabic, Persian, and Urdu Sufi texts and poetry, a reprint of Henry Corbin's *The Man of Light in Iranian Sufism*, and a set of CDs that includes recitations by American Sufi poet Coleman Barks, *The Hand of Poetry: Five Mystic Poets of Persia*. A separate web page (www.omegapub. com), a Facebook page ("Suluk Press/Omega Publications"), and an email newsletter supplement the order's digital bookstore, providing regular updates on forthcoming publications, programs, and book tours. Here again we see a symbiotic feedback loop between the virtual and analog realms. By design, Inayati digital media provide multidirectional pathways to the offline world of books, personalized teaching, community fellowship, and embodied ritual practices. And, in turn, Inayati public events increasingly incorporate digital texts and recorded programs into their curricula, augmenting offline pedagogy with a variety of virtual teaching tools.

Significantly, the themes of Pir Zia's public appearances are often tied to the order's latest print publications—and these live events are amplified through the adroit use of digital multimedia resources. On July 13, 2016, for example, Pir Zia used Facebook to announce the publication of an updated version of the first volume of Inayat Khan's collected works: *The Sufi Message of Hazrat Inayat Khan, Centennial Edition*.[17] "I am delighted to announce that the first volume of the Centennial Edition of the works of my grandfather is now in print," Pir Zia exclaimed. "We plan to bring out another volume every year over the next eleven years, God willing."[18] In September of that year, the order then launched an ambitious series of multi-part online courses, "The Inner Life." In four separate lectures, streamed live for free on successive weeks, Pir Zia led participants through a careful analysis of the volume's second book. Students were encouraged to purchase and read the printed text as the course progressed; they were also provided with a digital study guide with summaries and study questions to complement Pir Zia's live commentary on his grandfather's teachings.[19] This distance learning series continued in May 2017, with four additional talks focused on the third book of the new volume, "The Soul Whence and Whither."[20] A final cycle, "The Mysticism of Sound and Music," utilized a new digital technology, Zoom Webinar, to broadcast live lectures by Pir Zia and a host of scholars and musicians at the Astana in May 2018.[21]

For those unable to attend or stream these events live—or who simply wish to revisit the experience—digital recordings of these online classes were uploaded to the website's "Digital Media" link. Virtual viewers are encouraged to make a ten-dollar online donation before uploading each successive talk on Livestream. In a clear demonstration of the growing interconnectivity of Inayati digital media, a female disciple confirmed the efficacy of these online programs in an enthusiastic Facebook post. "I was listening on the website of the Inayati Order today to 'The Inner Life, Part IV,'" she exclaimed. "O, yes, I feel the call. And I follow it, best as I can. I feel so very thankful. There is no difference for me, listening to the teachings, doing the meditations, etc. with Pir Zia on the computer. It feels very real. What a gift. Thank you so much from far away, but closer than my heartbeat."[22] As this quote suggests, digital media can and do have real-world consequences. More and more, Inayati virtual spaces dovetail with its offline programming, expanding the boundaries of community and communicating an affective power that still manages to both edify and inspire.

As we have seen, an appeal to the common ground between the world's religious traditions was an essential component of Inayat Khan's message.

In that spirit, a commitment to interfaith conversations and collaborations remains a distinguishing feature of twenty-first-century Inayati identity. In both theory and practice, Inayati disciples are encouraged to see themselves as part of an inclusive, interconnected global family that transcends the parochial boundaries of their daily, local lives. In another Facebook post, Pir Zia publicly reminded his followers of this legacy, saying, "Murshid [Inayat Khan] intended his Order to be a nucleus of the worldwide human family, and more and more it is becoming so."[23] As Celia Genn notes, this inclusive and expansive notion of 'spiritual family' is a distinguishing feature of Inayati teachings:

> Even for those whose participation remains local, membership in a transnational spiritual organization, with more or less common perspectives and practices across space, creates a sense of global belonging or family. In the Inayati movement this often extends beyond the *pir-bhai* or community of a traditional Sufi order to a sense of kinship with other religious organizations and individuals who combine a specific spiritual commitment with a universalist or inclusive outlook. As a social process, it mirrors that in modern social movements such as environmentalism, in which the movement exceeds the boundaries of any single group or organization.[24]

With the past as precedent, interfaith dialogue and bridge-building are ubiquitous themes in twenty-first-century Inayati publications, programming, and digital media.

The Inayati Order's enduring commitment to cross-cultural and cross-creedal networking is evidenced in numerous platforms, both online and offline. In 2007, for example, Pir Zia founded the Seven Pillars House of Wisdom. This spiritual community is expressly modeled on historical institutions that sought to preserve knowledge, advance scholarship, and promote a cosmopolitan worldview through cross-cultural exchanges: the ancient library of Alexandria; the House of Wisdom (*bayt al-hikma*) of ninth-century Baghdad; the sixteenth-century House of Worship (*'ibadat khana*) founded by the Mughal emperor Akbar in Fatehpur Sikri; and the Platonic Academy of Renaissance Florence.[25] A detailed website, www.sevenpillarshouse.org, outlines the institution's mission: "Seven Pillars House of Wisdom brings together a diverse community of people devoted to cultivating a living wisdom for our time. We draw on the intelligence of the natural world, humanity's sacred heritage, and contemplative insight to inform and inspire this pursuit. Through gatherings, media and the arts, we explore ways to respond with integrity and beauty to the needs of the world."[26] From 2008 through 2015, this interfaith group sponsored a variety of public programs—in both the United States and Europe—led by spiritual teachers from multiple religious traditions. The website's online bookstore offers a catalogue of books (many in digital format) on global spirituality and mysticism, organized around four primary areas: cosmology, revelation, mysticism, and chivalry. A lively Facebook page, "Seven Pillars House of Wisdom," provides yet another platform to draw spiritual seekers into the Inayati fold, with frequent posts offering an eclectic mix of inspirational quotes, poetry, music videos, advertisements for local events, as well as questions, comments, and advice.

In service of his grandfather's legacy, Pir Zia remains actively involved in numerous interfaith organizations. In his travels in the United States and around the world, he frequently appears at events with spiritual teachers from other religious backgrounds, including leaders from other Sufi communities.[27] To take one prominent example, in May 2017, Suluk Press published Pir Zia's book, *Mingled Waters: Sufism and the Mystical Unity of Religions*. As a prelude to its publication, the order launched an ambitious series of three-day seminars entitled "The Wisdom of the Prophets." Beginning in November 2015—with a new course offered every six months thereafter— this extended program surveyed the intersections of Sufism with six world religions: Hinduism, Buddhism, Zoroastrianism, Judaism, Christianity, and Islam. Not coincidentally, these are also the spiritual traditions at the center of the Universal Worship service initiated by Inayat Khan. In each successive seminar, Pir Zia engaged directly with teachers from the respective religious communities, drawing on the themes of his forthcoming book to explore shared histories, parallel rituals, and theological common ground. According to the order's website: "This six-part course offers the opportunity to study and practice the inner teachings of the prophets as enshrined in the wisdom traditions that derive from their revelations. Drawing on material from classic texts as well as his forthcoming book, Pir Zia Inayat Khan will invite special guests from each tradition to add depth to each section of the course."[28]

While the first four courses took place at the Abode in upstate New York, the November 2017 installment, "Wisdom of the Prophets: Sufism and Christianity," was held at the Astana—the first major public event at the new Richmond headquarters. A seminar on "Sufism and Islam" completed the series in May 2018. For this final program, Pir Zia was joined by four special guests: Shaykh Ghassan Manasra of the Qadiri Order in the Holy Land (Nazreth); Shaykha Fariha al-Jerrahi from the Nur Ashki Jerrahi Community in New York City; Cheikh Sufi, an American Sufi teacher based in Atlanta and trained in the Muridiyya Order in Senegal; and Dr Omid Safi, a professor of Islamic Studies at Duke University. In a four-day program that combined formal lectures and informal discussions with Islamic ritual practices (*salat* prayers and Sufi *zikr*), the teachers explored "the gnosis of Islam as it has been lived and described by Sufi mystics through the centuries."[29]

For each of these live seminars, participants paid tuition, plus room and board. Every course also featured a parallel online option, with live-streaming access to the daily events. Further, all of these programs were digitally recorded and uploaded for purchase via the website's "Digital Media" link. This is now a common pattern that continues to evolve and expand each month with new Inayati programs. By integrating live talks and ritual performances with printed texts and digital media archives into a seamless package, the Inayati community is creating a nexus of interdependent outlets for personal experience, public interface, and interfaith outreach.

FUNDRAISING AND POLITICAL ENGAGEMENT

As a complex, multidimensional corporate institution, the Inayati Order incurs significant financial obligations to fund its in-house staff, maintain its real estate holdings, support its training programs, operate its public events, and coordinate its many moving parts. Sales from its digital bookstore, tuition from its live offline and online programs, and access fees for its digital archive—all of which are available on the website's "Shop" link—help to pay the bills. To supplement these revenue streams, the community also solicits public donations through numerous fundraising campaigns. Another link, "Donate," allows supporters to make either one-time or recurring contributions by submitting their credit card and billing information online. Major gifts (a commitment of $5,000 per year for five years), monthly gifts, and estate gifts are also encouraged. Any financial contribution can be earmarked to support various causes based on five categories: "General Appeal," "Online Courses,"

"Monthly Tithe," "Inayati General Scholarships," and "Inayati Young Adult Scholarships." A note at the bottom of the donation page reminds potential donors that "the Inayati Order is a Non-Profit, 501c3 organization. All donations are fully tax deductible."[30] In another sign of the organization's administrative complexity and transparency, a public document, "North America Keynotes 2018" (posted on the "Donate" link), outlines all the Inayati Order's activities in 2018, and provides granular details on 2019 budget outlays for income and expenses (with accompanying colored pie charts). The 2019 budget projects a total income of just over $900,000—with 42.5 % coming from program fees, 42 percent from donations, and the remainder from a combination of grants and sales.[31]

In addition to the open solicitation of digital donations, the community also organizes a fundraising drive every fall. This is in fact common practice among non-profit institutions in the United States, where tax deductions for charitable contributions are tagged to the end of each calendar year. A web page announcement from Tajalli Roselli, the Inayati Board Secretary, outlines the annual "2018 Fall Appeal":

> Our beloved Murshid, Hazrat Inayat Khan, said, "Harmony is the source of manifestation, the cause of its existence, and the medium between God and humanity." Last year at this time, we were settling into our new home at the Astana after a year of sorting, packing, moving and renovating. With our successful transition behind us, we have begun fine-tuning our priorities and harmonizing our operations to determine just what chords we want to strike and what songs we want to sing . . . This year a major focus for our Order has been to listen deeply to our different voices, as there is no music without different notes. We have begun to harmonize with respect to diversity, generational integration, and the balance of tradition with innovation, in the hope of addressing the desire to, instead of run away, approach the world in a spirit of beauty and creativity.
>
> We are deeply grateful for all the contributions we have relied upon to support our many accomplishments this year. If the Inayati Order and Murshid's teachings have helped you to find a measure of love, harmony and beauty, to stand firm in this world without running away, or maybe even to sing out loud, please consider making a generous donation this year.[32]

In an effort to reach this annual goal, the order organizes a special call for support on 'Giving Tuesday' each year after the Thanksgiving holiday. A November 2017 post, for example, invoked the words of Inayat Khan to solicit support for the order's ongoing work and new initiatives:

> In *The Alchemy of Happiness*, Hazrat Inayat Khan tells us that "happiness is in giving," for giving frees us from the bonds of selfishness. In the same spirit, Giving Tuesday was established in 2012 to remind us of our highest and most cherished values in a season which often seems dominated by commercialism and consumerism. Thus, we give on this day as a statement of those values, in support of the things about which we care most. For many of us, that is the Sufi Message of Love and Unity taught in our lineage. This Giving Tuesday, please consider giving in one of the following four ways, in support of our new North American Headquarters, called the Astana, and the vision of Pir Zia as he focuses his worldwide work to serve all *murids* and seekers drawn to this mystical lineage of Sufism.[33]

As all these online donation campaigns illustrate, the Inayati Order cannot escape the dollars and cents realities of bills and debts. Like most other religious groups in the United States, the community responds to contemporary American consumer culture by packaging, marketing, and commodifying Sufi knowledge and spiritual guidance in exchange for financial viability and institutional stability.[34]

What about politics? Given the Inayati Order's expansive public profile, how does the community position itself amid the changes and challenges of contemporary American political life? A thorough search of its digital media outlets leads to the overall impression that the Inayati Order is a resolutely apolitical organization. As a religious institution focused on the spiritual growth of its own followers—and networking with other like-minded faith communities—its digital documents and public pronouncements are largely devoid of overt political commentary. In this sense, today's Inayati community follows in the footsteps of its Indo-Muslim Chishti Sufi predecessors who tended to avoid the sphere of political power and courtly intrigue. Even so, there are recent indications of a possible shift in attitude and approach, particularly on social media.

In the wake of the chaotic and combative 2016 presidential election, Pir Zia utilized Facebook on several occasions to voice his own political opinions. After Donald Trump's victory—and the wave of xenophobic, racist, and Islamophobic incidents that followed—numerous disciples expressed their anger and concerns on the order's Facebook page. On November 9, Pir Zia broke with past precedent to offer his own public words of encouragement, reminding his followers of the basic beliefs and ethical values that should guide their thoughts and actions in the face of doubt, ambiguity, anxiety, and fear:

> The election is over, and life goes on.
> We will keep bearing witness to the One Being.
> We will keep honoring the legacies of the prophets and prophetesses of all lands.
> We will keep revering the sacredness of the Earth.
> We will keep following the way of remembrance which all religions share.
> We will keep pursuing justice for all people.
> We will keep recognizing people of all races and persuasions as our sisters and brothers.
> We will keep extending our hearts' goodwill toward everyone, excluding no one.
> We will keep witnessing the beauty that is all around us and within us.
> We will keep learning the truth of our being.
> We will keep working to draw back the curtains of egoism from our eyes.
> Life goes on, and we will keep going.[35]

This pattern continued in the ensuing days and months. On November 12, for example, Pir Zia responded to the violence against protesters at the Standing Rock reservation in North Dakota, with a post declaring, "I call upon the President-elect to immediately denounce racism." This brief statement was accompanied by a photograph of his wife and son holding a sign with the words, "We stand with Standing Rock," followed by the hashtag #NoDAPL (No Dakota Access Pipeline).[36]

Other overtly political messages followed. In January 2017, a video was uploaded to the order's website in which Pir Zia expressed support and solidarity for the Women's March on Washington. In his words, "Hazrat

Inayat Khan said, 'I see as clear as daylight that the hour is coming when women will lead humanity to a higher evolution.' Today in Washington DC and across the world, women are preparing to march. God bless them. May the marches be filled with and surrounded by peace, and may the voices of the marchers resound."[37] A transcription of this video message was subsequently linked to the community's website under the title, "Women Will Lead."[38]

In mid-August 2017, in the aftermath of the violent street protests and the murder of a young woman, Heather Heyer, by neo-Nazi sympathizers in Charlottesville, Virginia, Pir Zia once again took to Facebook to address the Inayati community. His online post notes that Charlottesville "is just an hour's drive from Richmond, where our new North American headquarters is located." Richmond too, he acknowledges, has its own Confederate monuments and a long history of racial strife. "Our nation," he states, "is now struggling to find an adequate response, not only to the presence of Lee's image, but to the shadows of American history, encompassing the dispossession of native people, the brutal practice of slavery, and the subordination of women." Yet amidst his grief, Pir Zia emphasizes America's enduring legacy as "a land of vision and promise, where much has been, and may yet be, achieved." While acknowledging the persistence of social injustice in the United States, he ends his message by affirming the enduring relevance of the Inayati mission as an antidote to societal divisions:

> Lost souls grasp desperately for belonging and forge factional identities premised on assumed superiority in the hope of shoring up self-esteem. Sooner or later, however, the illusion of separateness must crumble. Murshid [Inayat Khan] says, "The one who will not take in the idea of unity will be taken in by unity one day." How much better it would be for the whole of the world to take in the idea of unity now. It is for this reason that the Inayati Order exists: to realize and spread the knowledge of unity so that hearts overflow with love and hatred based on distinctions and differences is rooted out. We intend to always be a community of equality between people of all races, religions, and kinds, and to spread the message of unity. This requires of us continuous vigilance, uprooting the traces of divisiveness whenever they appear in our own minds and hearts.[39]

In similar fashion, Pir Zia included a revealing statement in the March 2018 issue of the digital monthly newsletter, The Zephyr—a message that was immediately uploaded to the community's Facebook page as well. While updating the Inayati community on recent travels, workshops, and publications, he comments on the horrific school shooting at Marjory Stoneman Douglas High School in Parkland, Florida on February 14. In his words:

> Soul power is certainly needed in the U.S. right now as the nation mourns the victims of another senseless tragedy. Times of collective reckoning such as this can be significant turning points. Clearly, the students sense this. Change is possible. And by this I mean something still more fundamental than the reform of laws and policies: I mean the elevation of the human spirit and the expansion of the human heart. This is where, as an Order, our essential work lies. And as we know, it begins with each one of us ourselves.[40]

Here Pir Zia describes "soul power" as a prerequisite to social and political change in American society. This path of personal moral and ethical cultivation, he asserts, is the real, foundational work of the Inayati Order's ongoing spiritual (and social) mission.

In the October 2018 edition of The Zephyr, Pir Zia responded yet again to the daily news headlines. Reaffirming his personal concerns with gender equality and social justice, he reflects on the broader implications of the contentious debates over Judge Brett Kavanaugh's nomination to the US Supreme Court:

> Here in the U.S., over the last weeks the confirmation of a new Supreme Court Justice accused of sexual assault has riveted the nation, sparking fierce debates about what fairness demands—toward the accuser and the accused alike. So intense at times was the contention that basic human empathy seemed almost completely eclipsed by sectarian zeal, bringing to mind George Washington's prescient warnings about the dangers of partisanship. Underscoring our fraught national conversation is the dawning realization of the scale on which sexual harassment and assault exists in our society, and the pressing need to address it directly. There is growing recognition of the necessity of a collective ethical renewal rooted in what the heart knows.

In the same posting, Pir Zia links this call for ethical renewal and social activism to the issue of global climate change, emphasizing the Inayati Order's lasting commitment to environmental stewardship:

> The need to reimagine our individual and collective lives was recently brought home in a still more encompassing context by the new report of the International Panel on Climate Change. The report warns that Earth will become a drastically less hospitable planet, for ourselves and for innumerable species, as early as 2040—unless a civilizational shift is swiftly achieved. A hundred years ago, Murshid [Inayat Khan] and the Murshidas [the group of prominent female teachers in the early Inayati community] saw that sacred nature is the mother of all books, that Earth is a vital organic unity, and that humankind is an interconnected whole. Another century must not pass before these crucial realizations become the substance of the spirit of the age. *May we be among those who are to bring about the transfiguration of the Earth.*[41]

Whether these kinds of emotive, pointed, and poignant messages signal a new and purposeful realignment of the Inayati Order's political engagement in the public sphere or are simply spontaneous and heartfelt responses to a series of extraordinary events remains to be seen. What is perfectly clear, however, is that Pir Zia fully recognizes the utility of social media as a powerful communication device to preserve the Inayati Order's communal identity and protect its internal cohesion in an era of profound (and, at times, disorienting) social change.

CONCLUSION

Although there is often a great deal of internal debate and hand-wringing over the utility and permissibility of digital media, the trend lines are clear: more and more religious communities around the world are going 'all in' on the digital revolution. It is clear that cyberspace is hard to resist. In unprecedented ways, it opens new pathways for religious identity, community, and practice.

Digital media most certainly do not replace the lived-in world of everyday experience—but when skillfully used, they can complement, amplify, and extend it. As Heidi Campbell notes in a summary of the scholarship on digital religion: "It is true that offline religious practitioners and organizations often fear that Internet-based community is in some way inauthentic, impoverished, deceptive, or holds the seductive potential power to lead people out of the pew and away from face-to-face community. Yet this research showed that, for most, online religious community is not a substitute, but rather a supplement to extend offline relationships and communication in unique and novel ways."[42]

As this chapter has demonstrated, cyberspace cements relationships and builds connections between multiple audiences. There is a feedback loop—a direct and symbiotic relationship—between digital and analog worlds. As Pauline Hope Cheong and Charles Ess argue, "Very clearly, digital media facilitate and mediate social relations, including people's notion of relationship, pattern of belonging, and community—and in doing so, digital media thus immediately intersect with, and significantly impact, central religious concerns with (re)establishing right relationship or harmony in these various communities."[43] The Inayati Order's revitalized website and social media outlets provide a bridge to its myriad live, public events—drawing outsiders into the orbit of its public Activities, print publications, social welfare projects, and interfaith programs. By design, Inayati digital media speak to multiple audiences simultaneously: both insiders (*murids*) and outsiders (religious seekers of all backgrounds, potential converts and allies, and curious but uninformed cybernauts of all stripes). Narrating an ethic of inclusion, openness, and reciprocity, Inayati digital texts and images aim to expand the definitions and boundaries of 'community' itself.

These three case-study chapters have illustrated how cyberspace now plays a vital role in the Inayati Order's ambitious, multidimensional project of reimagining and realignment. By adopting a new name, relocating its headquarters, and renovating its institutional architecture, the organization has repositioned itself for the twenty-first century. Through careful and coordinated planning, today's Inayati community is pivoting into the Internet Age: strategically deploying digital media to broadcast its message, solidify the bonds of community, experiment with new spaces for pedagogy and ritual performance, and broaden its social networks.

As scholars and students of American Sufism, how do we make sense of Inayati identity in the face of all this change? In their own studies, Alan Godlas and Mark Sedgwick both characterize the Inayati Order as a "non-Islamic" outgrowth of New Age religiosity.[44] Marcia Hermansen, by contrast, frames the community as "a perennialist movement" that has become "ever less Islamic and South Asian over time."[45] In my view, such essentialist categories ultimately fail to fully capture the full complexity, nuance, and dynamism of today's Inayati Order under Pir Zia's leadership. In an effort to understand the community on its own terms, I have consciously avoided reductive labels and taxonomies. Narrowing the analytical frame, I opted instead for a deep-dive exegesis of the words and images of Inayati digital media. An exploration of websites and social media reveals the persistence of both strands of Inayat Khan's message and mission: his universalist and perennialist philosophy, coupled with a deep and enduring connection to Islamic history and Chishti Sufi pedagogy and piety. Going one step further, we have also traced the complex interplay between the order's online and offline worlds, documenting how the contemporary Inayati Order remains firmly grounded in the Indo-Muslim past while adapting to the contingencies of the twenty-first-century American present.

Inayati digital media narrate a story of both continuity and change. The organization's reformulated websites and social media presence mark a clear symmetry in both substance and style between the founder (Hazrat Inayat Khan) and current spiritual leader (Pir Zia Inayat Khan). In a video recorded at the 2017 Sufi Healing Order leadership retreat—and uploaded to Facebook—Pir Zia offered an insightful reflection on his grandfather's practical approach to Sufi tradition. In his words:

Then you come to the time of Hazrat Pir-o Murshid Inayat Khan himself, and you see that there is a certain selectivity in his application of the traditional practices. There are ones that kind of fall away, or ones that were initially given by him and were found to be too foreign. For instance, practices involving a lot of Arabic recitations weren't easily absorbed in the West. If you study his instructions to Rabia Martin and certain others, in the beginning his giving of practices was very copious and included a lot of traditional methods which proved not so easy to assimilate in the Western world.

So over time, he selected, he simplified the focus in certain areas. And all the while also he became not only an editor, so to speak, of that inheritance of practices but he became a channel of knowledge through his own inspiration. Prayers came through him that became part of the methods he taught. Prayers, movements, the way that he reformulated practices represents the distinctness of a new dispensation—taking the old material, remolding it, transmitting essential things and providing a repertoire that becomes the basis of his school.[46]

This is an important and revealing statement. In Pir Zia's reading of institutional history, his grandfather's main challenge—and most important legacy—was to translate Sufism for a Western audience. To do so, he argues, Inayat Khan consciously modified traditional Sufi beliefs and practices to fit the needs of the time. Inayat Khan's teachings and practices, Pir Zia insists, were also continuously shaped by his own religious experiences. The end result was a highly original spiritual path—a unique amalgam Pir Zia describes in the title of his doctoral dissertation as "a hybrid Sufi order at the crossroads of modernity."

Echoing this innovative spirit, today's Inayati Order is once again retuning its message, reformulating its organizational structure, and amending its ritual repertoire. And in direct response to the current age, the community is mobilizing cyberspace to attract a new generation of spiritual seekers. Celia Genn describes this program of institutional reformation as "reworking tradition." As she notes, the Inayati community has "adopted a variety of elements from Western culture, including a formal organization and the new communications technologies that appeared over the twentieth century, to coordinate its worldwide activities and groups. Adopting this formal, transnational organizational pattern, unprecedented in Indian Sufi orders, has both potentiated and constrained the group's development."[47]

Where this ongoing process will ultimately lead remains unclear, and raises a host of questions for the future: Will the organization's experiments with digital media create permanent pathways for ritual experience, pedagogy, and performance? If so, how will the Inayati leadership maintain control over these rapidly evolving virtual spaces? Will the renewed emphasis on the order's Islamic and Chishti Sufi roots attract new Muslim disciples in new places—and perhaps also drive some non-Muslim devotees away? In what ways will the new Astana headquarters in Richmond reshape the boundaries and dynamics of the Inayati community? Will the order continue to focus its efforts and energy on the local American context, or push outward into new global territory in Europe, Asia, Africa, the Middle East, and beyond? Will Inayati interfaith programs bear fruit, leading to new cross-cultural connections and cross-creedal networks? How will the community respond to the momentous changes and challenges of American political life in the decades ahead? And in the long term, will the Inayati Order remain a hereditary tradition, or will future successors to Pir Zia (whether male or female) be appointed from outside the family?

Whatever the future brings, one thing seems certain: given its own institutional history, the Inayati Order will continue to embrace change and reinvent itself. Adaptation to new cultural environments and the appropriation of new media technologies are, after all, long-standing hallmarks of the Chishti Order that profoundly shaped Inayat Khan's spiritual life. As Carl Ernst and Bruce Lawrence remind us:

> The Chishti response to the colonial experience involved the appropriation of new communications media, beginning with print, soon to be followed by sound recordings, occasional appearance in government films and on television programs, and most recently on Internet sites. These new forms of communications have been used to respond to ideological challenges from Orientalists, fundamentalists, and secular modernists. In the process, they are contributing to new forms of community that reconfigure the spiritual practices inherited from the spiritual lineages that connect the Chishtis to their past.[48]

With this past as a guidepost, the Inayati Order's ongoing metamorphosis within the American cultural milieu and across the virtual continuum of the Internet represents the latest chapter in an old, ever-evolving story.

While the Inayati Order offers an especially useful test case to examine how digital media are now transforming Sufi identity, piety, and practice, the full story of Cyber Sufis in America is far more complex. Returning to a macroscopic analysis, chapter 7 identifies key tropes, themes, and trajectories in American Cyber Sufism more broadly. This meta-analysis focuses on a pair of long-term, 'big picture' questions: As we move inexorably towards Web 3.0, how might Sufis respond to the exponential growth and ubiquity of digital technologies in the years ahead? And what are the lessons for scholars and students who hope to keep pace with the accelerating pace of digital religion in twenty-first-century America and beyond?

7

Contextualizing American Cyber Sufism

In researching this book, I traveled far and wide through an ocean of American Sufi digital multimedia. During those online sojourns, I spent countless hours immersed in Sufi web pages, Facebook posts, Twitter feeds, YouTube videos, and other virtual spaces. For the purposes of this study, I ultimately decided to spotlight the Inayati Order as an illustrative case study of Cyber Sufism in practice. I could just as easily have gone in other directions. As any basic Google search will confirm, Sufism is alive and well in cyberspace. Today, there are dozens of institutional Sufi orders in the United States, many with multiple sub-branches. Almost all of them are active on the World Wide Web—and clearly spend a good deal of time, energy, and resources maintaining their digital footprints. In addition, an array of self-styled Sufi masters and self-professed Sufi 'experts' operate online, offering (and often selling) Sufi-inflected teachings, poetry, and products via websites and social media. Amid this bewildering cacophony and chaos, one thing is abundantly clear: there is no single, seamless narrative for American Cyber Sufism.

Within the virtual ecosystem, hybridity, fluidity, and adaptability are hardly unique to the Inayati Order. As a microcosm of American's vast and varied kaleidoculture, Sufi communities display a variegated mix of identities, beliefs, and practices: a panoply of ethnicities and localized cultural traditions, blending Islamic language and symbols with other intellectual currents and spiritual streams. I would argue that variety and vibrancy are, in fact, *the* distinguishing features of contemporary American Sufism. As David Damrel notes:

American Islamic mysticism is the product and project of two comple-
mentary forces in contemporary North American society and culture.
One of these generative forces is the diverse vitality of the substantial
multi-ethnic and multi-generational US and Canadian Muslim communities. A second powerful factor is a more general modern American
interest in a broadly conceived 'spirituality' that investigates and
sometimes incorporates religious beliefs, symbols and rituals from a
dizzying host of sources, including Islam and Islamic mysticism. For
many individuals pursuing this brand of integrative spirituality, Islamic
mysticism, conveniently described by the term 'Sufism', does not
require a Muslim identity. Understanding this interaction—between
Muslim and non-Muslim practitioners of mysticism in the Americas—is
a crucial element in interpreting the shape and trajectory of Islamic
mysticism in the Americas.[1]

Given the hardwired heterogeneity and intrinsic dynamism of American
Sufism, what (if anything) do today's Cyber Sufis have in common? And
looking to the future, where does digital Sufism go from here? This concluding
chapter ponders these perplexing questions. I begin with brief synopses of
seven additional American Sufi communities whose digital media exploits
offer alternative perspectives on the massive shifts in today's virtual landscape.
Returning to a wide-angle view, I then trace key tropes, common themes,
and divergent patterns amid the incredible multiplicity of American Cyber
Sufism while revisiting some of the underlying theoretical and methodological
questions in the study of digital religion. In anticipation of the technological
promises of Web 3.0—the uncharted frontier of augmented reality, virtual
reality, and artificial intelligence—I conclude with a speculative prognosti-
cation on the future of American Cyber Sufism, marking some important
trends and unresolved questions that scholars will need to be attuned to in
the years ahead.

OTHER VOICES, OTHER STORIES

In the virtual landscape of American Cyber Sufism, there are many other
voices to hear and many other stories to tell. To that end, I offer a snapshot

of seven additional American Sufi orders that offer interesting comparisons to the Inayati Order. Both online and offline, each of these groups display a distinct style of Sufi identity, piety, and practice. This list is certainly not comprehensive and these brief summaries are far from exhaustive. Instead, these examples are meant to provide interested readers with a foothold for new investigations. Using these vignettes as a springboard, curious cyber surfers can compare and contrast these remarkably different expressions of the American Muslim experience—and then, more importantly, venture further into the vast virtual terrain on their own.

BAWA MUHAIYADDEEN FELLOWSHIP (www.bmf.org)[2]

Bawa Muhaiyaddeen (birthdate unknown–1986) was a Tamil-speaking, ascetic holy man from Sri Lanka. According to hagiographical accounts, he emerged from the jungles near Jaffna in the early 1940s and established an *ashram* for Hindu devotees (who referred to him as *swami* and *guru*). He subsequently cultivated a following among Muslims in Columbo. Arriving in the United States in 1971, he quickly developed an eclectic, ethnically diverse community of South Asian immigrants, African Americans, and New Age American seekers in Philadelphia, Pennsylvania. During the last fifteen years of his life, Bawa gradually integrated Islamic and Sufi rituals into his hybrid teachings. This included the introduction of formal prayers (*salat*), *dhikr* practices, and the construction of a mosque. Affiliated with the Qadiri Order, the Fellowship today has multiple branches in the United States, Canada, Australia, and the United Kingdom, in addition to long-standing Sri Lankan enclaves in Jaffna and Colombo.

The Fellowship's multilayered website and social media accounts (Facebook, Twitter, Instagram, YouTube, Shoutcast Audio Stream) document its beliefs, rituals, and evolving history. Since Bawa never designated a successor, in a very real sense his teachings and presence are virtually preserved. The website contains multiple audio and video recordings of Bawa—a small sampling of thousands of hours of his live teachings (using stories, parables, poems, and songs) archived by his American disciples. In addition, the Fellowship publishes an impressive range of books—mostly translations of Bawa's myriad discourses—which are available for purchase online. Digital media also connect curious web seekers to the living community offline. The urban mosque—built according to Bawa's instructions in 1984—integrates the Fellowship into the broader Philadelphia Muslim community. As the website illustrates, the saint's tomb (*mazar*) is located on the Fellowship Farm in rural Chester County, forty miles east of the city. As Sufi sacred space on American soil, the shrine serves as a focal point of ritual practice for both Fellowship disciples and, intriguingly, significant numbers of American Muslim pilgrims of South Asian descent.

JERRAHI ORDER OF AMERICA (www.jerrahi.org) AND THE NUR ASHKI JERRAHI COMMUNITY (www.nurashkijerrahi.org)[3]

Shaykh Muzaffer Ashki Ozak al-Jerrahi (1916–1985) was a renowned Turkish spiritual master in the Halveti-Jerrahi Order. From 1978 to 1984, Shaykh Ozak made more than a dozen extended trips to America from his home in Istanbul, attracting large audiences to his public lectures and events, and cultivating a core group of diverse and devoted American *murids*. Over the past forty years, two separate Sufi communities that each lay claim to Shaykh Ozak's legacy have followed divergent trajectories in the United States. By comparing and contrasting these two separate branches of a single genealogical tree, we see how even American Sufi communities that share a common heritage can deploy digital media in remarkably different ways in order to reimagine Sufi identity, redefine the boundaries of community, and respond to the contingencies of twenty-first-century American life.

From 1977 until his death, Shaykh Tosun Bayrak (1926–2018) served as the spiritual guide of the Jerrahi Order of America. A former artist and professor of art history, Shaykh Tosun met Muzaffer Ozak in Turkey in 1970, became his disciple, and was subsequently named a teaching *shaykh* and one of Ozak's designated successors (*khalifa*). Under his guidance, a community of predominantly Turkish immigrants preserved the continuity of Halveti-Jerrahi identity and tradition from the order's headquarters in upstate New York. The *tariqa* has four additional locations in the United Sates along with centers in Canada, Argentina, Chile, Brazil, Spain, Italy and Australia.

The order's refurbished website outlines the community's teachings, texts, and practices. This includes a monthly calendar of events, links to numerous articles and books, selected audio clips and YouTube videos of *khutbas* (weekly sermons that accompany Friday congregational prayers), and audio files with accompanying Turkish transliteration and English translations of *ilahis* (a distinctly Turkish form of *dhikr* practice). The website emphasizes the order's commitment to relief work, with descriptions and photos of a variety of social welfare programs that combat poverty and provide aid to victims of war and disaster around the world (in Afghanistan, Pakistan, Bangladesh, Turkey, Palestine, Bosnia, Syria, Iraq, and elsewhere). The simple and streamlined website is complemented by other digital media outlets, including a community Facebook page ("Jerrahi Order of America"), as well as Shaykh Tosun's personal web page (http://tosunbayrak.com), which features colorful reproductions of his paintings, descriptions of his translations of Sufi works, and selections of his Turkish poetry.

By contrast, the Nur Ashki Jerrahi Community displays a markedly different version of Halveti-Jerrahi tradition under the leadership of its current spiritual guide: Shaykha Fariha Fatima al-Jerrahi (b. 1947), a female Sufi teacher with an ethnically diverse group of devotees in New York City. The order is named in honor of both Muzaffer Ashki Ozak and its eponymous founder, Lex Hixon (1941–1995)—a Muslim convert and another of Shaykh Ozak's direct successors, known as Shaykh Nur al-Anwar al-Jerrahi. Shaykha Fariha was born Philippa De Menil and raised in a prominent Catholic family in Houston, Texas. She met Ozak in 1976, was named a *khalifa* in 1980, and together with Shaykh Nur established the community which she now leads. Every Thursday evening, Shaykha Fariha (along with her husband, Ali) leads a "ceremony of remembrance" (a Jerrahi *dhikr* performance) at the Dergah al-Farah in Tribeca, Lower Manhattan. The community welcomes "seekers and students of all religious paths into our gatherings," although they do ask visitors to email them beforehand to express their interest and intentions. Beyond the New York City headquarters, the *tariqa* is affiliated with fifteen additional "dervish communities" in the United States, as well as groups in Mexico, Australia, and Germany.

The Nur Ashki Jerrahi website is a sophisticated, multidimensional, and multisensorial digital document. Web links provide access to voluminous resources: a detailed weekly events calendar; lengthy biographies and images of the lineage's spiritual masters; myriad articles and book selections outlining key beliefs and practices; and an expansive media library (much of it available for free on iTunes) featuring podcasts and videos of Shaykha

Fariha's discourses (*sohbet* in Turkish), prayers, and sermons, along with audio files with accompanying texts of English versions of Jerrahi *ilahis*. There is a link to a separate web page for the order's publishing house, Pir Press, which sells an array of books and translations by Shaykh Ozak, Shaykh Nur, and numerous scholars of Sufism, along with CDs of live performances of *dhikr* and *ilahis* led by Shaykh Ozak. This rich material is augmented by an active community Facebook account and Shaykha Fariha's own Facebook page. Combining text with multimedia displays (sound clips, photographs, videos), Nur Ashki Jerrahi digital media narrate a vision of Sufi community based on emotional experience (love, intimacy, ecstasy), individuality, ethnic and gender diversity, and openness to all (including non-Muslims). In sharp contrast with the Jerrahi Order of America, Nur Ashki Jerrahi digital media frame Islamic language and symbols within the order's universalist mysticism, all communicated in a cosmopolitan American idiom.

MURID ISLAMIC COMMUNITY IN AMERICA (www.toubamica.org)[4]

Within the cultural and ethnic mosaic of Islam in the United States, Black Muslims comprise approximately a third of the American *umma*. This community is incredibly diverse and defies easy categorization. It includes both native-born African Americans—adherents of the Nation of Islam and its offshoots, along with followers of numerous Sunni and Shi'a groups—as well as diasporic African immigrants.

The Muridiyya Order was founded in Senegal, West Africa, in 1883 by Shaykh Amadou Bamba (1853–1927). Renowned for his piety, miracles, and resistance to the French colonial regime, he was buried in the great mosque of Touba which now comprises a vast pilgrimage center that serves as the hub of the global Muridiyya movement. A hereditary Sufi brotherhood, the Muridiyya have been led by eight successive male descendants of Amadou Bamba. Since his installation in January 2018, Serigne Mountakha Mbacké (b. 1933) currently serves as the order's Grand Marabout from his seat in Touba. Today, the Muridiyya Order impacts nearly every dimension of public life in Senegal: from culture to politics to economics. Beyond West Africa, a sophisticated diasporic network also provides support to Senegalese immigrant communities in numerous Western cities. In both Paris and New York City, Muridiyya followers are often easy to spot in public—with significant numbers of disciples working as small-scale street merchants.

The Murid Islamic Community in America (MICA) was established in New York City in 1989 to "unite all Murids in the United States under the umbrella of brotherhood to preserve and spread the teachings of Shaykh Amadou Bamba and to promote the expansion of Islam." The community's website and social media accounts (Facebook, Twitter, Google+) outline MICA's concerted efforts to preserve the continuity of Senegalese Sufi tradition in the American context. A rich multimedia library provides audio, photo, and video archives of cultural events and the lectures of Muridiyya *shaykhs*, as well as links to the order's radio and television broadcasts. Another web link, "Our Services," documents the community's religious activities, Qur'an courses, marriage and funeral services, and social outreach programs.

NAQSHBANDI HAQQANI SUFI ORDER OF AMERICA (www.naqshbandi.org)[5]

The Naqshbandi *tariqa* emerged in fourteenth-century Central Asia (near the city of Bukhara, in modern-day Uzbekistan), and over the centuries spread throughout the Indian subcontinent and the broader Middle East, all the way to China. Today, the Naqshbandi Haqqani Sufi Order of America is one node in a sprawling and dynamic transnational Sufi network with an expansive global reach and diverse cross-cultural following. The order's eponymous founder, Shaykh Muhammad Nazim al-Haqqani (1922–2014), was a Turkish Cypriot scholar and renowned Naqshbandi Sufi master. His successor, Shaykh Muhammad Hisham Kabbani (b. 1945), was born in Lebanon but relocated to the United States in 1991. Under his tireless leadership, the order has established twenty-eight mosques, centers, and retreats across America, anchored by a convention and retreat center in Fenton, Michigan.

The Naqshbandi Haqqani community is distinguished by its technological savvy. The order utilizes a plethora of interconnected digital multimedia to amplify its message, document its history, teachings and rituals, answer its critics, and expand its ranks. The *tariqa*'s multidimensional website, linked to a bevy of social media (Facebook, Google+, Twitter, YouTube, Flickr), reveals a complex bureaucratic and administrative architecture. The website also pushes the boundaries of online ritual, allowing cyber seekers to take virtual *bay'at* (initiation). Shaykh Hisham Kabbani's personal Facebook page and website each spotlight his *shari'a* and *sunna*-centric teachings and document his peripatetic lifestyle. A related site, www.sufilive.com, provides a massive multimedia library filled with images and streaming videos of the *shaykh's* lectures, sermons (*khutbahs*), ritual performances, and public events in the United States, Europe, and around the world. A number of associated organizations serve the order's commitment to political activism, social outreach, and interfaith dialogue. This includes https://eshaykh.com (a repository of online Naqshbandi *fatwas* that answer practical questions about Muslim piety and practices), as well as the Islamic Supreme Council of America (www.islamicsupremecouncil.org), a "non-profit, non-governmental religious organization dedicated to educating Muslims and non-Muslims alike, and developing good citizenry through the teaching of moral excellence."

NIMATULLAHI SUFI ORDER
(www.nimatullahi.org)[6]

The Nimatullahi Order traces its origins to fourteenth-century Iran. Originally a Sunni *tariqa*, it became Shi'i during the Safavid Empire in the sixteenth century. Under the remarkable leadership of Dr Javad Nurbakhsh (1926–2008)—a psychiatrist, writer, poet, and Sufi master—the order was revitalized and expanded, attracting a large number of devotees from across the globe. Following the 1979 Iranian Revolution, Dr Nurbakhsh migrated to the United States before eventually settling in England. His son and designated successor, Dr Alireza Nurbakhsh—who holds a doctorate in philosophy and practices law in London—now oversees a broad network of Nimatullahi centers across Europe, Africa, Australia and New Zealand, and the Americas (with a dozen locations in the United States).

The order's website charts this complex institutional history, highlighting in particular the teachings and voluminous writings of Dr Javad Nurbakhsh. A multimedia library contains videos of interviews with the *shaykh*, compilations of his poetry, and audio tracks of selections from his wide-ranging lectures on Sufi doctrine and ritual practice, as well as Nimatullahi musical performances (*sama'*) with accompanying Persian lyrics. The organization's diverse publications include *Sufi Journal*, a bi-annual English language magazine—available in both print and digital formats—which "explores the diverse aspects of mysticism, spiritual thought and practice through articles, interviews, poetry, narratives, art, reviews and much more." The flagship website also spotlights the community's social welfare programs, in particular its patronage of health clinics and hospitals in West Africa (Benin and Ivory Coast).

THE THRESHOLD SOCIETY (https://sufism.org/)[7]

Even if most Americans know little of Sufism's diverse history and spiritual practices, they are likely to encounter the world's most famous Sufi master: Jalal ad-Din Rumi (1207–1273). Rumi's luminous (and voluminous) Persian poetry is readily accessible via the best-selling English translations/interpretations of the American poet (and disciple of Bawa Muhaiyaddeen), Coleman Barks. Branching outward from Rumi's shrine complex in Konya, Turkey, the Mevlevi Order today encompasses an expansive global Sufi network, and is perhaps best known for its distinct ritual dance (*sema'*), known colloquially as the 'Whirling Dervishes.'

Under the leadership of Shaykh Kabir Helminski (b. 1947), the Threshold Society draws on this rich legacy, communicating Rumi's message to Western audiences by "integrating the classical methods with modern needs." Initiated into the Mevlevi tradition in 1980, Helminski was formally recognized as a teaching *shakyh* in 1990 by the order's leader in Istanbul. Working in tandem with his wife, Camille, he established the Threshold Society, which is now headquartered in Louisville, Kentucky, with a dozen affiliated "study groups" in the United States, Canada, Mexico, England, the Netherlands, Pakistan, and Indonesia. The official website includes an expansive online bookstore, along with a digital library with links to a range of articles, videos, audio files, and podcasts that explore Mevlevi teachings and Rumi's poetry. In combination with other social media—Facebook, Twitter, YouTube, Instagram, and a cellphone app, "Heart Space"—the community's digital resources include multisensorial platforms for ritual practice, including formal Muslim prayers (*salat*), Mevlevi *dhikr* recitations, hymns (*ilahis*), and prayers (*wird*). Prolific authors and constant travelers, the Helminskis offer a range of annual teaching forums (both offline and online) in the United States and abroad. As the website events page illustrates, these include lectures, musical performances, spiritual retreats, and e-courses, including the 99 Day Program: a formal training program developed by Shaykh Kabir Helminski that explores "Sufism and spiritual psychology."

Like the Inayati Order, all of these American Sufi communities are well-known public entities, firmly grounded in local communities and contexts yet, at the same time, connected to premodern antecedents and global networks. Each of these groups has a heterogeneous membership, comprised of immigrants, indigenous Muslims, and converts (and, in several cases, non-Muslims). Most importantly for this study, they all have a significant and easily accessible digital footprint on the World Wide Web. Despite these similarities, however, all of these Sufi orders are different and distinct. On closer examination, they each display a unique constellation of historical trajectories, cultural identities, internal dynamics, and core issues that shape their institutional identity and public profile. And each *tariqa* navigates its own particular path through the pitfalls and possibilities of cyberspace. The lesson here is clear: every institutional Sufi order in the United States has its own particular story to tell. Following the model and methods I used to analyze the contemporary Inayati Order, thematic case studies would detail how each one of these Sufi orders harnesses cyberspace to narrate identity, bolster pedagogy and ritual practices, and expand its social outreach and public networks. That task is for another time (and other books), however.

As for this intervention, we are left to ask: amid all this dizzying diversity, what discernable patterns, common tropes, and shared trajectories mark twenty-first-century Cyber Sufism as a whole? And, more broadly, what are the lessons and challenges for scholars and students who seek to make sense of the seismic shifts in religious life in the globalized, hypermediated Digital Age?

PATTERNS, TROPES, AND TRAJECTORIES

Sufism in the twenty-first-century United States is both paradigmatic and protean. For every Sufi community, the past is always present. Each Sufi order is molded by the weight of tradition—its own unique amalgamation of sacred history and geography, cultural assemblages and aesthetic expressions, genealogy and spiritual heroes, canonical texts and pedagogical methods, ritual performances and embodied practices. While history matters, however, past precedent is not fully determinative. To keep pace with changing times, a Sufi *tariqa* cannot remain static, inflexible, and ossified. If it is to adapt to new environments and social circumstances, it must constantly evolve across the generations—adopting new idioms, new forms of expression, and even new media technologies to reach new audiences.

In everyday practice, every Sufi *tariqa* is shaped by the vision, talents, energy, creativity, and agency of its own *shaykhs* (and/or *shaykhas*). As the living embodiment of sacred history, spiritual knowledge, and authority, it is the spiritual guide who ultimately makes Sufism real for his/her devotees. Like their spiritual ancestors before them, today's American Sufi masters teach according to audience, altering the style and sometimes even the substance of piety and practice to fit their devotees' personal needs. Within the rich pageantry of Islam in America, Sufi orders also demonstrate an array of American cultural inflections. They follow divergent paths, influenced by the shifts, flows, confluences, and dislocations of America's kaleidoscopic social, political, cultural, and religious topography. To borrow Tom Tweed's aquatic metaphor, American Sufism is "a flowing together of currents—some enforced as 'orthodox' by institutions," others blending with divergent intellectual and religious paths to create new, hybrid "spiritual streams."[8] As living communities embedded in local contexts, American Sufi orders display a diverse bricolage of accumulated traditions, evolving discourses, morphing practices, and reimagined identities.

Across the centuries and around the globe, Sufism has always been distinguished by its fluidity, malleability, and heterogeneity. Of course, this protean nature is precisely what many of its modern-day Muslim detractors find confusing, threatening, and even dangerous about Sufism. As we have seen, Sufism's inherent elasticity and hybridity challenges the essentialist claims of many Islamist ideologues who assert a timeless, universal, and monolithic vision of Islamic normativity, which they claim the exclusive right to define, mediate, and control. History, however, is on Sufism's side. Any thorough and objective assessment of fourteen hundred years of history confirms that diversity and dynamism are the defining hallmarks of Islamic civilization itself. As Shahab Ahmed argues in his posthumous work, *What Is Islam?*, "Islam is a *process*, that is a process of human discursive and social activity, and that discourse is characterized by a multiplicity of voices."[9] As a small but vital subset of Islam in America, Sufi communities in the United States are polyvocal, multivalent, and capacious. Blending diasporic immigrant traditions (from Africa, Asia, and the Middle East) with the experiences of native-born Muslims and local converts, contemporary American Sufism mirrors the geographic, linguistic, socio-economic, ethnic, and cultural diversity of the global *umma* itself.

The variety and vibrancy of American Sufism has profound implications for scholarship. In order to track the diversity within and between Sufi communities, the concepts and paradigms scholars employ need to be both flexible and nuanced. Any comparative study of Sufism, I argue, needs to account for both continuity and change, similarity and difference. To do so, scholars must be careful to avoid purity tests and the authenticity trap: the impulse to distinguish between—and thereby authorize—various strands of 'real Islam' and 'real Sufism.' As Kambiz GhaneaBassiri argues:

> If we begin with the premise that diversity rather than unity is to be expected in the way in which religions are practiced, then to understand Islamic praxis in the United States we need to ask how certain practices and beliefs are signified as Islamic and not how a unified understanding of Islam is diversified by its practice in the United States. Put differently, we need to approach Islamic normativity not so much in terms of orthodoxy and orthopraxy but in terms of the means or structures by which Muslims deem certain beliefs and performances as Islamic. This approach allows us to move beyond reified or idealized understandings of Islam to inquire how religious authority and normativity are practically negotiated in relation to changing circumstances.[10]

As this quote suggests, by focusing on the continuously changing *process* of identity construction, scholars gain a much more accurate picture of Muslim life in America.

GhaneaBassiri's methodological mantra, I argue, is especially relevant for the study of the history and practice of Sufism in the United States, both online and offline. Measuring American Sufism against some 'top down,' universal, and static model of Islamic normativity can only lead to confusion, distortion, and erasure. It is not sufficient for scholars to simply peg Sufi ideas and practices along a sliding scale of 'orthodox,' '*fiqh*-centric,' or '*shari'a*-compliant.' In doing so, we are apt to miss the myriad ways that different Sufis assert and enact their own unique path to God via distinct aesthetic expressions, methodologies, and ritual devotions. To capture the full spectrum of Sufi piety, it is far more productive to begin from the 'bottom up,' documenting how particular Sufi communities continuously reimagine and reconstitute their own traditions within the local, embedded, and embodied context of twenty-first-century American life.

Throughout this book, I have been careful to avoid rigid and reified taxonomies. In my view, catch-all categories like "Islamic," "quasi-Islamic," and "non-Islamic"—or even "hybrids," "perennials," and "transplants"—can obscure the nuance, complexity, and intersectionality of identities expressed in American Sufi cyberspaces.[11] As explanatory devices, such essentializing terms are too simplistic and reductive, and often fail to capture the fluidity, multivalence, and overlaps in many Sufi beliefs and practices. If we hope to give voice to Sufis, we must allow them to speak and learn to listen. To this end, scholars should aim to first encounter and then *re-present* American Sufi communities on their own terms. As Dickson concludes in his own study of North American Sufi movements:

> In light of these findings, I suggest that Sufism is better understood as an inherently fluid and diverse tradition that takes a multiplicity of forms in North America based on the choices Sufi teachers make regarding: (1) the degree to which Sufism can or should be adapted to suit the North American context, and (2) the degree to which Sufism is connected to Islamic practice. With Sufism's living diversity and dynamism in mind, none of the varied forms that Sufism takes in North America need be written off as inauthentic simply because they are in some way innovative or alternative to more mainstream Islamic discourses and practices. As scholars, we can more accurately represent the phenomenon by abandoning essentialist understandings of Sufism that narrowly conceive its possibilities as limited to conventional Islamic frameworks. This emphasis on Sufism's inherent

multiplicity allows us to form a more complete and nuanced picture of Sufism in North America (and Sufism in general), a picture that includes the full range of shape the tradition can take.[12]

In the end, all Sufism is local and contextual. Since there is no 'one size fits all' model that can encapsulate the full range of American Sufi experience, scholars should aim to ensure that the granular details of local Sufi traditions are never dismissed, downplayed, or lost in translation.

Amid all the dazzling diversity and difference of American Sufi communities, what (if anything) unifies today's American Sufi Cyberscapes? Are there any shared patterns, tropes, and trajectories in the digital profiles of disparate American Sufi orders? I believe so. Based on the selective case studies I document in this book, I see common ground in three interdependent dimensions: forms, audiences, and boundaries.

FORMS

American Sufi Cyberscapes articulate specific histories, identities, and practices. Each *tariqa* communicates its own virtual story. Even so, most Sufi digital media share a number of pervasive forms, styles, and characteristics. These include:

- Multidimensional, multilayered, and multisensorial web page displays.
- The expanding integration of multimedia, including audio files, photographs, videos, and live-streaming events.
- An increasingly sophisticated interface across multiple social media platforms (with a particular affinity for Facebook and YouTube)
- A dual emphasis on individual piety and collective identity. Most American Sufi sites display devotees engaged in both intense ritual practices (with images of disciples and teachers, for example, immersed in prayer and meditation) and social activities (with images of groups of smiling and laughing disciples). This affective imagery portrays American *turuq* as open, diverse, and welcoming

communities that offer individual spiritual transformation as well as a strong social support network.

- A spotlight on the personality, piety, and charisma of individual *shaykhs*. In this context, the importance of mobility, travel, and accessibility is often foregrounded, with peripatetic Sufi teachers traveling constantly to meet with their disciples and interact with new audiences.
- A focus on public programming (lectures, retreats, workshops, conferences), with multiple touchpoints for public outreach, social engagement, and interfaith dialogue.
- Multiple commercial dimensions, including live tuition-based events (both online and offline) and archived 'pay per view' audio and video programs, along with digital bookstores, online shopping, and digital donation and fundraising campaigns.

Amid the remarkable variety of American Sufism, these common patterns point to an emerging consensus on the utility of digital media. The trend line is clear: year by year, even month by month, Sufi web pages and social media become increasingly more expansive, sophisticated, integrated, and multidimensional. By combining digital words, sounds, and images to produce ever more complex narratives, American Sufis are discovering new ways to deploy digital media to amplify their messages and expand their networks.

AUDIENCES

Sufi digital media are carefully constructed to tell a story. A critical reading of these digital documents reveals a great deal about each American Sufi order's sense of its own identity and, more importantly, how it wants to be perceived and received by the outside world. In both form and function, Sufi websites and social media are designed to appeal to multiple audiences simultaneously.

For the internal audience of Sufi devotees, digital media effectively serve as a virtual encyclopedia and digital archive. Websites, linked to active social media accounts, promote a Sufi community's shared values, cement its collective identity, and preserve its institutional memory. Hyperlinked websites provide instant access to a comprehensive digital library that documents the order's collective wisdom, genealogy, and sacred history. Wherever they are, disciples can log on to access information on the *tariqa*'s key beliefs, foundational texts, and ritual performances. A website's updated events calendar helps members organize their everyday, secular lives around the community's public religious events. YouTube videos and archived digital recordings allow disciples to experience a program or event they may have missed in person, or to study a Sufi teacher's lecture more carefully on their own—stopping, rewinding, or fast-forwarding the video as an at-home teaching tool. Facebook posts provide real-time updates, inspirational quotes, and a live platform for personal inquiries and engagement. Most importantly, Sufi digital media can be easily and instantaneously shared with others—providing, in effect, an easily accessible digital brochure that can be circulated among friends, colleagues, or curious outsiders. "If you want to know who we are," a Sufi disciple can tell a friend at school or work, "check us out online, and then come and join us in person."

Although they rarely expressly say so, Sufis deploy digital media as tools for missionary *da'wah* (proselytizing and preaching) as well. To this end, American Sufi Cyberscapes are designed to cultivate allies and attract potential converts. For external audiences, Sufi digital media are primarily a public relations and advertising platform. For non-Muslim outsiders, they convey basic information about foundational Sufi beliefs, rituals, practices, and history. Web page narratives also endeavor to clarify fears, misperceptions, and misunderstandings about Sufi tradition. Aimed at a weary and wary American public, barraged with Islamophobic rhetoric and negative impressions of Islam and Muslims, digital media typically portray Sufism as a safe, familiar, and naturalized version of American religiosity. In the face of increasing political persecution and social marginalization, American Sufis actively engage digital media to demonstrate that they are critics of Islamist ideology and victims of *jihadi* terrorism, open to dialogue with other religious communities, and fellow citizens worthy of empathy, sympathy, and support.

I would argue that Sufi digital media are consciously aimed at another external American audience as well: non-Sufi Muslims. Pushing back against critics and detractors, most American Sufi Cyberscapes stake a claim to Islamic authority and authenticity. For Muslim cybernauts already familiar with the 'guideposts' of Islam—the scripture (the Qur'an), the moral exemplar (the Prophet), and the law (the *shari'a*)—Sufi digital media present a vision of Sufi identity and piety consistent with Islamic norms, values, and symbols. Whether explicitly or implicitly, digital media narratives assert the legitimacy of Sufi institutional structures, historical genealogy, and religious authority, beliefs, and ritual performances. At times, this requires some creative posturing. Like any extended family, every Sufi order must at times deal with internal personality conflicts and stark differences of opinion. Internal debates over the parameters of tradition, succession disputes, and the permissibility of particular social practices, however, are typically 'cleaned up' in public digital spaces. Putting on their best face, Sufi orders utilize cyberspace to brand themselves, to appeal to multiple audiences, to defend their tradition, and to assert their rightful place at the table of American religious life.

BOUNDARIES

While there is a symbiotic relationship between online and offline worlds, all of the Sufi organizations I highlight in this book are clearly attuned to boundaries. Reading between the proverbial lines, the producers of these virtual spaces appear singularly concerned with controlling digital narratives and delimiting digital engagement. As we have seen, Sufi digital media provide a 'taste' (in Sufi parlance, *dhawq*) of Sufi piety in practice via evocative images, sounds, and narratives. Even so, surprisingly few American Sufi orders have taken full advantage of the capabilities of today's digital technologies, especially in regard to virtual rituals. At present, the vast majority of Sufi websites are *not* flat space, open-source forums with chat rooms, expansive social media platforms, or unlimited interactive spaces for ritual performance and experience. Instead, they are largely static, one-way spaces, with fixed barriers to access and prescribed limits to participation. At best, contemporary American Sufi digital media offer an invitation to practice and a bridge to direct, personal engagement with the living community offline.

This pervasive concern with control is understandable. As digital technologies continue to push the envelope, creating ever-faster, more integrated, multidimensional pathways for people to meet, express ideas, build relationships, and share experiences, Sufi communities face unprecedented challenges. Although most American Sufi leaders clearly recognize the powerful and potentially transformative affordances of digital media, they appear wary of the trade-offs to unbridled freedom. After all, the disruptions of digital media threaten to unsettle Sufi tradition in novel and potentially radical ways. Cyberspace complicates established institutional modes of religious authority, intimacy, and the dynamics of ritual exchange. An open, untethered, and unrestricted digital landscape therefore problematizes the normative structures, geographic orientation, pedagogical dynamics, and ritual rules of a traditional Sufi order.

Upon entering the virtual realm, a Sufi *tariqa* is immediately faced with a host of daunting questions: How is Sufi sacred space altered in cyberspace? What exactly does it mean to be virtually 'there'? Can the interpersonal connections and shared identity of a Sufi community be transferred to online forums? Does virtual initiation (*bay'at*) into a Sufi community—as the Naqshbandi Haqqani *tariqa* already allows—undermine the fundamental dynamics of the master–disciple relationship? Are virtual interactions with a *shaykh* efficacious? Can a spiritual master's presence and charisma be digitally replicated? Is the divine energy (*faizan*) experienced during Sufi pilgrimage to the shrines of saints (*ziyarat*) accessible to someone sitting in front of a computer screen? What about the Hajj pilgrimage? Does virtual *zikr* convey tangible spiritual benefits? Can *baraka* (divine blessing) be digitized and delivered over fiber-optic cables? In short: what is both gained and lost in cyberspace? The tension, ambiguity, and anxiety that surround such pressing (and unprecedented) questions, I argue, partly explains why American Sufis have been relatively late to fully embrace digital culture. Even a cursory Google search confirms that Sufis lag far behind other religious groups in the United States as well as many of their fellow Muslims across the world—*'ulama* scholars, media preachers, *jihadi* organizations—who have proved to be much more willing to dive headlong into virtual life.

Among individual American Sufi orders, we see a diverse range of attitudes and approaches to cyberspace. Although there is no simple formulaic rule, there seems to be a general correlation between cultural adaptation and technological innovation. To return to Marcia Hermansen's taxonomy,

Sufi communities that demonstrate (or combine) the traits of "hybrids" and "perennials" tend to be the most ambitious Internet producers and consumers in today's digital ecosystem. To varying degrees, this would include the Inayati Order, the Naqshbandi Haqqani Sufi Order of America, the Nur Ashki Jerrahi Community, and the Threshold Society. Despite their distinct approaches to Islamic identity and piety, these Sufi orders demonstrate a number of common traits:

- They are founded and led by immigrant Sufi masters—or their family descendants or designated successors (*khalifas*), which in prominent cases include white converts to Islam.
- In the interest of reaching new audiences and potential converts, they maintain relatively low barriers to digital access.
- They embrace malleable definitions and expressions of Sufi tradition—with less fixed notions of a geographical homeland and cultural practices.
- They are ethnically diverse and gender inclusive, receptive to women in prominent leadership roles.
- They actively pursue social outreach, communication, and collaboration with other American religious communities, emphasizing interfaith dialogue.
- They are fundamentally global in perspective, with broad diasporic networks and diverse groups of local American followers.
- Most importantly, they are at the same time fully integrated into the American context, communicating in English and drawing on local idioms, vernacular culture, and political rhetoric to shape their message.

By contrast, more traditionalist, conservative, and insular "transplant" Sufi orders catering mostly to immigrant communities—like the Jerrahi Order of America, the Murid Islamic Community in America, and the Nimatullahi Sufi Order—are relatively less open, pliable, and responsive to the American cultural milieu, and (so far) less bold, creative, and assertive in their use of digital media. Once again, however, there are important exceptions to these general rules. For example, with its eclectic teachings, diverse membership, and lack of a living spiritual guide—combined with its ambitious use of digital media—the contemporary Bawa Muhaiyaddeen Fellowship is an outlier that upends the standard paradigm.

In the end, I would argue that the single most important determining factor in a Sufi community's approach to cyberspace is its leadership. Regardless of background and biography, it is the individual Sufi master who ultimately charts the course for his/her community, navigating between the boundaries of online and offline worlds. Despite the many challenges, for those Sufi leaders who choose to embrace technological innovation, cyberspace now offers a powerful tool to help reach new audiences, to root Sufi tradition deeper in American soil, and to prepare the next generation of spiritual seekers for the tantalizing (if at times unsettling) possibilities of the digital future.

THE FUTURE OF AMERICAN CYBER SUFISM

Sufism is, above all, a system of moral and ethical training. Sufis learn by doing, and in their pursuit of inner, experiential knowledge (*ma'rifa*), *presence* is paramount. Sufi pedagogy is mediated through a direct, personal relationship with a spiritual master, extended and strengthened in community, and experienced through the daily discipline of ritual practices. These bedrock foundations have shaped the Sufi path across the world and throughout history. In the twenty-first century, cyberspace offers tantalizing new channels for communication and contact. Even so, American Sufi communities have yet to go 'all in' on the digital revolution. There remains an underlying conservatism in their approach to cyberspace—a pervasive hesitancy to let go of the reins and allow digital media to run free and unfettered. I predict, however, that this reluctance will not last long. With an eye to the future, I anticipate that most American Sufi communities will rapidly expand their use of cyberspace for three reasons: historical precedent; Sufism's internal resources; and the promises and possibilities of Web 3.0.

HISTORICAL PRECEDENT

Religions have always been mediated. From oral culture to handwritten manuscripts, from the printing press to radio, television, and film, successive media technologies have continuously transformed the ways in which religious knowledge and authority are confirmed and conveyed. Today, however, cyberspace is upending the rules of the game. With unprecedented speed and reach, digital media are transforming discursive space. In the Digital Age, media flows are increasingly multidirectional. As a result, the boundaries between public and private, insiders and outsiders, center and periphery, and the local and the global are no longer so clearly demarcated. "New forms of communication and their increased rapidity allow 'peripheries' and audiences to talk back and can infuse new life to local and regional traditions," argues Dale Eickelman. "The new political geography of communications may actually facilitate pluralism. In the sense that symbolic and political connections across national and other political boundaries are encouraged, conventional understandings of 'external' and 'internal' become increasingly blurred."[13] Digital media stimulate new conversations, facilitate new connections and, in the process, reconfigure individual and group identities. By altering both the form and function of communication, cyberspace is fundamentally rewiring how religious practitioners disseminate knowledge, interpret their faith, and encounter the sacred. "The central question to ask, therefore," Nabil Echchaibi notes, "is not how the media cover religion or even how religious subjects use modern media, but how transformations in religious mediation generate new formats and styles of devotional communication and consequently create and sustain new religious subjectivities."[14]

As chapter 1 illustrated, technological innovation is hardwired into Islamic history, and technological appropriation is part of Sufism's DNA. Sufis have historically been among the earliest Muslim adopters of new technologies, especially in times and places when their tradition has been criticized and attacked by both outsiders (such as Christian missionaries in the colonial era) or insiders (like Islamist ideologues and *jihadi* militants). Since there is a long and established track record of Sufis adapting to new media innovations there is every reason to see the past as predictive. The very things that attracted Sufis to previous media technologies now informs their approaches to cyberspace, and I predict these tendencies will only accelerate and intensify in coming decades.

Why? Like previous technologies, digital media offer a powerful platform to forcefully and effectively counter critics in defense of Sufi tradition—but with exponentially wider reach and deeper impact. As a double minority community in today's United Sates (a relatively small sector of Muslims within the American Muslim minority), Sufis are particularly marginalized and vulnerable. In this unsettled, liminal position, cyberspace offers American Sufis leverage. Digital media provide open spaces where the rules are not set, expectations are not fixed, and where tech-savvy users can break free from the grasp of the gatekeepers of traditional media outlets (editors, publishers, corporate media conglomerates). Within the fluid landscape of cyberspace, the modes of discourse are reconstituted, and experimentation and creativity are unleashed.

In similar fashion, digital media allow Sufis to access new audiences, but exponentially larger ones, at infinitely greater speed and reduced cost. The Internet has a unique capacity to streamline a Sufi community's internal communication while also expanding its outward reach—unbound by national borders, gender boundaries, geographic barriers, or the monopoly of entrenched religious elites. As Stewart Hoover argues:

> Above all, the media age has empowered audiences, or at least has invested audience practice with a claim of autonomy and empowerment, and that has radically changed the grounds on which religious and spiritual meanings and symbols are now articulated and circulated. These are practices of construction, not only of reception. Authorities can no longer assume a unitary and instrumental flow of meaning and influence from received doctrine through medium to waiting adherents. Those adherents are now active (or imagine themselves to be active) in the process, and that has changed things substantially.[15]

Here, Hoover makes an important point that reveals a final, compelling incentive for American Sufis to join the digital media revolution. After all, no single audience is more receptive to, active in, and empowered by the virtual realm than America's youth. As every parent and teacher knows all too well, young people today are fully enmeshed in digital culture, moving seamlessly, without angst or anxiety, between online and offline worlds. By operating in cyberspace, therefore, American Sufis open the door to the most important constituency for their future survival: the next generation of spiritual seekers. In this sense, what is true for a university professor in the classroom is no less true for American Sufi leaders; to attract and keep their attention, you need to meet your students/disciples where they are. And where the kids are in the twenty-first century is online. Since cyberspace is the new game in town, today's American Sufis have a powerful incentive to follow the old adage: "if you can't beat them, join them."

SUFISM'S INTERNAL RESOURCES

American Sufis are the heirs to a wealth of resources that can (and, I predict, will) influence their response to future digital media innovations. Throughout the centuries, and in myriad cultural settings, Sufis have demonstrated a pliable and expansive approach to religious texts. Beyond the foundational canon that shapes all Muslims' lives (Qur'an, *hadith*, and law), Sufis have always remained open to diverse genres of religious expression. From Morocco to Indonesia, Sufi teachers have for centuries used poetry, music, dance, and the visual arts to reach new audiences. If digital texts can help Sufis to bridge cultural gaps in new social contexts, why not make full use of them? In the same vein, Sufis have long embraced an inclusive understanding of sacralized space. They distinguish between the lived-in, flesh-and-blood, terrestrial, and 'secular' world of the calendar and the clock (*al-dunya*), and the transcendent, unseen realm of divine secrets (*al-ghayab*). At certain times and places, however, the boundaries between these worlds collapse. The map of Sufi sacred geography marks a terrain punctuated with holy sites: portals where divine blessings (*baraka*) are accessible to human beings. For all Muslims everywhere, Mecca, Medina, and Jerusalem are such miraculous, extraordinary places. But for Sufis, so too are the constellation of shrines and tomb complexes of holy men and women that draw legions of pious pilgrims around the globe. Wherever a *wali Allah* ('friend of God,' or saint) dies and is buried is remembered and memorialized as holy ground. Given this imaginative, capacious approach to spiritual geography, why not a virtual sacred space? If powerful, life-altering things can and do happen in the digital realm, Sufis have every reason to be there.

In other intriguing ways, Sufism's inherent worldview and ritual practices make it compatible with cyberspace. In both theory and practice, Sufis have always engaged the non-material realm of the imagination. Indeed, there is an entire lexicon of Islamic and Sufi terminology that resonates with the basic idea of a *virtual reality*. In keeping with Qur'anic teachings, Sufi theology, ontology, and epistemology emphasize the symbiotic nature of both the outward/manifest (*zahir*) and inward/hidden (*batin*) dimensions of reality. In Islamic eschatology, the *barzakh* ('obstacle,' 'separation,' or 'barrier') defines a liminal, purgatorial space between the material and spiritual dimensions. For the renowned theologian, jurist, philosopher, and Sufi master, Abu Hamid al-Ghazali (1058–1111 CE), the metaphor of the *dihliz* ('the threshold position') marks an interstitial space between divergent yet interdependent realities.[16] And inspired by the neo-Platonism of Ibn Sina (980–1037 CE), both the influential philosopher Shihab ad-Din Suhrawardi (1154–1191 CE) and the Sufi luminary Ibn 'Arabi (1165–1240 CE) employ the concept of *'alam al-mithal*: an archetypal 'imaginal world' that mediates between human reason and divine being.[17] All of these terms form a semantic field that describes 'in between' spaces beyond the limits of worldly, material life where real, powerful, and sacred things happen. While I do not mean to suggest there is a one-to-one correspondence, I do think that it is a small logical leap for American Sufis to apply this same terminology and reasoning to the virtual landscape of digital Cyberscapes.

Less abstractly, 'virtual' experiences are central to Sufi ritual practice as well. For Sufis, the barriers between the living and the dead, between the material and spiritual realms, between heaven and earth, and between Allah and humanity are porous and permeable. Sufi rituals endeavor to make the invisible visible, tangible, tactile, and real. Across a vast historical and cultural continuum, for example, the hagiographical accounts of Sufi luminaries abound with stories of dreams and visions. For Muslims both past and present, visionary experiences are much more than hallucinations. As a medium for both revelation and inspiration, they impart vital ontological, epistemological, and spiritual truths. In dreams and visions, the boundaries of time and space are erased, and long-dead prophets and saints become visible, alive, and accessible. As flashes of ultimate reality, spiritual dreams and visions serve a dual function in Sufi pedagogy: they inspire the Sufi adept and simultaneously provide the *shaykh* who interprets them with a barometer to assess the disciple's progress along the path.[18] In this sense, visionary experiences serve as models for Muslim selfhood and sainthood, tools for spiritual development, and markers of mystical attainment. At the same time, they often have immediate, tangible, real-world consequences that change lives. In actual practice, dreams and visions may help a Sufi adept to decide who to marry, what job to take, or even where to find their rightful spiritual master. The prevalence of such 'virtual' rituals in Sufism, I argue, resonates with the logic and practice of cyberspace: a parallel, non-material, virtual realm that spurs the creative imagination and, at the same time, does real work in the everyday, offline world.

In similar fashion, I see intriguing overlaps between cyber life and Sufism in the image of the circle (in Arabic, *al-halqa*). Take one resonant example: Google+.[19] This social networking platform contains a feature, Circles, that allows cyber surfers to post messages, photos, and status updates to friends, and to share information with larger groups (or, 'circles') based on shared interests and common relationships. The parallels here with Sufism are obvious. In Sufi piety and practice, the circle is an important symbol for the dynamics of mystical pedagogy, ritual practice, and spiritual community. Indeed, Sufi teaching networks can be mapped as a series of concentric circles that radiate outward from a central hub: the teaching *shaykh*. For Sufis, however, the circle is not simply a visual metaphor. In everyday practice, Sufi masters often teach in a circle, surrounded by their disciples. Likewise, the practice of *zikr* meditation is typically performed in a circle (in Persian, *halqa-e zikr*, or 'circle of remembrance'), with the *shaykh* encircled by followers. And who can forget the indelible image of the famous ritual *sema'* ceremony of the Mevlevi Order which reenacts the ecstatic states of the poet Jalal ad-Din Rumi via a ritualized dance—with the *shaykh* encircled by his 'whirling dervish' disciples who spin in their own turning circles as they move methodically around him? Circles upon circles, both literal and symbolic, both analog and digital. In my view, all these examples suggest a natural affinity between the logic and practice of Sufi piety in cyberspace—an alternative universe where the interplay between the 'virtual' and the 'real' creates enticing possibilities for new forms of Sufi experience and expression.

THE PROMISES AND POSSIBILITIES OF WEB 3.0

While predicting the future of technology is a fool's errand, it is safe to say that the Internet is not going away, and that digital media will only become

increasingly powerful and omnipresent in the years ahead. Current trajectories, common sense, and Moore's Law all suggest that we are at the tip-
ping point of another major technological and social paradigm shift, with
momentous changes already underway.[20] Tech giants (Facebook, Apple,
Google, Amazon, Microsoft), Silicon Valley venture capital firms, and global
corporate media conglomerates continue to pour massive financial investments into big data analytics; metadata mining and digital advertising;
mobile, cloud, and social applications; virtual and augmented reality; and
artificial intelligence.[21] Exactly where all this energy, effort, and expense
leads—and what mindblowing, game-changing, and life-altering gadgets we
will carry (or wear) in five, ten, or twenty years as a result—is impossible to
say. More broadly, the ubiquity of the digital economy raises a host of vexing
(and unresolved) ethical questions surrounding the proper balance between
unbridled capitalism, government oversight and regulation, and individual
privacy. But if, as the tech pundits and prognosticators suggest, we are in
fact moving inexorably towards an increasingly integrated, interactive, and
immersive Web 3.0, I am willing to predict that American Sufis will quickly
adapt to the next wave of emergent digital technologies to keep pace with
changing times.[22]

In this book, I have described American Sufi Cyberscapes as a virtual
imaginarium and digital sensorium. The Internet's architecture and affordances provide Sufis an alternative universe where they are free to imagine
and enact new forms of religious identity, new connections in elastic social
networks, and new multimodal forms of representation and communication.
In their provocative work, Stewart Hoover and Nabil Echchaibi describe
cyberspace as an interstitial 'third space' for religious life: an entirely new
arena where all things are possible, where the fixed habits and patterns of the
established order are shattered, and where radically different expressions of
religious community, identity, and subjectivity are already operational. I fully
agree that cyberspace has this innate capacity and transformative potential.
At present, however, I argue that institutional Sufi orders in the United States
are not quite there yet.

In the early decades of the twenty-first century, Sufi Cyberscapes remain
partially formed, contingent, and 'under construction.' In this moment of creative tension and transition, boundaries are slowly but steadily being tested,
probed, and stretched in new directions. During the past decade, Sufi digital
media have shown tangible signs of experimentation with, for example, the

increasing integration of video, social media posts, and live-streaming events. While mapping these changes in American Sufi Cyberscapes, however, my analysis has also noted an underlying anxiety and pervasive ambivalence in Sufi attitudes towards digital media. Many American Sufi orders remain hesitant to fully immerse themselves in digital culture, reluctant to completely unlock and unleash the wizardry of cyberspace. Despite the technical wonders and incredible capacities of today's Web 2.0, Sufi digital media have yet to duplicate the intimacy, face-to-face interactions, and hands-on instruction at the heart of the master–disciple relationship. They have not yet replaced the relationships, friendships, and interpersonal networks that cement a living Sufi community. And, as presently constituted, they are no substitute for the intensity, affective power, and visceral experience of embodied ritual performance. I doubt they ever will be. Not entirely. Even so, I still anticipate a bright future for American Cyber Sufism. Reading the tea leaves, I predict that the technological transformations of Web 3.0 will eventually tip the scales. As digital media platforms exponentially improve, there is every reason to think that Sufi Cyberscapes will continue to adapt, expand, and evolve, propelling American Sufi communities into new frontiers.

Painting with broad analytical brushstrokes, I see today's American Sufis pushed and pulled in opposite directions by two simultaneous forces: a centrifugal force that propels them outward, and a centripetal force that directs them inward. Both these forces have inherent benefits and dangers. The centrifugal force pushes a Sufi community further into the public sphere and towards a more open, accommodating, and cosmopolitan worldview—but at the risk of unbinding tradition, upsetting established norms, and engendering fears of a loss of control. By contrast, the centripetal force promotes tighter interpersonal bonds, stronger internal networks, and a more local perspective. At the same time, it tends to create an echo chamber, pulling a Sufi community towards insulation, isolation, and even ossification. Though the exact form that Web 3.0 technologies will take is anyone's guess, they will certainly be faster, more integrated, and more deeply immersive. If so, I assert, the digital media of the future will help to align (or at least ameliorate) these independent forces, facilitating a deeper complementarity and increased symbiosis between Sufism's online and offline worlds.

Letting the imagination run wild, we can envision a time when today's science-fiction fantasy becomes tomorrow's ordinary lived reality. Picture a scene: sitting on her living-room couch in Bethlehem, Pennsylvania, a young

Sufi *murid* slips on her Virtual Reality glasses. With a simple voice command, she uploads a live, three-dimensional image of her Chishti *shaykh* (who is at that moment in his own home in Lahore, Pakistan) seated in front of her. After exchanging greetings and *salaams*, she asks him to interpret a puzzling dream she had the night before. Soon other disciples join them for virtual *suhbat*, listening to the master's discourses and chiming in, one by one, with questions of their own. To illustrate particular points, the *shaykh* displays images of texts, shares selections of *qawwali* music, and uploads a streaming 3D video of the live *'urs* celebrations at the sacred Sufi shrine of Ajmer Sharif in Rajasthan, India. With the day's lesson at an end, the group forms a virtual circle and the *shaykh* leads them in a meditative performance of virtual *zikr*. Bidding farewell to her teacher and friends, the young woman logs off—and heads towards the kitchen where her robot housekeeper is waiting to serve her a late-night snack.

Given the dizzying pace of technological change, this scene—and probably something far stranger and unimaginable—is an increasingly likely scenario in a not-so-distant future. In such a world, the two-dimensional experience of Web 2.0 would be turbocharged. Immersed in the interactive hyper-reality of Web 3.0, a Sufi disciple would encounter an augmented sensorium via a seamless and multidimensional integration of oral, aural, textual, visual, and tactile materials. All the senses would be simultaneously stimulated, the limits of space and time would fall away, and new aesthetic, affective, and bodily expressions of devotional piety would be actualized. Whatever the future brings, American Sufi communities will have massive incentives to expand their online presence if they want to grow, evolve, and not get left behind in the competitive arena of the American spiritual marketplace. The constant challenge, however, will be to negotiate the interface between Sufism's virtual and analog worlds without surrendering control, ceding authority, loosening the bonds of community, or jettisoning the past.

CONCLUSION: THE ROAD AHEAD

Setting aside futuristic fantasies, what remains abundantly clear is that in the twenty-first century the *Net* does real *work*. Across the globe, the cyber networks of digital religion are flourishing as tech-savvy explorers venture deeper into the virtual ecosystem. The unmapped and yet undiscovered terrain of the cyberspace jungle is definitely not for the faint of heart. But for intrepid adventurers it holds tantalizing possibilities for religious transformation. American Sufis today stand on the precipice of this digital borderline. Although some Sufi communities have made tentative inroads, most have yet to mount major expeditions and stake their own permanent territorial claims in the virtual landscape. In this current historical moment, digital media constitute a contingent, secondary space for American Cyber Sufis. Yet there are clear signs that Sufi communities are beginning to see cyberspace as a potential third space for piety and practice, with vast untapped resources to help build religious community, bolster religious identity, and augment ritual experience.

This book began as a simple thought experiment: what would it mean to approach Sufi digital media as a distinct genre of religious text and a unique formation of sacred space? By focusing on online experiences and expressions, I aimed to document some of the ways that American Sufis reimagine identity, reassemble tradition, and recast the practice of piety in cyberspace. In doing so, however, I have admittedly told only half the story. In keeping with Heidi Campbell's model of digital religion, what is not fully fleshed out in this study is the complex interplay between Sufism's online and offline worlds. As Campbell argues:

> the term 'digital religion' describes the technological and cultural space that is evoked when we talk about how online and offline religious spheres have become blended or integrated. We can think of digital religion as a bridge that connects and extends online religious practices and spaces into offline religious contexts, and vice versa. This merging of new and established notions of religious practice means digital religion is imprinted by both the traits of online culture (such as interactivity, convergence, and audience-generated content) and traditional religion (such as patterns of belief and ritual tied to historically grounded communities).[23]

Following Campbell's logic, a complete portrait of American Sufism will ultimately require more detailed, comprehensive ethnographic research to account for the reciprocity, complementarity, and symbiosis between the online and offline worlds. After all, even within the virtual, imaginative realm of cyberspace, Sufism remains firmly implanted in the embodied, sensual, affective, material stuff of everyday life.

This book is hardly the last word on Cyber Sufis. It is instead meant to be an experimental intervention that will, I hope, serve as a catalyst for further scholarly investigations. At the moment, the field is wide open, primed for new voices and alternative perspectives. Future research will require more granular, 360-degree studies of the reciprocal flows between online digital Sufism and the day-to-day, 'on the ground' dynamics of American Sufi community life. To that end, scholars will need to better illustrate how digital media help American Sufi communities forge offline relationships, build networks, and transcend geographic and cultural boundaries—and how the 'real world,' in turn, reinforces or reformulates cyber experiences. Detailed studies that combine online ethnography with interviews and interactions with the producers and users of these spaces will help illuminate the gaps between the 'ought to be' and 'is' of Sufi Cyberscapes: the divergences between digital fantasies and lived realities. Most importantly, the field will benefit from alternative methodological approaches to digital narratives and practices, as well as more nuanced theoretical frameworks to explain precisely how religious subjectivity, identity, and experience are augmented or altered in cyberspace.

I leave all that important, unfinished work for another research project—and to other interlocutors. With the ground already moving under our feet, digital religion will no doubt remain a growth industry in the years ahead, allowing ample room for future contributions from students and scholars fascinated by the virtual expressions of the American Muslim experience.

Bibliography

Abdullah, Zain. *Black Mecca: The African Muslims of Harlem*. New York: Oxford University Press, 2010.

———. "American Muslims in the Contemporary World: 1965 to the Present." In *The Cambridge Companion to American Islam*, eds. Juliane Hammer and Omid Safi, pp. 65–82. Cambridge: Cambridge University Press, 2013.

Adi, Mohammad-Munir. *The Usage of Social Media in the Arab Spring: The Potential of Media to Change Political Landscapes Throughout the Middle East and Africa*. Berlin: LIT Verlag, 2014.

Adib-Moghaddam, Arshin. *A Metahistory of the Clash of Civilisations: Us and Them Beyond Orientalism*. New York: Columbia University Press, 2011.

Aggarwal, Neil Krishan. *The Taliban's Virtual Emirate: The Culture and Psychology of an Online Militant Community*. New York: Columbia University Press, 2016.

Ahmed, Shahab. *What Is Islam?: The Importance of Being Islamic*. Princeton: Princeton University Press, 2017.

Aidi, Hisham. *Rebel Music: Race, Empire, and the New Muslim Youth Culture*. New York: Pantheon Books, 2014.

Akbarzadeh, Shahram, ed. *Routledge Handbook of Political Islam*. New York: Routledge, 2011.

Akhtar, Shabbir. *Islam as Political Religion: The Future of an Imperial Faith*. New York: Routledge, 2010.

Alatas, Ismail Fajrie. "Sufi Sociality in Social Media." In "Piety, Celebrity, Sociality: A Forum on Islam and Social Media in Southeast Asia," eds. Carla Jones and Martin Slama. *American Ethnologist*, November 8, 2017. http://americanethnologist.org/features/collections/piety-celebrity-sociality/sufi-sociality-in-social-media

Algar, Hamid. *Wahhabism: A Critical Essay*. Oneonta, NY: Islamic Publications International, 2002.

Ali, Kecia. "Redeeming Slavery: The 'Islamic State' and the Quest for Islamic Morality." *Mizan*, Vol. 1, No. 1 (2016), "The Islamic State in Comparative and Historical Perspective": pp. 1–19. www.mizanproject.org/journal-post/redeeming-slavery

Ali, Wajahat, Eli Clifton, Matthew Duss, Lee Fang, Scott Keyes, and Faiz Shakir. "Fear, Inc.: The Roots of the Islamophobia Network in America." Center for American Progress, August 26, 2011. https://www.americanprogress.org/issues/religion/reports/2011/08/26/10165/fear-inc/

Alkousaa, Riham. "How Facebook Hurt the Syrian Revolution." *al-Jazeera*, December 4, 2016. http://www.aljazeera.com/indepth/opinion/2016/12/facebook-hurt-syrian-revolution-161203125951577.html

Allen, Chris. *Islamophobia*. New York: Routledge, 2016.

Alsultany, Evelyn. *Arabs and Muslims in the Media: Race and Representation After 9/11*. New York: New York University Press, 2012.

Aly, Anne, Stuart Macdonald, Lee Jarvis, and Thomas Chen, eds. *Violent Extremism Online: New Perspectives on Terrorism and the Internet*. New York: Routledge, 2016.

Aminrazavi, Mehdi, ed. *Sufism and American Literary Masters*. Albany: State University of New York Press, 2014.

Amos, Deborah. "Saudi Women Can't Drive to Work, So They're Flocking to the Internet." *National Public Radio*, May 11, 2015. http://www.npr.org/sections/parallels/2015/05/11/405885958/saudi-women-cant-drive-to-work-so-theyre-flocking-to-the-internet

Anderson, Benedict. *Imagined Communities: Reflections on the Origin and Spread of Nationalism*. London: Verso, 1983.

Anderson, Jon W. "'Cyberites': Knowledge Workers and New Creoles on the Superhighway." *Anthropology Today*, Vol. 11, No. 4 (August 1995): pp. 13–15.

———. "Cybernauts of the Arab Diaspora: Electronic Mediation in Transnational Cultural Identities." March 1997. www.naba.org.uk/content/articles/diaspora/cybernauts_of_the_arab-diaspora.htm

———. "Globalizing Politics and Religion in the Muslim World." *Journal of Electronic Publishing*, Vol. 3, No. 1, September 1997. http://quod.lib.umich.edu/j/jep/T3336451.0003.116?view=text;rgn=main

———. "The Internet and Islam's New Interpreters." In *New Media in the Muslim World: The Emerging Public Sphere*, eds. Dale F. Eickelman and Jon W. Anderson, pp. 41–56. Bloomington: Indiana University Press, 1999.

———. "Technology, Media and the Next Generation in the Middle East." A paper delivered at the Middle East Institute, Columbia University, September 28, 1999. http://www.mafhoum.com/press3/104T45.htm

———. "Muslim Networks, Muslim Selves in Cyberspace: Islam in the Post-Modern Public Sphere." NMIT Working Papers, 2001. www.mafhoum.com/press3/102S22.htm

———. "Internet Islam: New Media of the Islamic Reformation." In *Everyday Life in the Muslim Middle East*, eds. Donna Lee Bowen and Evelyn A. Early, pp. 300–305. Bloomington: Indiana University Press, 2002.

———. "New Media, New Publics: Reconfiguring the Public Sphere of Islam." *Social Research*, Vol. 70, No. 3 (Fall 2003): pp. 887–906.

———. "Wiring Up: The Internet Difference for Muslim Networks." In *Muslim Networks: From Hajj to Hip Hop*, eds. miriam cooke and Bruce B. Lawrence, pp. 252–263. Chapel Hill: University of North Carolina Press, 2005.

Anderson, Scott. "Fractured Lands: How the Arab World Came Apart." *New York Times Magazine*, August 11, 2016. http://www.nytimes.com/interactive/2016/08/11/magazine/isis-middle-east-arab-spring-fractured-lands.html

Apolito, Paolo. *The Internet and the Madonna: Religious Visionary Experience on the Web*. Chicago: University of Chicago Press, 2005.

Appadurai, Arjun. *Modernity at Large: Cultural Dimensions of Globalization*. Minneapolis: University of Minnesota Press, 1996.

Asad, Talal. "The Idea of an Anthropology of Islam." In *Occasional Paper Series*, by the Center for Contemporary Arab Studies, Georgetown University. Washington, D.C.: Georgetown University Press, March 1986, pp. 1–23.

Aydin, Cemil. *The Idea of the Muslim World: A Global Intellectual History*. Cambridge, MA: Harvard University Press, 2017.

Babou, Cheikh Anta. *Fighting the Greater Jihad: Amadu Bamba and the Founding of the Muridiyya of Senegal, 1853–1913*. Athens: Ohio University Press, 2007.

Bacevich, Andrew. *America's War for the Greater Middle East: A Military History*. New York: Random House, 2017.

Bail, Christopher. *Terrified: How Anti-Muslim Fringe Organizations Became Mainstream*. Princeton: Princeton University Press, 2015.

Bakalian, Anny and Mehdi Bozorgmehr. *Backlash 9/11: Middle Eastern and Muslim Americans Respond*. Berkeley: University of California Press, 2009.

Baldwin, Shauna Singh. *The Tiger Claw*. Toronto: Vintage Canada, 2005.

Bashir, Shahzad. *Sufi Bodies: Religion and Society in Medieval Islam*. New York: Columbia University Press, 2011.

Basu, Shrabani. *Spy Princess: The Life of Noor Inayat Khan*. New York: Omega Publications, 2007.

Bauman, Zygmunt. *Liquid Modernity*. Cambridge, UK: Polity Press, reprint edition, 2012.

Bayat, Asef. *Revolution Without Revolutionaries: Making Sense of the Arab Spring*. Palo Alto: Stanford University Press, 2017.

Bayoumi, Moustafa. *How Does It Feel to Be a Problem?: Being Young and Arab in America*. New York: Penguin Press, 2008.

———. *This Muslim American Life: Dispatches from the War on Terror*. New York: New York University Press, 2015.

Beinart, Peter. "The Denationalization of American Muslims." *The Atlantic*, March 19, 2017. https://www.theatlantic.com/politics/archive/2017/03/frank-gaffney-donald-trump-and-the-denationalization-of-american-muslims/519954/

Bell, Catherine. *Ritual Theory, Ritual Practice*. New York: Oxford University Press, 1992.

Bell, Matthew. "Even at His Funeral, Muhammad Ali Wanted to Share His Muslim Faith With the World." *Public Radio International*, June 9, 2016. http://www.pri.org/stories/2016-06-09/even-his-funeral-muhammad-ali-wanted-share-his-muslim-faith-world

Benard, Cheryl. "Five Pillars of Democracy: How the West Can Promote an Islamic Reformation." *RAND Corporation*, Spring 2004. https://www.rand.org/pubs/periodicals/rand-review/issues/spring2004/pillars.html

Bernal, Victoria. "Eritrea Online: Diaspora, Cyberspace and the Public Sphere." *American Ethnologist*, Vol. 32, No. 4 (2005): pp. 660–675.

———. "Diaspora, Cyberspace and Political Imagination: The Eritrean Diaspora Online." *Global Networks*, Vol. 6, No. 2 (2006): pp. 161–179.

Beydoun, Khaled. *American Islamophobia: Understanding the Roots and Rise of Fear*. Oakland: University of California Press, 2018.

Bhabha, Homi. *The Location of Culture*. New York: Routledge, 1994.

Bilici, Mucahit. *Finding Mecca in America: How Islam is Becoming an American Religion*. Chicago: University of Chicago Press, 2012.

Blank, Jonah. *Mullahs on the Mainframe: Islam and Modernity Among the Daudi Bohras*. Chicago: University of Chicago Press, 2001.

Blann, Gregory. *Lifting the Boundaries: Muzaffer Effendi and the Transmission of Sufism to the West*. Nashville: Four Worlds Publishing, 2005.

Brandon, James. *Virtual Caliphate: Islamic Extremists and Their Websites*. London: Centre for Social Cohesion, 2008.

Brasher, Brenda. *Give Me That Online Religion*. New Brunswick: Rutgers University Press, 2001.

Brinkerhoff, Jennifer. *Digital Diasporas: Identity and Transnational Engagement*. Cambridge: Cambridge University Press, 2009.

Bunt, Gary R. *Virtually Islamic: Computer-Mediated Communication and Cyber Islamic Environments*. Cardiff: University of Wales Press, 2000.

———. *Islam in the Digital Age: E-Jihad, Online Fatwas and Cyber Islamic Environments*. London: Pluto Press, 2003.

———. "Defining Islamic Interconnectivity." In *Muslim Networks: From Hajj to Hip Hop*, eds. miriam cooke and Bruce B. Lawrence, pp. 235–251. Chapel Hill: University of North Carolina Press, 2005.

———. *iMuslims: Rewiring the House of Islam*. Chapel Hill: University of North Carolina Press, 2009.

———. "Surfing the App Souq: Islamic applications for mobile devices." *CyberOrient*, 2010.

———. "#islam, social networking and the cloud." In *Islam in the Modern World*, eds. Jeffrey Kenney and Ebrahim Moosa, pp. 177–208. New York: Routledge, 2014.

———. *Hashtag Islam: How Cyber-Islamic Environments Are Transforming Religious Authority*. Chapel Hill: University of North Carolina Press, 2018.

Burke, Daniel. "Threats, Harassment, Vandalism at Mosques Reach Record High." CNN, December 15, 2015. http://www.cnn.com/2015/12/10/living/mosques-attack-study-2015/index.html

Buturovic, Amila. "Between the *Tariqa* and the *Shari'a*: The Making of the Female Self." In *Feminist Poetics of the Sacred: Creative Suspicions*, eds. Frances Devlin-Glass and Lyn McCredden, pp. 135–150. Oxford: Oxford University Press, 2001.

Cainkar, Louise A. *Homeland Insecurity: The Arab American and Muslim American Experience After 9/11*. New York: Russell Sage Foundation, 2009.

Callimachi, Rukmini. "To the World They Are Muslims. To ISIS, Sufis Are Heretics." *New York Times*, November 25, 2017. https://www.nytimes.com/2017/11/25/world/middleeast/sufi-muslims-isis-sinai.html?hp&action=click&pgtype=Homepage&clickSource=story-heading&module=first-column-region&region=top-news&WT.nav=top-news&_r=0 Th

Campbell, Heidi A. "Considering Spiritual Dimensions Within Computer-Mediated Communication Studies." *New Media and Society*, Vol. 7, No. 1 (February 2005): pp. 110–134.

―――. *Exploring Religious Community Online: We Are One in the Network*. New York: Peter Lang, 2005.

―――. "Spiritualizing the Internet: Uncovering Discourses and Narratives of Religious Internet Usage." *Online Heidelberg Journal of Religions on the Internet*, Vol. 1, No. 1 (September 2005).

―――. *When Religion Meets New Media*. New York: Routledge, 2010.

―――. "How Religious Communities Negotiate New Media Religiously." In *Digital Religion, Social Media and Culture: Perspectives, Practices and Futures*, eds. Pauline Hope Cheong, Peter Fischer-Nielsen, Stefan Gelfgren, and Charles Ess, pp. 81–96. New York: Peter Lang, 2012.

―――. "Understanding the Relationship Between Religion Online and Offline in a Networked Society." *Journal of the American Academy of Religion*, Vol. 80, No. 1 (March 2012): pp. 64–93.

―――. "Community." In *Digital Religion: Understanding Religious Practice in New Media Worlds*, ed. Heidi Campbell, pp. 57–71. New York: Routledge, 2013.

―――, ed. *Digital Religion: Understanding Religious Practice in New Media Worlds*. New York: Routledge, 2013.

―――. "Introduction: The Rise of the Study of Digital Religion." In *Digital Religion: Understanding Religious Practice in New Media Worlds*, ed. Heidi Campbell, pp. 1–22. New York: Routledge, 2013.

―――, ed. *Digital Judaism: Jewish Negotiations With Digital Media and Culture*. New York: Routledge, 2015.

Cantwell, Christopher D. and Hussein Rashid. "Religion, Media, and the Digital Turn." A report for the Social Science Research Council's Program on Religion and the Public Sphere, December 2015. https://www.ssrc.org/publications/view/religion-media-and-the-digital-turn/

Casanova, Jose. *Public Religions in the Modern World*. Chicago: University of Chicago Press, 1994.

Cassidy, Christina. "FBI: Hate Crimes Against Muslims Up By 67 Percent in 2015." Associated Press, November 15, 2016. https://www.apnews.com/f699eb3597 2949c8b8861e2185fe43c7/FBI:-Hate-crimes-against-Muslims-up-by-67-percent-in-2015

Castells, Manuel. *The Power of Identity: The Information Age: Economy, Society and Culture, Volume II*, Second Edition. Oxford: Blackwell, 1997.

―――. *End of Millennium: The Information Age: Economy, Society and Culture, Volume III*, Second Edition. Oxford: Blackwell, 2000.

―――. *The Rise of the Network Society: The Information Age: Economy, Society and Culture, Volume I*, Second Edition. Oxford: Blackwell, 2000.

―――. *The Internet Galaxy: Reflections on the Internet, Business and Society*. Oxford: Oxford University Press, 2001.

Cesari, Jocelyne. *When Islam and Democracy Meet: Muslims in Europe and in the United States*. New York: Palgrave Macmillan, 2004.

―――, ed. *Encyclopedia of Islam in the United States*. 2 Volumes. Santa Barbara: ABC-CLIO/Greenwood, 2007.

―――. *Muslims in the West After 9/11: Religion, Politics and Law*. New York: Routledge, 2009.

————. *What Is Political Islam?* Boulder: Lynne Rienner Publishers, 2017.

Chakrabarty, Dipesh. *Provincializing Europe: Postcolonial Thought and Historical Difference.* Princeton: Princeton University Press, 2000.

————. *Habitations of Modernity: Essays in the Wake of Subaltern Studies.* Chicago: University of Chicago Press, 2002.

Chan-Malik, Sylvia. *Being Muslim: A Cultural History of Women of Color in American Islam.* New York: New York University Press, 2018.

Cheong, Pauline Hope. "Authority." In *Digital Religion: Understanding Religious Practice in New Media Worlds,* ed. Heidi Campbell, pp. 72–87. New York: Routledge, 2013.

Cheong, Pauline Hope and Charles Ess. "Introduction: Religion 2.0?: Relational and Hybridizing Pathways in Religion, Social Media, and Culture." In *Digital Religion, Social Media and Culture: Perspectives, Practices and Futures,* eds. Pauline Hope Cheong, Peter Fischer-Nielsen, Stefan Gelfgren, and Charles Ess, pp. 1–24. New York: Peter Lang, 2012.

Cheong, Pauline Hope, Peter Fischer-Nielsen, Stefan Gelfgren, and Charles Ess, eds. *Digital Religion, Social Media and Culture: Perspectives, Practices and Futures.* New York: Peter Lang, 2012.

Chiabotti, Francesco, Eve Feuillebois-Pierunek, Catherine Mayeur-Jaouen, and Luca Patrizi, eds. *Ethics and Spirituality in Islam: Sufi Adab,* Leiden: Brill, 2017.

Chih, Rachida, Catherine Mayeur-Jaouen, and Rüdiger Seesemann, eds. *Sufism, Literary Production, and Printing in the Nineteenth Century.* Wurzburg: Ergon Verlag, 2015.

Cho, Kyong James. "New Media and Religion: Observations on Research." *Communication Research Trends,* Vol. 30, No. 1 (March 2011). http://www.biomedsearch.com/article/New-media-religion-observations-research/252449215.html

Choueiri, Youssef. *Islamic Fundamentalism: The Story of Islamist Movements.* New York: Continuum, 2010.

Cockburn, Patrick. *The Rise of Islamic State: ISIS and the New Sunni Revolution.* London: Verso, 2015.

cooke, miriam and Bruce B. Lawrence. "Introduction." In *Muslim Networks: From Hajj to Hip Hop,* eds. miriam cooke and Bruce B. Lawrence, pp. 1–30. Chapel Hill: University of North Carolina Press, 2005.

————, eds. *Muslim Networks: From Hajj to Hip Hop.* Chapel Hill: University of North Carolina Press, 2005.

Commins, David. *The Wahhabi Mission and Saudi Arabia.* London: I.B.Tauris, 2006.

Corbett, Rosemary. *Making Moderate Islam: Sufism, Service, and the 'Ground Zero Mosque' Controversy.* Palo Alto: Stanford University Press, 2017.

Corbin, Henry. *Creative Imagination in the Sufism of Ibn 'Arabi.* Princeton: Princeton University Press, 1969/1981.

————. *The Man of Light in Iranian Sufism.* Omega Publications, 1994.

Cornell, Rkia E. *Early Sufi Women: Dhikr an-niswa al-muta 'abbidat as-sufiyyat.* Louisville, KY: Fons Vitae, 1999.

Council on American-Islamic Relations (CAIR). "Confronting Fear: Islamophobia and its Impact in the United States." http://islamophobia.org/reports/179-confronting-fear-islamophobia-and-its-impact-in-the-u-s-2013-2015.html

Cowan, Douglas E. *Cyberhenge: Modern Pagans on the Internet*. New York: Routledge, 2005.

Crawford, Michael. *Ibn 'Abd al-Wahhab*. Oxford: Oneworld Publications, 2014.

Csordas, Thomas J. "Embodiment as a Paradigm for Anthropology." *Ethos*, Vol. 18, No. 1 (March 1990): pp. 5–47.

———, ed. *Embodiment and Experience: The Existential Ground of Culture and Self*. Cambridge: Cambridge University Press, 1994.

Curry, John J. *The Transformation of Muslim Mystical Thought in the Ottoman Empire: The Rise of the Halveti Order, 1350–1650*. Edinburgh: Edinburgh University Press, 2012.

Curtis, Edward E. IV. *Islam in Black America: Identity, Liberation and Difference in African-American Islamic Thought*. Albany: State University of New York Press, 2002.

———. *Black Muslim Religion in the Nation of Islam, 1960–1975*. Chapel Hill: University of North Carolina Press, 2006.

———. *The Columbia Sourcebook of Muslims in the United States*. New York: Columbia University Press, 2007.

———. *Muslims in America: A Short History*. Oxford: Oxford University Press, 2009.

———, ed. *Encyclopedia of Muslim-American History*. 2 Volumes. New York: Facts On File, 2010.

———. "The Study of American Muslims: A History." In *The Cambridge Companion to American Islam*, eds. Juliane Hammer and Omid Safi, pp. 15–27. Cambridge: Cambridge University Press, 2013.

———. *The Call of Bilal: Islam in the African Diaspora*. Chapel Hill: University of North Carolina Press, 2014.

Dahlgren, Peter. "The Public Sphere and the Net: Structure, Space and Communication." In *Mediated Politics: Communication in the Future of Democracy*, eds. W. Lance Bennett and Robert M. Entman, pp. 33–55. Cambridge: Cambridge University Press, 2001.

———. "The Internet, Public Spheres and Political Communication: Dispersion and Deliberation." *Political Communication*, Vol. 22 (April–June 2005): pp. 147–162.

Damrel, David W. "Aspects of the Naqshbandi-Haqqani Order in North America." In *Sufism in the West*, eds. Jamal Malik and John Hinnells, pp. 115–126. New York: Routledge, 2006.

Dawson, Lorne. "Researching Religion in Cyberspace: Issues and Struggles." In *Religion on the Internet: Prospects and Promises*, eds. J. K. Hadden and D. E. Cowan. Amsterdam: Elsevier Science, 2000.

———. "Religion and the Internet: Presence, Problems and Prospects." In *New Approaches to the Study of Religion*, eds. P. Antes, A. Geertz, and R. Warne. Berlin: Verlag de Gruyter, 2002.

Dawson, Lorne and Douglas E. Cowan, eds. *Religion Online: Finding Faith on the Internet*. New York: Routledge, 2004.

De Jong, Frederick and Bernd Radtke, eds. *Islamic Mysticism Contested: Thirteen Centuries of Controversies and Polemics*. Leiden: Brill, 1999.

DeLong-Bas, Natana. *Wahhabi Islam: From Revival and Reform to Global Jihad*. London: I.B.Tauris, 2004.

Devji, Faisal. *Landscapes of the Jihad: Militancy, Morality, Modernity*. Ithaca: Cornell University Press, 2005.

———. *The Terrorist in Search of Humanity: Militant Islam and Global Politics*. New York: Columbia University Press, 2008.

Dickson, William Rory. "An American Sufism: The Naqshbandi-Haqqani Order as a Public Religion." *Studies in Religion* 43 (2014): pp. 411–424.

———. *Living Sufism in North America: Between Tradition and Transformation*. Albany: State University of New York Press, 2015.

Dickson, William Rory and Meena Sharify-Funk. *Unveiling Sufism: From Manhattan to Mecca*. Bristol, CT: Equinox, 2017.

Diouf, Sylviane A. *Servants of Allah: African Muslims Enslaved in the Americas*. New York: New York University Press, 1998.

Dressler, Markus. "Pluralism and Authenticity: Sufi Paths in Post-9/11 New York." In *Sufis in Western Society: Global Networking and Locality*, eds. Ron Geaves, Markus Dressler, and Gritt Klinkhammer, pp. 77–96. New York: Routledge, 2009.

———. "Between Legalist Exclusivism and Mysticist Universalism: Contested Sufi Muslim Identities in New York." *The Muslim World*, Vol. 100 (October 2010): pp. 431–451.

Duss, Matthew, Yasmine Taeb, Ken Gude, and Ken Sofer. "Fear, Inc. 2.0: The Islamophobia Network's Efforts to Manufacture Hate in America." Center for American Progress, February 11, 2015. https://www.americanprogress.org/issues/religion/reports/2015/02/11/106394/fear-inc-2-0/

Echchaibi, Nabil. "From Audio Tapes to Video Blogs: The Delocation of Authority in Islam." *Nations and Nationalism*, Vol. 17, No. 1 (January 2001), pp. 25–44.

———. "Hyper-Islamism?: Mediating Islam from the Halal Website to the Islamic Talk Show." *Journal of Arab and Muslim Media Research*, Vol. 1, No. 3 (April 2009): pp. 199–214.

———. "Gendered Blueprints: Transnational Masculinities in Muslim Televangelist Cultures." In *Circuits of Visibility: Gender and Transnational Media Cultures*, ed. Radha Hegde, pp. 80–102. New York: New York University Press, 2011.

———. "Alt-Muslim: Muslims and Modernity's Discontents." In *Digital Religion: Understanding Religious Practice in New Media Worlds*, ed. Heidi Campbell, pp. 119–138. New York: Routledge, 2013.

———. "American Muslims and the Media." In *The Cambridge Companion to American Islam*, eds. Juliane Hammer and Omid Safi, pp. 299–311. Cambridge: Cambridge University Press, 2013.

———. "Taming the West: Mediations of Muslim Modernities." In *Religion Across Media: From Early Antiquity to Late Modernity*, ed. Knut Lundby, pp. 137–152. New York: Peter Lang, 2013.

———. "Muslimah Media Watch: Muslim Media Activism and Social Change." *Journalism: Theory, Practice and Criticism*, Vol. 14, No. 7 (2014), pp. 852–867.

———. "Post-Islamist Sounds: *Nasheed* and Qur'anic Recitation on YouTube and the Triangulation of Islamic Preaching." An unpublished paper delivered to a faculty forum at Lehigh University, February 18, 2017.

Edwards, Brian. *After the American Century: The Ends of U.S. Culture in the Middle East*. New York: Columbia University Press, 2016.

Eickelman, Dale F. "Communication and Control in the Middle East: Publication and Its Discontents." In *New Media in the Muslim World: The Emerging Public Sphere*, eds. Dale F. Eickelman and Jon W. Anderson, pp. 19–32. Bloomington: Indiana University Press, 1999.

——— and Jon W. Anderson. "Redefining Muslim Publics." In *New Media in the Muslim World: The Emerging Public Sphere*, eds. Dale F. Eickelman and Jon W. Anderson, pp. 1–18. Bloomington: Indiana University Press, 1999.

——— and Armando Salvatore. "The Public Sphere and Muslim Identities." *European Journal of Sociology*, Vol. 43, No. 1 (2002): pp. 92–115.

Eisenstadt, S. N. "Multiple Modernities." *Daedalus*, Vol. 129, No. 1 (2000): pp. 1–29.

El Fadl, Khaled M. Abou. *The Great Theft: Wrestling Islam From the Extremists*. New York: Harper Collins, 2005.

Elias, Jamal. "Female and the Feminine in Islamic Mysticism." *The Muslim World*, Vol. 78, Nos. 3–4 (1988): pp. 209–224.

el-Nawawy, Mohammed and Sahar Khamis. *Islam Dot Com: Contemporary Islamic Discourses in Cyberspace*. New York: Palgrave Macmillan, 2009.

Ernst, Carl W. *The Shambhala Guide to Sufism*. Boston: Shambhala Publications, 1997.

———. "Between Orientalism and Fundamentalism: Problematizing the Teaching of Sufism." in *Teaching Islam*, ed. Brannon M. Wheeler, pp. 108–123. New York: Oxford University Press, 2003.

———. "Ideological and Technological Transformations of Contemporary Sufism." In *Muslim Networks: From Hajj to Hip Hop*, eds. miriam cooke and Bruce B. Lawrence, pp. 191–207. Chapel Hill: University of North Carolina Press, 2005.

———. "Sufism, Islam, and Globalization in the Contemporary World: Methodological Reflections on a Changing Field of Study." *In Memoriam: The 4th Victor Danner Memorial Lecture*. Bloomington, Indiana: Department of Near Eastern Languages and Cultures, 2009.

———, ed. *Islamophobia in America: The Anatomy of Intolerance*. New York: Palgrave Macmillan, 2013.

——— and Bruce B. Lawrence. *Sufi Martyrs of Love: The Chishti Order in South Asia and Beyond*. New York: Palgrave Macmillan, 2002.

Esposito, John L. and Ibrahim Kalin, eds. *Islamophobia: The Challenge of Pluralism in the 21st Century*. Oxford: Oxford University Press, 2011.

Euben, Roxanne. *Enemy in the Mirror: Islamic Fundamentalism and the Limits of Modern Rationalism*. Princeton: Princeton University Press, 1999.

——— and Muhammad Qasim Zaman, eds. *Princeton Readings in Islamist Thought: Texts and Contexts from al-Banna to Bin Laden*. Princeton: Princeton University Press, 2009.

Ewing, Katherine. *Arguing Sainthood: Modernity, Psychoanalysis, and Islam*. Durham: Duke University Press, 1997.

Faris, David M. and Babak Rahimi, eds. *Social Media in Iran: Politics and Society After 2009*. Albany: State University of New York Press, 2015.

Freedom House. "Silencing the Messenger: Communication Apps Under Pressure." Freedom on the Net, 2016 report. https://freedomhouse.org/report/freedom-net/freedom-net-2016

Fuller, Jean Overton. *Noor-un-nisa Inayat Khan*. Rotterdam: East-West Publications, 1971.

Garner, Tom. "Digital Trends: Why 2017 Will be Shaped by VR, AR, AI and Personalized Digital Assistants." *Newsweek*, January 3, 2017. http://www.newsweek.com/virtual-reality-virtual-reality-sets-phones-technology-537969

Geaves, Ron. "The Bawa Muhaiyaddeen Fellowship." In *New Religions, A Guide: New Religious Movements, Sects and Alternative Spiritualities*, ed. Christopher Partridge, pp. 144–146. Oxford: Lion Publishing, 2004.

Geaves, Ron, Markus Dressler, and Gritt Klinkhammer, eds. *Sufis in Western Society: Global Networking and Locality*. New York: Routledge, 2009.

Gelvin, James L. and Nile Green, eds. *Global Muslims in the Age of Steam and Print*. Berkeley: University of California Press, 2014.

Genn, Celia A. "The Development of a Modern Western Sufism." In *Sufism and the 'Modern' in Islam*, eds. Martin van Bruinessen and Julia Day Howell, pp. 257–277. New York: I.B.Tauris, 2007.

Gerges, Fawaz. *ISIS: A History*. Princeton: Princeton University Press, 2016.

GhaneaBassiri, Kambiz. *A History of Islam in America*. Cambridge: Cambridge University Press, 2010.

———. "Religious Normativity and Praxis Among American Muslims." In *The Cambridge Companion to American Islam*, eds. Juliane Hammer and Omid Safi, pp. 208–227. Cambridge: Cambridge University Press, 2013.

Ghonim, Wael. *Revolution 2.0: The Power of the People is Greater than the People in Power*. Boston: Mariner Books, 2012.

Giddens, Anthony. *The Consequences of Modernity*. Palo Alto: Stanford University Press, 1991.

———. *Modernity and Self-Identity: Self and Society in the Late Modern Age*. Palo Alto: Stanford University Press, 1991.

Godlas, Alan. "Sufism-Sufis-Sufi Orders." http://islam.uga.edu/sufismwest.html

Gomez, Michael A. *Black Crescent: The Experience and Legacy of African Muslims in the Americas*. Cambridge: Cambridge University Press, 2005.

Gottschalk, Peter and Gabriel Greenberg. *Islamophobia: Making Muslims the Enemy*. Lanham, Maryland: Rowan and Littlefield, 2007.

Gould, Mark. "Toward a Theory of 'Islamist Movements.'" *Sociology of Islam*, Vol. 2 (2014): pp. 21–59.

Gowins, Phillip. *Practical Sufism: A Guide to the Spiritual Path Based on the Teachings of Pir Vilayat Inayat Khan*. Wheaton, IL: Quest Books, 2010.

Graham, Donald A. Sharif. "Spreading the Wisdom of Sufism: The Career of Pir-o-Murshid Inayat Khan in the West." In *A Pearl in Wine: Essays on the Life, Music and Sufism of Hazrat Inayat Khan*, ed. Zia Inayat Khan, pp. 257–278. New Lebanon, NY: Omega Publications, 2001.

Graham, Terry. "Shah Ni'matullah Wali: Founder of the Ni'matu'llahi Sufi Order." In *The Heritage of Sufism, II: The Legacy of Medieval Persian Sufism*, ed. Leonard Lewisohn, pp. 173–190. Oxford: Oneworld Publications, 1999.

Green, Nile. *Sufism: A Global History*. Chichester, UK: Wiley-Blackwell, 2012.

Green, Todd. *The Fear of Islam: An Introduction to Islamophobia in the West*. Minneapolis: Fortress Press, 2015.

Grewal, Zareena. *Islam Is a Foreign Country: American Muslims and the Global Crisis of Authority*. New York: New York University Press, 2013.

Grieve, Gregory Price. "Religion." In *Digital Religion: Understanding Religious Practice in New Media Worlds*, ed. Heidi Campbell, pp. 104–118. New York: Routledge, 2013.

———. *Cyber Zen: Imagining Authentic Buddhist Identity, Community, and Practices in the Virtual World of Second Life*. New York: Routledge, 2017.

——— and Daniel Veidlinger, eds. *Buddhism, the Internet, and Digital Media: The Pixel in the Lotus*. New York: Routledge, 2015.

Grossberg, Lawrence. "Identity and Cultural Studies: Is That All There Is?" In *Questions of Cultural Identity*, eds. Stuart Hall and Paul du Gay, pp. 87–107. London: Sage Publications, 1997.

Habermas, Jürgen. *The Structural Transformation of the Public Sphere: An Inquiry Into a Category of Bourgeois Society*. Boston: MIT Press, 1991.

Hadden, Jeffrey K. and Douglas E. Cowan, eds. *Religion on the Internet: Prospects and Promises*. Amsterdam: Elsevier Science, 2000.

Hallaq, Wael. *The Impossible State: Islam, Politics, and Modernity's Moral Predicament*. New York: Columbia University Press, 2013.

Hamid, Shadi. *Temptations of Power: Islamists and Illiberal Democracy in a New Middle East*. Oxford: Oxford University Press, 2014.

——— and Rashid Dar. "Islamism, Salifism and Jihadism: A Primer." *Markaz: Middle East Politics and Policy*, July 15, 2016. http://www.brookings.edu/blogs/markaz/posts/2016/07/15-islamism-salafism-jihadism-primer-hamid-dar

Hammer, Juliane. *American Muslim Women, Religious Authority and Activism: More Than a Prayer*. Austin: University of Texas Press, 2012.

——— and Omid Safi. "Introduction: American Islam, Muslim Americans, and the American Experiment." In *The Cambridge Companion to American Islam*, eds. Juliane Hammer and Omid Safi, pp. 1–14. Cambridge: Cambridge University Press, 2013.

———, eds. *The Cambridge Companion to American Islam*. Cambridge: Cambridge University Press, 2013.

Hammer, Olav. "Sufism for Westerners." In *Sufism in Europe and North America*, ed. David Westerlund, pp. 127–143. New York: Routledge Curzon, 2004.

Helland, Christopher. "Online Religion/Religion Online and Virtual Communitas." In *Religion on the Internet: Prospects and Promises*, eds. Jeffrey K. Hadden and Douglas E. Cowan, pp. 205–224. Amsterdam: Elsevier Science, 2000.

———. "Popular Religion and the World Wide Web: A Match Made in (Cyber) Heaven." In *Religion Online: Finding Faith on the Internet*, eds. Lorne Dawson and Douglas Cowan, pp. 23–36. London: Routledge, 2004.

———. "Online Religion as Lived Religion: Methodological Issues in the Study of Religious Participation on the Internet." *Online Heidelberg Journal of Religions on the Internet*, Vol. 1, No. 1 (2005). http://archiv.ub.uni-heidelberg.de/volltextserver/5823/1/Helland3a.pdf

———. "Ritual." In *Digital Religion: Understanding Religious Practice in New Media Worlds*, ed. Heidi Campbell, pp. 25–40. New York: Routledge, 2013.

———. *Virtual Religion: A Case Study of Virtual Tibet*. Oxford Handbooks Online. New York: Oxford University Press, 2015. http://www.oxfordhandbooks.com/view/10.1093/oxfordhb/9780199935420.001.0001/oxfordhb-9780199935420-e-43

Helminski, Camille Adams, ed. *Women of Sufism: A Hidden Treasure*. Boston: Shambhala Publishers, 2003.

Hendrick, Joshua. *Gülen: The Ambiguous Politics of Market Islam in Turkey and the World*. New York: New York University Press, 2013.

Hermansen, Marcia. "In the Garden of American Sufism Movements: Hybrids and Perennials." In *New Trends and Developments in the World of Islam*, ed. Peter Clarke, pp. 155–178. London: Luzac, 1996.

———. "Visions as 'Good to Think': A Cognitive Approach to Visionary Experience in Islamic Sufi Thought." *Religion*, Vol. 27 (January 1997): pp. 25–43.

———. "Hybrid Identity Formations in Muslim America: The Case of American Sufi Movements." *The Muslim World*, Vol. 90, No. 1–2 (2000): pp. 158–197.

———. "Common Themes, Uncommon Contexts: The Sufi Movements of Hazrat Inayat Khan and Khwaja Hasan Nizami." In *A Pearl in Wine: Essays on the Life, Music and Sufism of Hazrat Inayat Khan*, ed. Zia Inayat Khan, pp. 322–353. New Lebanon, NY: Omega Publications, 2001.

———. "What's American About American Sufi Movements?" In *Sufism in Europe and North America*, ed. David Westerlund, pp. 36–63. London: Routledge, 2004.

———. "The Other Shadhilis of the West." In *The Shadhiliyya-Une voie Soufi dans le monde*, ed. Eric Geoffroy, pp. 481–499. Paris: Maisonneuve et Larose, 2005.

———. "Literary Productions of Western Sufi Movements." In *Sufism in the West*, eds. Jamal Malik and John Hinnels, pp. 28–48. New York: Routledge, 2006.

———. "Global Sufism: 'Theirs and Ours.'" In *Sufism in Western Society: Global Networking and Locality*, eds. Ron Geaves, Markus Dressler, and Gritt Linkhammer, pp. 26–45. New York: Routledge, 2009.

———. "Sufism." In *Encyclopedia of Muslim-American History*, Volume 2, ed. Edward E. Curtis IV, pp. 539–542. New York: Facts on File, 2010.

———. "South Asian Sufism in America." In *South Asian Sufis: Devotion, Deviation, and Destiny*, eds. Clinton Bennett and Charles M. Ramsey, pp. 247–268. New York: Bloomsbury, 2012.

———. "Sufism and American Women." *World History Connected* 4 (1) http://worldhistoryconnected.press.illinois.edu/4.1/hermansen.html

———. "The Emergence of Media Preachers: Yusuf al-Qaradawi." In *Islam in the Modern World*, eds. Jeffrey Kenney and Ebrahim Moosa, pp. 301–318. New York: Routledge, 2014.

Herrera, Linda and Asef Bayat, eds. *Being Young and Muslim: New Cultural Politics in the Global South and North*. Oxford: Oxford University Press, 2010.

Hirshkind, Charles. "Experiments in Devotion Online: The YouTube *Khutba*." *International Journal of Middle East Studies*, Vol. 44, No. 1 (February 2012): pp. 5–21.

Hjarvard, Stig. "Three Forms of Mediatized Religion: Changing the Public Face of Religion." In *Mediatization and Religion: Nordic Perspectives*, eds. Stig Hjarvard and Mia Lovheim, pp. 21–44. Göteborg, Sweden: Nordicom, 2012.

Hoesterey, James Bourk. *Rebranding Islam: Piety, Prosperity, and a Self-Help Guru*. Palo Alto: Stanford University Press, 2015.

Hodgson, Marshall G. S. *The Venture of Islam: Conscience and History in a World Civilization* (Volumes 1–3). Chicago: University of Chicago Press, 1974.

Hoffmann, Thomas and Goran Larsson, eds. *Muslims and the New Information and Communication Technologies: Notes From an Emerging and Infinite Field*. New York: Springer, 2013.

Hoffman, Valerie J. "The Role of Visions in Contemporary Egyptian Religious Life," *Religion*, Vol. 27 (January 1997): pp. 45–64.

Hofheinz, Albrecht. "The Internet in the Arab World: Playground for Political Liberalization." March 2005. http://library.fes.de/pdf-files/id/ipg/02941.pdf

Hogan, Bernie and Barry Wellman, "The Immanent Internet Redux." In *Digital Religion, Social Media and Culture: Perspectives, Practices and Futures*, eds. Pauline Hope Cheong, Peter Fischer-Nielsen, Stefan Gelfgren, and Charles Ess, pp. 115–130. New York: Peter Lang, 2012.

Hojsgaard, Morten T. "Cyber-Religion: On the Cutting Edge Between the Virtual and the Real." In *Religion and Cyberspace*, eds. Morten T. Hojsgaard and Margit Warburg, pp. 50–63. London: Routledge, 2005.

——— and Margit Warburg, eds. *Religion and Cyberspace*. New York: Routledge, 2005.

Holpuch, Amanda, Ed Pilkington, and Jared Goyette. "Muslims in Trump's America: Realities of Islamophobic Presidency Begin to Sink In." *The Guardian*, November 17, 2016. https://www.theguardian.com/us-news/2016/nov/17/muslim-americans-donald-trump-hate-crimes-surveillance?CMP=Share_iOSApp_Other

Hooley, Tristam, John Marriott, and Jane Wellens. *What Is Online Research?: Using the Internet for Social Science Research*. London: Bloomsbury, 2011.

Hoover, Stewart M. *Religion in the Media Age*. New York: Routledge, 2006.

———. "Concluding Thoughts: Imagining the Religious In and Through The Digital." In *Digital Religion: Understanding Religious Practice in New Media Worlds*, ed. Heidi Campbell, pp. 266–268. New York: Routledge, 2013.

———. "Evolving Religion in the Digital Media." In *Religion Across Media: From Early Antiquity to Late Modernity*, ed. Knut Lundby, pp. 169–184. New York: Peter Lang, 2013.

———. "Religious Authority in the Media Age." In *The Media and Religious Authority*, ed. Stewart M. Hoover, pp. 15–36. University Park, PA: Pennsylvania State University Press, 2016.

———, ed. *The Media and Religious Authority*. University Park, PA: Pennsylvania State University Press, 2016.

——— and Lynn Schofield Clark, eds. *Practicing Religion in the Age of the Media: Explorations in Media, Religion, and Culture*. New York: Columbia University Press, 2002.

———, Lynn Schofield Clark, and Lee Rainie. "Faith Online." Pew Internet and American Life Project, 2004. http://www.pewinternet.org/files/old-media/Files/Reports/2004/PIP_Faith_Online_2004.pdf

——— and Nabil Echchaibi. "Media Theory and the 'Third Spaces of Digital Religion.'" https://thirdspacesblog.files.wordpress.com/2014/05/third-spaces-and-media-theory-essay-2-0.pdf

Howard, Philip. *The Digital Origins of Dictatorship and Democracy: Information Technology and Political Islam*. Oxford: Oxford University Press, 2010.

——— and Muzammil M. Hussain. *Democracy's Fourth Wave?: Digital Media and the Arab Spring*. Oxford: Oxford University Press, 2013.

Huntington, Samuel. *The Clash of Civilizations and the Remaking of World Order*. New York: Touchstone, 1996.

Hutchings, Tim. "Creating Church Online: Networks and Collectives in Contemporary Christianity." In *Digital Religion, Social Media and Culture: Perspectives, Practices and Futures*, eds. Pauline Hope Cheong, Peter Fischer-Nielsen, Stefan Gelfgren, and Charles Ess, pp. 207–226. New York: Peter Lang, 2012.

Inge, Anabel. *The Making of a Salafi Muslim Woman: Paths to Conversion.* Oxford: Oxford University Press, 2016.

Jackson, Michael. "Knowledge of the Body." *Man*, Vol. 18, No. 12 (June 1983): pp. 327–345.

Jackson, Sherman A. *Islam and the Blackamerican: Looking Toward the Third Resurrection.* Oxford: Oxford University Press, 2005.

———. *Islam and the Problem of Black Suffering.* Oxford: Oxford University Press, 2009.

Jalal, Ayesha. *Partisans of Allah: Jihad in South Asia.* Cambridge, MA: Harvard University Press, 2008.

Jamal, Amaney and Liali Albana. "Demographics, Political Participation, and Representation." In *The Cambridge Companion to American Islam*, eds. Juliane Hammer and Omid Safi, pp. 98–118. Cambridge: Cambridge University Press, 2013.

Jamali, Reza. *Online Arab Spring: Social Media and Fundamental Change.* Waltham, MA: Chandos Publishing, 2015.

Jervis, James. "The Sufi Order in the West and Pir Vilayat Inayat Khan: Space-Age Spirituality in Contemporary Euro-America." In *New Trends and Developments in the World of Islam*, ed. Peter B. Clarke, pp. 211–260. London: Luzac Oriental Press, 1997.

Johnson, Chalmers. *Blowback: The Costs and Consequences of American Empire.* New York: Henry Holt, 2004.

Jones, Steven, ed. *Cybersociety.* London: Sage Publications, 1995.

———. *Virtual Culture: Identity and Communication in Cybersociety.* London: Sage Publications, 1997.

———. *Cybersociety 2.0: Revisiting Computer Mediated Community and Technology.* London: Sage Publications, 1998.

———. *Doing Internet Research: Critical Issues and Methods for Examining the Net.* London: Sage Publications, 1999.

Kadushin, Charles. *Understanding Social Networks: Theories, Concepts and Findings.* Oxford: Oxford University Press, 2011.

Kane, Ousmane Oumar. *The Homeland Is the Arena: Religion, Transnationalism, and the Integration of Senegalese Immigrants in America.* Oxford: Oxford University Press, 2011.

Karaflogka, Anastasia. *E-Religion: A Critical Appraisal of Religious Discourse on the World Wide Web.* London: Equinox, 2006.

Karamustafa, Ahmet. *God's Unruly Friends: Dervish Groups in the Islamic Middle Period 1200–1550.* Salt Lake City: University of Utah Press, 1994.

Karim, Jamillah. *American Muslim Women: Negotiating Race, Class, and Gender Within the Ummah.* New York: New York University Press, 2009.

Kaviraj, Sudipta. "The Imaginary Institution of India." In *Subaltern Studies VII: Writings on South Asian History and Society*, eds. Partha Chatterjee and Gyanendra Pandey, pp. 1–39. Delhi: Oxford University Press, 1992.

Keesing, Elisabeth. *Hazrat Inayat Khan: A Biography.* The Hague: East-West Publications, 1980.

Kepel, Gilles. *Jihad: The Trail of Political Islam.* Cambridge, MA: Belknap Press of Harvard University Press, 2003.

Khabeer, Su'ad Abdul and Maytha Alhassen, "Muslim Youth Cultures." In *The Cambridge Companion to American Islam*, eds. Juliane Hammer and Omid Safi, pp. 299–311. Cambridge: Cambridge University Press, 2013.

Khalil, Osamah F. *America's Dream Palace: Middle East Expertise and the Rise of the National Security State*. Cambridge, MA: Harvard University Press, 2016.

Khan, Inayat. *Biography of Pir-o Murshid Inayat Khan*. London: East-West Publications, 1979.

———. *The Sufi Message of Hazrat Inayat Khan, Centennial Edition: Volume 1—The Inner Life*. New Lebanon, NY: Suluk Press, 2016.

———. *The Sufi Message of Hazrat Inayat Khan, Centennial Edition: Volume 2—The Mysticism of Sound*. New Lebanon, NY: Suluk Press, 2018.

Khan, Khizr. "Attacks on American Muslims are un-American. Under Trump, They're on the Rise." *Washington Post*, July 21, 2017. https://www.washingtonpost.com/opinions/attacks-on-american-muslims-are-un-american-under-trump-theyre-on-the-rise/2017/07/21/fb7a0526-6cc7-11e7-9c15-177740635e83_story.html?hpid=hp_no-name_opinion-card-b%3Ahomepage%2Fstory&utm_term=.c168b1f54a31

Khan, Mahmood. "Hazrat Inayat Khan: A Biographical Perspective." In *A Pearl in Wine: Essays on the Life, Music and Sufism of Hazrat Inayat Khan*, ed. Zia Inayat Khan, pp. 65–126. New Lebanon, NY: Omega Publications, 2001.

Khan, Vilayat Inayat. *Toward the One*. New York: Harper and Row, 1974.

———. *In Search of the Hidden Treasure: A Conference of the Sufis*. New York: Jeremy P. Tarcher/Putnam, 2003.

Khan, Zia Inayat, ed. *A Pearl in Wine: Essays on the Life, Music and Sufism of Hazrat Inayat Khan*. New Lebanon, NY: Omega Publications, 2001.

———. "The 'Silsila-i Sufian': From Khwaja Mu'in ad-Din Chishti to Sayyid Abu Hashim Mandani." In *A Pearl in Wine: Essays on the Life, Music and Sufism of Hazrat Inayat Khan*, ed. Zia Inayat Khan, pp. 267–321. New Lebanon, NY: Omega Publications, 2001.

———. "A Hybrid Sufi Order at the Crossroads of Modernity: The Sufi Order and Sufi Movement of Pir-o-Murshid Inayat Khan." Unpublished doctoral dissertation, Duke University, 2006.

———, ed. *Caravan of Souls: An Introduction to the Sufi Path of Hazrat Inayat Khan*. New Lebanon, NY: Omega Publications, 2013.

———. *Mingled Waters: Sufism and the Mystical Unity of Religions*. New Lebanon, NY: Suluk Press, 2017.

Klinkhammer, Gritt. "Sufism Contextualized: The Mevlevi Tradition in Germany." In *Sufism Today: Heritage and Tradition in the Global Community*, eds. Catharina Raudvere and Leif Stenberg, pp. 209–228. New York: I.B.Tauris, 2009.

Knight, Michael Muhammad. *The Five Percenters: Islam, Hip Hop and the Gods of New York*. Oxford: Oneworld Publications, 2013.

Knysh, Alexander. *Sufism: A New History of Islamic Mysticism*. Princeton: Princeton University Press, 2017.

Korb, Scott. *Light Without Fire: The Making of America's First Muslim College*. Boston: Beacon Press, 2013.

Korom, Frank. "Charisma and Community: A Brief History of the Bawa Muhaiyaddeen Fellowship." *The Sri Lanka Journal of the Humanities*, Vol. 37 (2011): pp. 19–33.

———. "Longing and Belonging at a Sufi Shrine Abroad." In *Islam, Sufism and Everyday Politics of Belonging in South Asia*, eds. Deepra Dandekar and Torsten Tschacher, pp. 77–100. New York: Routledge, 2016.

Koszegi, Michael A. "The Sufi Order in the West: Sufism's Encounter With the New Age." In *Islam in North America: A Sourcebook*, eds. Michael A. Koszegi and J. Gordon Melton, pp. 211–249. New York: Garden Publishing, 1992.

Kozinets, Robert. *Netnography: Doing Ethnographic Research Online*. London: Sage Publications, 2010.

Kruger, Oliver. "Discovering the Invisible Internet: Methodological Aspects of Searching Religion on the Internet." *Online Heidelberg Journal of Religions on the Internet*, Vol. 1, No. 1 (September 2005): pp. 1–27.

Kugle. Scott A. "The Heart of Ritual is the Body: Anatomy of an Islamic Devotional Manual of the Nineteenth Century." *Journal of Ritual Studies*, Vol. 17, No. 1 (2003): pp. 42–60.

———. *Sufis and Saints' Bodies: Mysticism, Corporeality, and Sacred Power in Islam*. Chapel Hill: University of North Carolina Press, 2007.

———, ed. *Sufi Meditation and Contemplation: Timeless Wisdom from Mughal India*. New Lebanon, NY: Omega Publications, 2012.

Kumar, Deepa. *Islamophobia and the Politics of Empire*. Chicago: Haymarket Books, 2012.

Kundnani, Arun. *The Muslims are Coming!: Islamophobia, Extremism, and the Domestic War on Terror*. London: Verso, 2014.

Kurzman, Charles. *The Missing Martyrs: Why There Are So Few Muslim Terrorists*. Oxford: Oxford University Press, 2011.

Kurzweil, Ray. *The Age of Spiritual Machines: When Computers Exceed Human Intelligence*. New York: Penguin Books, 1999.

Larsson, Goran. "The Death of a Virtual Muslim Discussion Group: Issues and Methods in Analyzing Religion on the Net." *Online Heidelberg Journal of Religions on the Internet*, Vol. 1, No. 1 (September 2005): pp. 1–18.

———. "Cyber-Islamophobia?: The Case of WikiIslam." *Contemporary Islam*, Vol. 1 (2007): pp. 53–67.

———. *Muslims and the New Media: Historical and Contemporary Debates*. New York: Routledge, 2016.

Latour, Bruno. *Reassembling the Social: An Introduction to Actor-Network Theory*. Oxford: Oxford University Press, 2007.

Laude, Patrick. *Pathways to an Inner Islam: Massignon, Corbin, Guenon, and Schuon*. Albany: State University of New York Press, 2010.

Lavoie, Jeffrey D. *The Theosophical Society: The History of a Spiritualist Movement*. Boca Raton, FL: Brown Walker Press, 2012.

Lawrence, Bruce B. *Defenders of God: The Fundamentalist Revolt Against the Modern Age*. San Francisco: Harper and Row, 1989.

———. "Allah On-Line: The Practice of Global Islam in the Information Age." In *Practicing Religion in the Age of the Media: Explorations in Media, Religion, and Culture*, eds. Stewart M. Hoover and Lynn Schofield Clark, pp. 237–253. New York: Columbia University Press, 2002.

———. *New Faiths, Old Fears: Muslims and Other Asian Immigrants in American Religious Life*. New York: Columbia University Press, 2004.

———. "The Polite Islamophobia of the Intellectual." *Religion Dispatches*, June 1, 2010. www.religiondispatches.org/archive/politics/2635/the_polite/islamophobia_of_the_intellectual

———. "Islam: Unbound and Global." In *Islam in the Modern World*, eds. Jeffrey Kenney and Ebrahim Moosa, pp. 210–230. New York: Routledge, 2014.

Lean, Nathan. *The Islamophobia Industry: How the Right Manufactures Hatred of Muslims*. London: Pluto Press, 2012/2017.

Leonard, Karen Isaksen. *Muslims in the United States: The State of Research*. New York: Russell Sage Foundation, 2003.

———. "Organizing Communities: Institutions, Networks, Groups." In *The Cambridge Companion to American Islam*, eds. Juliane Hammer and Omid Safi, pp. 170–189. Cambridge: Cambridge University Press, 2013.

Lewis, Bernard. *What Went Wrong?: The Clash Between Islam and Modernity in the Middle East*. New York: Oxford University Press, 2002.

Lewis, Franklin D. *Rumi—Past and Present, East and West: The Life, Teachings, and Poetry of Jalal al-Din Rumi*. Oxford: Oneworld Publications, 2007.

Lewisohn, Leonard. "The Nimatullahi Order: Persecution, Revival and Schism." In *Bulletin of the School of Oriental and African Studies*, Vol. 61, No. 3 (October 1998): pp. 437–464.

———. "Persian Sufism in the Contemporary West: Reflections on the Nimatullahi Diaspora." In *Sufism in the West*, eds. Jamal Malik and John Hinnels, pp. 49–70. New York: Routledge, 2006.

Lim, Merlyna. *Islamic Radicalism and Anti-Americanism in Indonesia: The Role of the Internet*. Washington, D.C.: East West Center, 2005.

———. "Lost in Transition?: The Internet and *Reformasi* in Indonesia." In *Reformatting Politics: Information Technology and Global Civil Society*, eds. Jodi Dean, Jon Anderson, and Geert Lovink. London: Routledge, 2006.

Lipka, Michael. "Muslims Expected to Surpass Jews as Second-Largest U.S. Religious Group." Pew Research Center, April 14, 2015. http://www.pewresearch.org/fact-tank/2015/04/14/muslims-expected-to-surpass-jews-as-second-largest-u-s-religious-group/.

——— and Conrad Hackett. "Why Muslims are the Fastest-Growing Religious Group." Pew Research Center, April 6, 2017. http://www.pewresearch.org/fact-tank/2015/04/23/why-muslims-are-the-worlds-fastest-growing-religious-group/

Lizzio, Kenneth. *Embattled Saints: My Year With the Sufis of Afghanistan*. Wheaton, IL: Quest Books, 2014.

Lo, Mbaye and Taimoor Aziz. "Muslim Marriage Goes Online: The Use of Internet Matchmaking by American Muslims." *Journal of Religion and Popular Culture*, Vol. 21, No. 3 (2009).

Lock, Margaret. "Cultivating the Body: Anthropology and Epistemologies of Bodily Practice and Knowledge." *Annual Review of Anthropology*, Vol. 22 (1993): pp. 133–155.

Lofton, Kathryn. *Consuming Religion*. Chicago: University of Chicago Press, 2018.

Love, Erik. *Islamophobia and Racism in America*. New York: New York University Press, 2017.

Lovheim, Mia. "Young People, Religious Identity and the Internet." In *Religion Online: Finding Faith on the Internet*, eds. Lorne Dawson and Douglas Cowan, pp. 59–73. London: Routledge, 2004.

Lundby, Knut. "Media and Transformations of Religion." In *Religion Across Media: From Early Antiquity to Late Modernity*, ed. Knut Lundby, pp. 185–202. New York: Peter Lang, 2013.

———, ed. *Religion Across Media: From Early Antiquity to Late Modernity*. New York: Peter Lang, 2013.

Maguire, Musa. "The Islamic Internet: Authority, Authenticity and Reform." In *Media on the Move: Global Flow and Contra-Flow*, ed. Daya Thussu, pp. 237–250. London: Routledge, 2006.

Mahan, Jeffrey H., ed. *Media, Religion and Culture: An Introduction*. New York: Routledge, 2014.

Mahdi, Muhsin. "From the Manuscript Age to the Age of Printed Books." In *The Book in the Islamic World: The Written Word and Communication in the Middle East*, ed. George N. Atiyeh., pp. 1–15. Albany: State University of New York Press, 1995.

Mahmood, Saba. *Politics of Piety: The Islamic Revival and the Feminist Subject*. Princeton: Princeton University Press, 2005.

Malik, Jamal. "Introduction." In *Sufism in the West*, eds. Jamal Malik and John Hinnells, pp. 1–27. New York: Routledge, 2006.

——— and John Hinnells, eds. *Sufism in the West*. New York: Routledge, 2006.

Mamdani, Mahmood. *Good Muslim, Bad Muslim: America, the Cold War, and the Roots of Terror*. New York: Pantheon Books, 2004.

Mandaville, Peter. "Digital Islam: Changing the Boundaries of Religious Knowledge?" *ISIM Newsletter* 2, 1999.

———. *Transnational Muslim Politics: Reimagining the Umma*. New York: Routledge, 2001.

———. "Reimagining the *Ummah*?: Information Technology and the Changing Boundaries of Political Islam." In *Islam Encountering Globalization*, ed. Ali Mohammadi, pp. 61–90. London: Routledge, 2002.

———. "Communication and Diasporic Islam: A Virtual *Ummah*?" In *The Media of Diaspora*, ed. Karim H. Karim, pp. 135–147. London: Routledge, 2003.

———. *Global Political Islam*. New York: Routledge, 2007.

Marable, Manning. *Malcolm X: A Life of Reinvention*. New York: Penguin, 2011.

——— and Hishaam Aidi, eds. *Black Routes to Islam*. New York: Palgrave Macmillan, 2009.

Marcotte, Roxanne. "Gender and Sexuality Online on Australian Muslim Forums." *Contemporary Islam*, Vol. 4, No. 1 (April 2010): pp. 117–138.

Marranci, Gabriele. *Jihad Beyond Islam*. New York: Berg, 2006.

Masud, Muhammad, Armando Salvatore, and Martin van Bruinessen, eds. *Islam and Modernity: Key Issues and Debates*. Edinburgh: Edinburgh University Press, 2009.

McAlister, Melani. *Epic Encounters: Culture, Media, and US Interests in the Middle East, 1945–2000*. Berkeley: University of California Press, 2001/2005.

McCants, William. *The ISIS Apocalypse: The History, Strategy, and Doomsday Vision of the Islamic State*. New York: St. Martin's Press, 2015.

McCloud, Aminah Beverly. *African American Islam*. New York: Routledge, 1995.

McKinsey & Company, "Offline and Falling Behind: Barriers to Internet Adoption," report, 2013. https://www.mckinsey.com/industries/high-tech/our-insights/offline-and-falling-behind-barriers-to-internet-adoption.

Meijer, Roel, ed. *Global Salafism: Islam's New Religious Movement.* New York: Columbia University Press, 2009.

Menoret, Pascal. *The Saudi Enigma: A History.* London: Zed Books, 2005.

Metcalf, Barbara Daly. "Introduction." In *Moral Conduct and Authority: The Place of Adab in South Asian Islam*, ed. Barbara Daly Metcalf, pp. 1–20. Berkeley: University of California Press, 1984.

Meyer, Birgit, ed. *Aesthetic Formations: Media, Religion, and the Senses.* New York: Palgrave Macmillan, 2009.

———. "Material Mediations and Religious Practices of World-Making." In *Religion Across Media: From Early Antiquity to Late Modernity*, ed. Knut Lundby, pp. 1–19. New York: Peter Lang, 2013.

Milani, Milad and Adam Possamai. "The Nimatullahiya and Naqshbandiya Sufi Orders on the Internet: The Cyber-construction of Tradition and the McDonaldisation of Spirituality." In *Journal for the Academic Study of Religion*, Vol. 26, No. 1 (2013): pp. 51–75.

Miller, Vincent. *Consuming Religion: Christian Faith and Practice in a Consumer Culture.* London: Bloomsbury, 2005.

Mittermaier, Amira. *Dreams That Matter: Egyptian Landscapes of the Imagination.* Berkeley: University of California Press, 2011.

Mohammadi, Ali, ed. *Islam Encountering Globalization.* London: Routledge, 2002.

Molla, Rani. "These Are the Companies Investing Most Aggressively in VR and AR." *Recode*, April 28, 2017. https://www.recode.net/2017/4/28/15376268/facebook-augmented-virtual-reality-linkedin-jobs-charts

Morgan, David. *Visual Piety: A History and Theory of Popular Religious Images.* Berkeley: University of California Press, 1998.

———. *The Sacred Gaze: Religious Visual Culture in Theory and Practice.* Berkeley: University of California Press, 2005.

———, ed. *Religion and Material Culture: The Matter of Belief.* New York: Routledge, 2010.

———. *The Embodied Eye: Religious Visual Culture and the Social Life of Feeling.* Berkeley: University of California Press, 2012.

———. *Images at Work: The Material Culture of Enchantment.* Oxford: Oxford University Press, 2018.

Morgenstein Fuerst, Ilyse R. "Tracking Hate: Islam and Race After the Presidential Election." *Religion and Politics*, December 6, 2016. http://religionandpolitics.org/2016/12/06/tracking-hate-islam-and-race-after-the-presidential-election/

Moore, Kathleen. "Muslim Advocacy in America." In *Islam in the Modern World*, eds. Jeffrey Kenney and Ebrahim Moosa, pp. 369–388. New York: Routledge, 2014.

Moosa, Ebrahim. *Ghazali and the Poetics of Imagination.* Chapel Hill: University of North Carolina Press, 2005.

Mueller, John and Mark Stewart. *Chasing Ghosts: The Policing of Terrorism.* Oxford: Oxford University Press, 2016.

Murata, Sachiko. *The Tao of Islam: A Sourcebook on Gender Relationships in Islamic Thought.* Albany: State University of New York Press, 1992.

Nawa, Fariba. "American Sufi: From Texas the Taliban and Back." *Foreign Affairs*, October 12, 2016. https://www.foreignaffairs.com/articles/united-states/2016-10-12/american-sufi

Nawaz, Maajid. "Don't Let Madmen Like the Orlando Shooter Hijack Muhammad Ali's Legacy." *Daily Beast*, June 12, 2016. https://www.thedailybeast.com/dont-let-madmen-like-the-orlando-shooter-hijack-muhammad-alis-legacy

Nielsen, Richard A. *Deadly Clerics: Blocked Ambition and the Paths to Jihad*. Cambridge: Cambridge University Press, 2017.

Nielsen, Jorgen S., Mustafa Draper, and Galina Yemelianova. "Transnational Sufism: The Haqqaniyya." In *Sufism in the West*, eds. Jamal Malik and John Hinnells, pp. 103–114. New York: Routledge, 2006.

Nimer, Mohamed. *The North American Muslim Resource Guide: Muslim Community Life in the United States and Canada*. New York: Routledge, 2002.

Nizami, Khaliq Ahmad. "Chishtiyya." *Encyclopedia of Islam*, Vol. 11 Leiden: E. J. Brill, 1965, pp. 50–56.

———. *Tarikh-i mashayikh-i Chisht* [*The History of the Chishti Sufi Masters*]. Delhi: Idarah-i Adabiyyat-i Delli, 1980.

———. *The Life and Times of Shaikh Nizam-ud-Din Auliya*, Muslim Religious Thinkers of South Asia Series, No. 3, Delhi: Idarah-i Adabiyyat-i Delli, 1991.

Norland, Rod. "Cellphones in Hand, Saudi Women Challenge Notions of Male Control." *New York Times*, April 21, 2017. https://www.nytimes.com/2017/04/21/world/middleeast/saudi-arabia-women-male-guardianship-activists-social-media.html?rr ef=collection%2Fsectioncollection%2Fmiddleeast

Norris, Pippa. *Digital Divide: Civic Engagement, Information Poverty, and the Internet Worldwide*. London: Cambridge University Press, 2006.

Nunns, Alex and Nadia Idle, eds. *Tweets from Tahrir: Egypt's Revolution as It Unfolded, In the Words of the People Who Made It*. New York: OR Books, 2011.

Nurbakhsh, Javad. *Sufi Women*. New York: Khaniqahi-Nimatullahi, 1990.

O'Leary, S. D. "Cyberspace as Sacred Space: Communicating Religion on Computer Networks." *Journal of the American Academy of Religion*, Vol. 64, No. 4 (1996): pp. 781–808.

Orsi, Robert. *Between Heaven and Earth: The Religious Worlds People Make and the Scholars Who Study Them*. Princeton: Princeton University Press, 2006.

———. *The Madonna of 115th Street: Faith and Community in Italian Harlem, 1880–1950*. New Haven: Yale University Press, 2010.

———. *History and Presence*. Cambridge, MA: Belknap Press of Harvard University Press, 2016.

Oshan, Maryam. *Saudi Women and the Internet: Culture and Gender Issues*. Saarbrucken: VDM, 2009.

Osman, Tarek. *Islamism: What It Means for the Middle East and the World*. New Haven: Yale University Press, 2016.

Pape, Robert. *Dying to Win: The Strategic Logic of Suicide Terrorism*. New York: Random House, 2005.

Peek, Lori. *Behind the Backlash: Muslim Americans After 9/11*. Philadelphia: Temple University Press, 2011.

Pennington, Rosemary and Hilary E. Khan, eds. *On Islam: Muslims and the Media*. Bloomington: Indiana University Press, 2018.

Peskes, Esther, ed. *Wahhabism: Doctrine and Development*. London: Gerlach Press, 2015.

Pew Research Center. "Muslim Americans: No Signs of Growth in Alienation or Support for Extremism." U.S. Politics and Policy, August 30, 2011. http://www.people-press.org/2011/08/30/muslim-americans-no-signs-of-growth-in-alienation-or-support-for-extremism/

———. "America's Changing Religious Landscape." Religion and Public Life, May 12, 2015. http://www.pewforum.org/2015/05/12/americas-changing-religious-landscape/

———. "U.S. Muslims Concerned About Their Place in Society, but Continue to Believe in the American Dream." Religion and Public Life, July 26, 2017. http://www.pewforum.org/2017/07/26/findings-from-pew-research-centers-2017-survey-of-us-muslims/

Piela, Anna. *Muslim Women Online: Faith and Identity in Virtual Space*. New York: Routledge, 2012.

Piraino, Francesco. "Between Real and Virtual Communities: Sufism in Western Societies and the Naqshbandi Haqqani Case." *Social Compass* (2015): pp. 1–16.

Poole, Elizabeth and John Richardson, eds. *Muslims and the News Media*. New York: I.B.Tauris, 2006.

Poushter, Jacob. "Extremism Concerns Growing in West and Predominantly Muslim Countries." Pew Research Center, July 16, 2015. http://www.pewglobal.org/2015/07/16/extremism-concerns-growing-in-west-and-predominantly-muslim-countries/

Promey, Sally, ed. *Sensational Religion: Sensory Cultures in Material Practice*. New Haven: Yale University Press, 2014.

Prothero, Stephen. *The White Buddhist: The Asian Odyssey of Henry Steel Olcott*. Bloomington: Indiana University Press, 2010.

Qureshi, Emran and Michael Sells, eds. *The New Crusades: Constructing the Muslim Enemy*. New York: Columbia University Press, 2003.

Rabasa, Angel, Cheryl Benard, Lowell H. Schwartz, and Peter Sickle. "Building Moderate Muslim Networks." RAND Corporation, 2007. https://www.rand.org/pubs/monographs/MG574.html

Rahimi, Babak. "The Agonistic Social Media: Cyberspace in the Formation of Dissent and Consolidation of State Power in Post-Election Iran." *The Communication Review*, Vol. 14 (2011): pp. 158–178.

———. "The State of Digital Exception: Censorship and Dissent in Post-Revolutionary Iran." In *State Power 2.0: Authoritarian Entrenchment and Political Engagement Worldwide*, eds. Muzammil Hussain and Philip Howard, pp. 33–44. New York: Routledge, 2013.

———. "Censorship and the Islam Republic: Two Modes of Regulatory Measures for Media in Iran." *The Middle East Journal*, Vol. 69, No. 3 (Summer 2015): pp. 358–378.

———. "Rethinking Digital Technologies in the Middle East." *International Journal of Middle East Studies*, Vol. 47, No. 2 (2015): pp. 362–365.

Ramsay, Gilbert. *Jihadi Culture on the World Wide Web*. New York: Bloomsbury, 2013.

Rane, Halim, Jacqui Ewart, and John Martinkus. *Media Framing of the Muslim World: Conflicts, Crises and Contexts*. New York: Palgrave Macmillan, 2014.

Rashid, Ahmed. *Taliban: Militant Islam, Oil and Fundamentalism in Central Asia*. New Haven: Yale University Press, 2001.

———. *Jihad: The Rise of Militant Islam in Central Asia*. New Haven: Yale University Press, 2003.

Raudvere, Catharina and Leif Stenberg, eds. *Sufism Today: Heritage and Tradition in the Global Community*. New York: I.B.Tauris, 2009.

Rausch, Margaret J. "Encountering Sufism on the Web: Two Halveti-Jerrahi Paths and Their Missions in the USA." In *Sufism Today: Heritage and Tradition in the Global Community*, eds. Catharina Raudvere and Leif Stenberg, pp. 159–175. New York: I.B.Tauris, 2009.

Rawlinson, Andrew. *The Book of Enlightened Masters: Western Teachers in Eastern Traditions*. Chicago: Open Court, 1997.

Reinhertz, Shakina. *Women Called to the Path of Rumi: The Way of the Whirling Dervish*. Prescott, AZ: Hohm Press, 2001.

Rippin, Andrew. "The Qur'an on the Internet: Implications and Future Possibilities." In *Muslims and the New Information and Communication Technologies: Notes From an Emerging and Infinite Field*, eds., Thomas Hoffman and Goran Larsson, pp. 113–128. New York: Springer, 2014.

Rizvi, Saiyid Athar Abbas. *A History of Sufism in India*. Delhi: Munshiram Manoharlal Publishers, 1975.

Robinson, Francis. "Technology and Religious Change: Islam and the Impact of Print." *Modern Asian Studies*, Vol. 21, No. 1 (February 1993): pp. 229–251.

Robinson, William. *Global Capitalism and the Crisis of Humanity*. Cambridge: Cambridge University Press, 2014.

Roof, Wade Clark. *A Generation of Seekers: The Spiritual Journeys of the Baby Boom Generation*. San Francisco: Harper, 1994.

———. *Spiritual Marketplace: Baby Boomers and the Remaking of American Religion*. Princeton: Princeton University Press, 2001.

Roy, Olivier. *The Failure of Political Islam*. Cambridge, MA: Harvard University Press, 1996.

———. *Globalized Islam: The Search for a New Ummah*. New York: Columbia University Press, 2004.

Rozehnal, Robert. *Islamic Sufism Unbound: Politics and Piety in Twenty-First Century Pakistan*. New York: Palgrave Macmillan, 2007.

———. "Flashes of Ultimate Reality: Dreams of Saints and Shrines in a Contemporary Pakistani Sufi Community." *Journal of the Anthropology of the Contemporary Middle East and Central Eurasia*, Vol. 2, No. 1 (September 2014): pp. 67–80.

———, ed. *Piety, Politics and Everyday Ethics in Southeast Asian Islam: Beautiful Behavior*. London: Bloomsbury Publishing, 2019.

Rumi, Jalal ad-Din. *The Masnavi, Books 1–4*. Translation and commentary by Jawid Mojaddedi. Oxford: Oxford University Press, 2004, 2007, 2013, 2017.

Safi, Omid. *Memories of Muhammad: Why the Prophet Matters*. New York: Harper One, 2009.

———. "Good Sufi, Bad Muslims." University of Chicago Divinity School, The Martin Marty Center for the Advanced Study of Religion. January 27, 2011. https://divinity.uchicago.edu/sightings/good-sufi-bad-muslims-omid-safi

Said, Edward. *Orientalism*. New York: Vintage Books, 1979.

———. *Covering Islam: How the Media and the Experts Determine How We See the Rest of the World*. New York: Vintage Books, 1981.

Sajoo, Amyn, ed. *Muslim Modernities: Expressions of the Civil Imagination*. London: I.B.Tauris, 2009.

Salvatore, Armando. *Islam and the Political Discourse of Modernity*. Reading: Ithaca Press, 2000.

———— and Dale F. Eickelman, eds. *Public Islam and the Common Good*. Boston: Brill, 2006.

———— and Mark LeVine. "Introduction: Reconstructing the Public Sphere in Muslim Majority Societies." In *Religion, Social Practice, and Contested Hegemonies: Reconstructing the Public Sphere in Muslim Majority Societies*, eds. Armando Salvatore and Mark LeVine, pp. 1–26. New York: Palgrave Macmillan, 2016.

Sands, Kristin Zahra. "Muslims, Identity and Multimodal Communication on the Internet." *Contemporary Islam*, Vol. 4, No. 1 (April 2010): pp. 139–155.

Sargut, Cemalnur. *Beauty and Light: Mystical Discourses by a Contemporary Female Sufi Master*. Edited by Tehseen Thaver. Louisville, KY: Fons Vitae, 2018.

Scahill, Jeremy. *Dirty Wars: The World Is a Battlefield*. London: Serpent's Tail, 2014.

Schaebler, Birgit and Leif Stenberg. *Globalization and the Muslim World: Culture, Religion, and Modernity*. Syracuse: Syracuse University Press, 2004.

Schimmel, Annemarie. *Mystical Dimensions of Islam*. Chapel Hill: University of North Carolina Press, 1975.

————. *My Soul Is a Woman: The Feminine in Islam*. New York: Continuum Publishing, 1997.

Schmidt, Eric and Jared Cohen. *The New Digital Age: Transforming Nations, Businesses, and Our Lives*. New York: Vintage Books, 2014.

Schmidt, Garbi. "Sufi Charisma on the Internet." In *Sufism in Europe and North America*, ed. David Westerlund, pp. 109–126. New York: Routledge Curzon, 2004.

Schönbeck, Oluf. "Sufism in the USA: Creolisation, Hybridisation, Syncretisation?" In *Sufism Today: Heritage and Tradition in the Global Community*, eds. Catharina Raudvere and Leif Stenberg, pp. 177–188. New York: I.B.Tauris, 2009.

Seager, Richard Hughes. *The World's Parliament of Religions: The East/West Encounter, Chicago, 1893*. Bloomington: University of Indiana Press, 2009.

Sedgwick, Mark. "Western Sufism and Traditionalism," 2003. http://www.traditionalists. org/write/WSuf.htm

————. *Against the Modern World: Traditionalism and the Secret Intellectual History of the Twentieth Century*. New York: Oxford University Press, 2004.

————. "The Reception of Sufi and Neo-Sufi Literature." In *Sufism in Western Society: Global Networking and Locality*, eds. Ron Geaves, Markus Dressler, and Gritt Linkhammer, pp. 180–197. New York: Routledge, 2009.

————. *Western Sufism: From the Abbasids to the New Age*. Oxford: Oxford University Press, 2017.

Seesemann, Rüdiger. *The Divine Flood: Ibrahim Niasse and the Roots of a Twentieth-Century Sufi Revival*. Oxford: Oxford University Press, 2011.

Sells, Michael. *Early Islamic Mysticism: Sufi, Qur'an, Mi'raj, Poetic and Theological Writings*. Mahwah, New Jersey: Paulist Press, 1996.

————. "Wahhabist Ideology: What It Is and Why It's a Problem." *Huffington Post*, December 20, 2016. https://www.huffingtonpost.com/entry/585991fce4b014e7c7 2ed86e?timestamp=1482266088767

Shaheen, Jack. *Guilty: Hollywood's Verdict on Arabs After 9/11*. Northampton, MA: Olive Branch Press, 2008.

————. *Reel Bad Arabs: How Hollywood Vilifies a People*. Northampton, MA: Olive Branch Press, 2001/2009.

Shaikh, Sa'diyya. *Sufi Narratives of Intimacy: Ibn 'Arabi, Gender, and Sexuality*. Chapel Hill: University of North Carolina Press, 2012.

Sharify-Funk, Meena, William Rory Dickson, and Merin Shobhana Xavier. *Contemporary Sufism: Piety, Politics, and Popular Culture*. New York: Routledge, 2018.

Sheehi, Stephen. *Islamophobia: The Ideological Campaign Against Muslims*. Atlanta: Clarity Press, 2011.

Shirazi, Faegheh. *Brand Islam: The Marketing and Commodification of Piety*. Austin: University of Texas Press, 2016.

Silvers, Laury. "Early Pious, Mystic Sufi Women." In *The Cambridge Companion to Sufism*, ed. Lloyd Ridgeon, pp. 24–52. Cambridge: Cambridge University Press, 2014.

Sirriyeh, Elizabeth. *Sufis and Anti-Sufis: The Defence, Rethinking and Rejection of Sufism in the Modern World*. Richmond, Surrey: Curzon Press, 1999.

Sisler, Vit. "Cyber Counsellors: Online Fatwas, Arbitration Tribunals and the Construction of Muslim Identity in the UK." *Information, Communication and Society*, Vol. 14, No. 8 (2011): pp. 1136–1159.

———. "Play Muslim Hero: Construction of Identity in Video Games." In *Digital Religion: Understanding Religious Practice in New Media Worlds*, ed. Heidi Campbell, pp. 136–146. New York: Routledge, 2013.

Smith, Margaret. *Muslim Women Mystics: The Life of Rabi'a and Other Women Mystics in Islam*. Oxford: Oneworld Publications, 2001.

Somers, Jeffrey. "Whirling and the West: The Mevlevi Dervishes in the West." In *New Trends and Developments in the World of Islam*, ed. Peter B. Clarke, pp. 261–276. London: Luzac Oriental, 1997.

Stack, Liam. "American Muslims Under Attack." *New York Times*, February 15, 2016. http://www.nytimes.com/interactive/2015/12/22/us/Crimes-Against-Muslim-Americans.html?_r=0

Stjernholm, Simon. "A Translocal Sufi Movement: Developments Among Naqshbandi-Haqqani in London." In *Sufism Today: Heritage and Tradition in the Global Community*, eds. Catharina Raudvere and Leif Stenberg, pp. 83–101. New York: I.B.Tauris, 2009.

Sugich, Michael. *Signs on the Horizons: Meetings With Men of Knowledge and Illumination*. Self-published by Michael Sugich, 2013.

Suliman, Adela. "Sufi Sect of Islam Draws 'Spiritual Vagabonds' in New York." *New York Times*, September 23, 2016. https://www.nytimes.com/2016/09/25/nyregion/sufi-islam-new-york-converts.html?_r=0

Takim, Liyakat Nathani. *Shi'ism in America*. New York: New York University Press, 2009.

Taylor, Charles. *A Secular Age*. Cambridge, MA: Belknap Press of Harvard University Press, 2007.

Taylor, Ula Yvette. *The Promise of Patriarchy: Women and the Nation of Islam*. Chapel Hill: University of North Carolina Press, 2017.

Trimingham, J. Spencer. *The Sufi Orders in Islam*. London: Oxford University Press, 1971.

Turner, Richard Brent. *Islam in the African-American Experience*. Bloomington: Indiana University Press, 1997.

———. "African Muslim Slaves and Islam in Antebellum America." In *The Cambridge Companion to American Islam*, eds. Juliane Hammer and Omid Safi, pp. 28–44. Cambridge: Cambridge University Press, 2013.

Tweed, Thomas A. *Crossing and Dwelling: A Theory of Religion*. Cambridge, MA: Harvard University Press, 2008.

Ullah, Haroon. *Vying for Allah's Vote: Understanding Islamic Parties, Political Violence, and Extremism in Pakistan*. Washington, D.C.: Georgetown University Press, 2014.

van Beek, Wil. *Hazrat Inayat Khan: Master of Life, Modern Sufi Mystic*. New York: Vantage Press, 1983.

van Bruinessen, Martin and Julia Day Howell, eds. *Sufism and the 'Modern' in Islam*. New York: I.B.Tauris, 2007.

van Stolk, Sirkar and Daphne Dunlop. *Memories of a Sufi Sage: Hazrat Inayat Khan*. The Hague: East-West Publications, 1967.

Varisco, Daniel. "Virtual Dasein: Ethnography in Cyberspace." *Cyber Orient*, Vol. 2, No. 1, 2007. http://www.cyberorient.net/article.do?articleId=3698

———. "Muslims and the Media in the Blogosphere." *Contemporary Islam*, Vol. 4, No. 1 (April 2010): pp. 157–177.

Vine, David. *Base Nation: How U.S. Military Bases Abroad Harm America and the World*. New York: Metropolitan Books, 2015.

Wadud, Amina. *Inside the Gender Jihad: Women's Reform in Islam*. Oxford: Oneworld Publications, 2006.

Wagner, Rachel. *Godwired: Religion, Ritual and Virtual Reality*. New York: Routledge, 2012.

Walt, Stephen M. "The Unbearable Lightness of America's War Against the Islamic State." *foreignpolicy.com*, December 11, 2015. http://foreignpolicy.com/2015/12/11/the-unbearable-lightness-of-americas-war-against-the-islamic-state-obama-san-bernardino-us/

Washington, Peter. *Madame Blavatsky's Baboon: A History of the Mystics, Mediums, and Misfits Who Brought Spiritualism to America*. New York: Schocken Books, 1995.

Wasserstein, David. *Black Banners of ISIS: The Roots of the New Caliphate*. New Haven: Yale University Press, 2017.

Webb, Gisela. "Tradition and Innovation in Contemporary American Islamic Spirituality: The Bawa Muhaiyaddeen Fellowship." In *Muslim Communities in North America*, eds. Y. Haddad and J. I. Smith, pp. 75–108. Albany: State University of New York Press, 1994.

———. "Sufism in America." In *America's Alternative Religions*, ed. Timothy Miller, pp. 249–258. Albany: State University of New York Press, 1995.

———. "Third-Wave Sufism in America and the Bawa Muhaiyaddeen Fellowship." In *Sufism in the West*, eds. Jamal Malik and John Hinnells, pp. 86–102. New York: Routledge, 2006.

———. "Negotiating Boundaries: American Sufis." In *The Cambridge Companion to American Islam*, eds. Julianne Hammer and Omid Safi, pp. 190–207. Cambridge: Cambridge University Press, 2013.

Weismann, Itzchak. *The Naqshbandiyya: Orthodoxy and Activism in a Worldwide Sufi Tradition*. New York: Routledge, 2007.

Wellman, Barry. "Studying the Internet Through the Ages." In *The Handbook of Internet Studies*, eds. Mia Consalvo and Charles Ess, pp. 17–23. Chichester, UK: Wiley-Blackwell, 2012.

Wertheim, Margaret. *The Pearly Gates of Cyberspace: A History of Space from Dante to the Internet*. London: Virago, 1999.

Westerlund, David, ed. *Sufism in Europe and North America*. New York: Routledge Curzon, 2004.

Wheeler, Deborah. *The Internet in the Middle East: Global Expectations and Local Imaginations in Kuwait*. New York: State University of New York Press, 2005.

Wilson, Peter Lamborn, Christopher Bamford, and Kevin Townley. *Green Hermeticism: Alchemy and Ecology*. Great Barrington, MA: Lindisfarne Books, 2007.

Worth, Robert. *A Rage for Order: The Middle East in Turmoil, From Tahrir Square to ISIS*. London: Farrar, Straus and Giroux, 2016.

Wuthnow, Robert. *The Restructuring of American Religion*. Princeton: Princeton University Press, 1988.

———. *After Heaven: Spirituality in America Since the 1950s*. Berkeley: University of California Press, 1998.

———. *America and the Challenges of Religious Diversity*. Princeton: Princeton University Press, 2005.

———. *After the Baby Boomers: How Twenty- and Thirty-Somethings Are Shaping the Future of American Religion*. Princeton: Princeton University Press, 2007.

Xavier, Merin Shobhana. *Sacred Spaces and Transnational Networks in American Sufism: Bawa Muhaiyaddeen and Contemporary Shrine Cultures*. London: Bloomsbury, 2018.

Zaleski, Jeffrey. *The Soul of Cyberspace: How New Technology is Changing Our Spiritual Lives*. San Francisco: Harper Collins, 1997.

Zaman, Muhammad Qasim. *Modern Islamic Thought in a Radical Age: Religious Authority and Internal Criticism*. Cambridge: Cambridge University Press, 2012.

Zaman, Saminaz. "From Imam to Cyber Mufti: Consuming Identity in Muslim America." *The Muslim World*, Vol. 98 (October 2008): pp. 465–474.

Notes

INTRODUCTION: CYBER SUFIS IN THE DIGITAL AGE

1. Throughout this book, I use the term 'American' as a shorthand for the United States of America (the nation and its citizens). My analysis does not include Canada, Central America, or South America. Following standard usage, I define the 'Internet' as the global communication network—both hardware and software infrastructure—that links smaller computer networks around the globe. The 'World Wide Web' is the system of interlinked, hypertext websites that are accessed via the Internet. I use 'cyberspace,' a term invented by science-fiction writer William Gibson, to designate the more abstract, imaginative, virtual worlds enabled by digital multimedia technologies.

2. Roof, *Spiritual Marketplace*.

3. For examples of Muslim networks in theory and practice, see cooke and Lawrence, eds., *Muslim Networks*. On social network theory, see Kadushin, *Understanding Social Networks* and Latour, *Reassembling the Social*. On its application to social dynamics in the Digital Age, see especially the groundbreaking work of Castells. Campbell provides a useful summary of scholarship on digital religion that employs the concept of "networked community" ("Community," pp. 64–66). For a comprehensive overview of Islamic civilizational history, Hodgson's magisterial three-volume work, *The Venture of Islam*, remains essential reading.

4. Hogan and Wellman, "The Immanent Internet Redux," p. 55.

5. Schmidt and Cohen, *The New Digital Age*, p. 13.

6. McKinsey & Company, "Offline and Falling Behind," p. 2.

7. Lawrence, *New Faiths, Old Fears*, p. 104. On the persistent inequalities of Internet access, see also Norris, *Digital Divide*.

8. Freedom House, "Silencing the Messenger," p. 1.

9. Habermas, *The Structural Transformation of the Public Sphere*. For an intriguing discussion of Habermas' notion of the public sphere and its relevance to Islamic online discourse, see el-Nawawy and Khamis, *Islam Dot Com*, pp. 23–79.

10   Although I occasionally use the term 'Muslim world' in this book (or quote other scholars who do), I fully acknowledge its problematic nature. In no way do I mean to suggest that there is a separate 'world' occupied only by Muslims, or that Muslims (and Islam) are homogeneous. Islam is an incredibly diverse religious tradition, and around the globe Muslims live in pluralistic social, cultural, and religious societies. I use the term sparingly, therefore, and only as a convenient shorthand for the global Muslim *umma* (the approximately 1.8 billion Muslims on planet Earth). See Aydin, *The Idea of the Muslim World*.

11   http://www.azhar.edu.eg/en/

12   https://www.sistani.org/

13   Bhabha, *The Location of Culture*, p. 37.

14   See, for example, Karamah—Muslim Women Lawyers for Human Rights (www. karamah.org) and the Muslim Anti-Racism Collaborative (www.muslimarc.org).

15   www.sapelosquare.com and www.sufiwomen.org.

16   www.muslimahmediawatch.org

17   Oshan, *Saudi Women and the Internet*. See also Amos, "Saudi Women Can't Drive to Work, So They're Flocking to the Internet" and Norland, "Cellphones in Hand, Saudi Women Challenge Notions of Male Control."

18   For an overview of the 'Arab Spring' and its aftermath, see Worth, *A Rage for Order*. For the role of digital media in the Arab Spring, see Adi, *The Usage of Social Media in the Arab Spring*; Ghonim, *Revolution 2.0*; Howard and Hussain, *Democracy's Fourth Wave?*; Jamali, *Online Arab Spring*; Nunns and Idle, eds., *Tweets from Tahrir*.

19   Alkousaa, "How Facebook Hurt the Syrian Revolution."

20   In this book, I use ISIS as the popular shorthand for the self-proclaimed 'Islamic State of Iraq and Syria,' alternatively known as the Islamic State of Iraq and the Levant (ISIL). The group's Arabic name is *al-Dawla al-Islamiya fi al-Iraq wa al-Sham* (with the corresponding acronym, 'Daesh'). On the use of digital media by Islamist militant groups, see Aggarwal, *The Taliban's Virtual Emirate*; Aly, et al., eds., *Violent Extremism Online*.

21   Chakrabarty, *Habitations of Modernity*, p. xix.

22   There is a vast literature on both globalization and modernity. See especially Giddens, *The Consequences of Modernity* and *Modernity and Self-Identity*; Robinson, *Global Capitalism and the Crisis of Humanity*; Taylor, *A Secular Age*. On the connections between global modernity and religion, see Appadurai, *Modernity at Large* and Casanova, *Public Religions in the Modern World*. For discussions of Islam, see Gelvin and Green, eds., *Global Muslims in the Age of Steam and Print*; Lawrence, "Islam: Unbound and Global"; Mandaville, *Global Political Islam* and *Transnational Muslim Politics*; Masud, et al., eds., *Islam and Modernity*; Mohammadi, ed., *Islam Encountering Globalization*; Roy, *Globalized Islam*; Sajoo, ed., *Muslim Modernities*; Schaebler and Stenberg, eds., *Globalization and the Muslim World*.

23   Chakrabarty, *Provincializing Europe*, p. 4.

24   Salvatore, *Islam and the Political Discourse of Modernity*, p. 30. *What Went Wrong?* is the title of a best-selling book by the late Princeton historian Bernard Lewis.

25   Ewing, *Arguing Sainthood*, p. 4.

26   Bauman, *Liquid Modernity*, p. viii.

27   Appadurai, *Modernity at Large*, p. 32.

28 Ibid., p. 33.

29 Grossberg, "Identity and Cultural Studies," p. 89.

30 Kaviraj, "The Imaginary Institution of India," p. 33.

31 Appadurai, *Modernity at Large*, pp. 35–36.

32 I privilege the term 'American Muslims' rather than 'Muslim Americans' throughout this book. Scholars in the field use one or the other, often interchangeably. In contemporary public discourse, however, these terms have taken on an added (and politically charged) valence in debates about the contours and compatibility of national and religious identity. In exploring contemporary Sufi communities in the United States, I favor the term 'American Muslims' to locate Muslims in the United States as part of an expansive, global community of believers (*umma*).

33 Echchaibi, "Taming the West," p. 143. On 'multiple modernities,' see especially Eisenstadt. For a trenchant critique of the concepts of 'alternative modernities' and 'multiple modernities,' see Grewal, *Islam Is a Foreign Country*, pp. 59–60.

34 Schmidt, "Sufi Charisma on the Internet," p. 113. On the methodological and ethical challenges of Internet research, see Jones, ed., *Doing Internet Research*; Kozinets, *Netnography*; Varisco, "Virtual Dasein."

35 On the imaginative, emotional, aesthetic, and sensory dimensions of religious expression and experience, see especially Meyer, ed., *Aesthetic Formations*; Morgan, *The Embodied Eye*; Promey, ed., *Sensational Religion*.

1. MAPPING DIGITAL RELIGION AND CYBER ISLAM

1 Hogan and Wellman, "The Immanent Internet Redux," p. 57.

2 Anderson, *Imagined Communities*, p. 6, pp. 44–45. On the link between ideology and print media, see also Lawrence, *Defenders of God*, pp. 72–73.

3 Salvatore, *Islam and the Political Discourse of Modernity*, p. 138.

4 Damrel, "Aspects of the Naqshbandi-Haqqani Order in North America," p. 121.

5 Choeng and Ess, "Introduction: Religion 2.0?," p. ix.

6 For an overview of this scholarship, see especially Campbell, "Introduction" and "Understanding the Relationship Between Religion Online and Offline in a Networked Society"; Cho, "New Media and Religion"; Grieve, "Religion"; Hoover, "Evolving Religion in the Digital Media"; Wellman, "Studying the Internet Through the Ages."

7 Grieve, "Religion," p. 110. "First wave" scholarship includes Brasher, *Give Me That Online Religion*; O'Leary, "Cyberspace as Sacred Space"; Wertheim, *The Pearly Gates of Cyberspace*; Zaleski, *The Soul of Cyberspace*. For early ethnographic and methodological research on the Internet and social life, see also the multiple volumes edited by Steven Jones: *Cybersociety*; *Cybersociety 2.0*; *Doing Internet Research*; *Virtual Culture*.

8 Important contributions to this "Second Wave" scholarship include Dawson and Cowan, eds., *Religion Online*; Hadden and Cowan, eds., *Religion on the Internet*; Hojsgaard and Warburg, eds., *Religion and Cyberspace*; Hoover, *Religion in the Media Age*; Hoover and Clark, eds., *Practicing Religion in the Age of Media*; Hoover, Clark, and Rainie, "Faith Online"; Karaflogka, *E-Religion*; Kruger, "Discovering the Invisible Internet."

9   See Apolito, *The Internet and the Madonna*; Bernal, "Diaspora, Cyberspace and Political Imagination" and "Eritrea Online"; Blank, *Mullahs on the Mainframe*; Bunt, *Islam in the Digital Age*; Campbell, *Exploring Religious Community Online*; Cowan, *Cyberhenge*.

10 Grieve, "Religion," p. 113. Significant contributions of this "Third Wave" scholarship include a series of influential edited volumes: Campbell, ed., *Digital Judaism* and *Digital Religion*; Cheong et al., eds., *Digital Religion, Social Media and Culture*; Grieve and Veidlinger, eds., *Buddhism, the Internet, and Digital Media*; Hooley, Marriott, and Wellens, *What Is Online Research?*; Hoover, ed., *The Media and Religious Authority*; Mahan, ed., *Media, Religion and Culture*. See also the studies by Brinkerhoff, *Digital Diasporas*; Campbell, *When Religion Meets New Media*; Cantwell and Rashid, "Religion, Media, and the Digital Turn"; Grieve, *Cyber Zen*; Helland, *Virtual Religion*; Wagner, *Godwired*.

11 Hjarvard, "Three Forms of Mediatized Religion"; Lundby, "Media and Transformations of Religion."

12 Hoover, "Evolving Religion in the Digital Media," p. 173.

13 Lundby, "Media and Transformations of Religion," p. 199.

14 Hoover, "Evolving Religion in the Digital Media," p. 173.

15 See Morgan, *Images at Work, The Embodied Eye, The Sacred Gaze*, and *Visual Piety*; Morgan, ed., *Religion and Material Culture*; Orsi, *Between Heaven and Earth*.

16 Meyer, "Material Mediations and Religious Practices of World-Making," p. 8.

17 Helland, "Online Religion/Religion Online and Virtual Communities," pp. 205–223.

18 Hoover, "Evolving Religion in the Digital Media," p. 175.

19 Ibid., p. 171.

20 www.colorado.edu/cmrc/

21 Hoover and Echchaibi, "Media Theory and the 'Third Spaces of Digital Religion,'" p. 11.

22 Hoover, "Evolving Religion in the Digital Media," p. 181.

23 http://digitalreligion.tamu.edu

24 Campbell, "How Religious Communities Negotiate New Media Religiously," p. 84. This article summarizes the theoretical model that informs Campbell's 2010 monograph, *When Religion Meets New Media*.

25 Ibid., pp. 84–85.

26 Ibid., p. 85. See also *When Religion Meets New Media*, pp. 60–62. In his study of online Christian churches, Tim Hutchings offers a salient critique of Campbell's model, arguing it gives insufficient attention to the dynamics of contestation, resistance, and renegotiation within religious communities ("Creating Church Online," p. 213).

27 Campbell, *When Religion Meets New Media*, pp. 127–156.

28 Abdullah, "American Muslims in the Contemporary World," p. 78.

29 On the history of print media in the Muslim world, see Francis Robinson, "Technology and Religious Change."

30 cooke and Lawrence, "Introduction," p. 27.

31 Eickelman and Anderson, "Redefining Muslim Publics," p. 2. On media, Islam, and the public sphere, see also Anderson, "New Media, New Publics"; Dahlgren, "The Internet, Public Spheres and Political Communication" and "The Public Sphere

and the Net"; Eickelman and Salvatore, "The Public Sphere and Muslim Identities"; Salvatore and Eickelman, eds., *Public Islam and the Common Good*; Salvatore and Levine, "Introduction."

32   Anderson, "'Cybarites'", "Cybernauts of the Arab Diaspora."

33   Anderson, "The Internet and Islam's New Interpreters," p. 49.

34   Anderson, "Internet Islam," p. 301.

35   Anderson, "The Internet and Islam's New Interpreters," pp. 49–50. See also "Muslim Networks, Muslim Selves in Cyberspace"; "New Media, New Publics"; "Wiring Up."

36   Anderson, "Globalizing Politics and Religion in the Muslim World."

37   Anderson, "Technology, Media and the Next Generation in the Middle East," p. 10.

38   Bunt's most recent work, *Hashtag Islam*, was published after this book went to press. Though it appears to be another important contribution to the field, I did not have the opportunity to review it for this present study. For a full listing of Bunt's publications, see his professional web page: www.virtuallyislamic.com.

39   In *iMuslims*, Bunt provides a visual diagram outlining the interdependent spaces of "Cyber Islamic Environments," pp. 44–45. For reviews of *iMuslims*, see Vit Sisler, *Cyber Orient*, Vol. 7, No. 1 (2013) and Rozehnal, *The Middle East Journal*, Vol. 64, No. 1 (Winter 2010): pp. 152–153.

40   Bunt, *iMuslims*, p. 276.

41   Bunt, *Virtually Islamic*, pp. 18–30; *iMuslims*, pp. 81–87.

42   Ibid., pp. 33–36.

43   Ibid., pp. 108–131; *Islam in the Digital Age*, pp. 114–118, 124–183.

44   Ibid., pp. 104–108; *iMuslims*, pp. 87–129.

45   Ibid., pp. 30–33.

46   Bunt, *iMuslims*, pp. 45–53.

47   See Bunt, "Surfing the App Souq"; *iMuslims*, pp. 64–68.

48   Bunt, *iMuslims*, pp. 131–176.

49   Ibid., pp. 117–120.

50   Bunt, *Virtually Islamic*, pp. 37–47.

51   Ibid., pp. 47–57; *Islam in the Digital Age*, pp. 184–198.

52   Ibid., pp. 58–65; *Islam in the Digital Age*, pp. 198–200. See also "#Islam, Social Networking and the Cloud," pp. 187–191.

53   Ibid., pp. 66–103.

54   Ibid., pp. 135–138; *Islam in the Digital Age*, pp. 37–66. See also *iMuslims*, pp. 69–75; "#Islam, Social Networking and the Cloud," pp. 196–200.

55   See Bunt, "Defining Islamic Interconnectivity." See also *Islam in the Digital Age*, pp. 25–36, 67–111; *iMuslims*, pp. 177–274; "#Islam, Social Networking and the Cloud," pp. 191–196.

56   Bunt, *iMuslims*, p. 247.

57   el-Nawawy and Khamis, *Islam Dot Com*.

58   See Echchaibi, "Alt-Muslim"; Larsson, "Cyber-Islamophobia?"; Lawrence, "Allah On-Line"; Zaman, "From Imam to Cyber Mufti."

59   See, for example, the research of Rahimi, including: "Censorship and the Islam Republic"; "Rethinking Digital Technologies in the Middle East"; "The Agonistic Social Media"; "The State of Digital Exception." See also Faris and Rahimi, eds., *Social Media in Iran*.

60 Hofheinz, "The Internet in the Arab World"; Wheeler, *The Internet in the Middle East.*

61 Alatas, "Sufi Sociality in Social Media"; Hoesterey, *Rebranding Islam*; Lim, "Lost in Transition?"

62 See Echchaibi, "Muslimah Media Watch"; Marcotte, "Gender and Sexuality Online on Australian Muslim Forums"; Piela, *Muslim Women Online.*

63 Khabeer and Alhassen, "Muslim Youth Cultures," p. 309.

64 Maguire, "The Islamic Internet."

65 Rippin, "The Qur'an on the Internet."

66 See Echchaibi, "From Audio Tapes to Video Blogs" and "Gendered Blueprints"; Hermansen, "The Emergence of Media Preachers"; Hirshkind, "Experiments in Devotion Online"; Larsson, *Muslims and the New Media*; Sisler, "Cyber Counsellors."

67 See Echchaibi, "Hyper-Islamism?"; Howard, *The Digital Origins of Dictatorship and Democracy*; Mandaville, "Communication and Diasporic Islam," "Digital Islam," and "Reimagining the *Ummah*?".

68 See Brandon, *Virtual Caliphate*; Lim, *Islamic Radicalism and Anti-Americanism in Indonesia*; Ramsay, *Jihadi Culture on the World Wide Web.*

69 Larsson, "The Death of a Virtual Muslim Discussion Group"; Varisco, "Muslims and the Media in the Blogosphere"; Sands, "Muslims, Identity and Multimodal Communication on the Internet."

70 Lo and Aziz, "Muslim Marriage Goes Online."

71 Sisler, "Play Muslim Hero."

72 See http://www.digitalislam.eu/ (managed by Vit Sisler) and http://www.cyberorient.net/ (maintained and edited by Daniel Martin Varisco).

73 Mahdi, "From the Manuscript Age to the Age of Printed Books," pp. 6–7.

74 For resonant examples, see the edited volume by Chih, Mayeur-Jaouen, and Seesemann: *Sufism, Literary Production, and Printing in the Nineteenth Century.*

75 Ernst, *The Shambhala Guide to Sufism*, pp. 215–220. See also Ernst, "Between Orientalism and Fundamentalism," p. 120. On the use of media by a contemporary Sufi order in Pakistan, see Rozehnal, *Islamic Sufism Unbound*, pp. 93–127.

76 Ernst, "Ideological and Technological Transformations of Contemporary Sufism," p. 203. Echoing Ernst, Green observes, "In the globalized environments of the twenty-first century, what unites all of the Sufi movements now active in Europe and North America, no less than in older Muslim regions, is their effective adaptation of new technologies and organizational formats to disseminate their message" (*Sufism: A Global History*, p. 227).

77 Echchaibi, "Taming the West," p. 145.

78 Email communication to research assistant Ryan Stillwagon, July 1, 2011.

2. (MIS)INTERPRETING SUFISM

1 Ernst, *The Shambhala Guide to Sufism*, p. 9. For the classic critique of Orientalist scholarship, see Said, *Orientalism.*

2 For an influential example of the prevalent historical model of Sufism, see Trimingham, *The Sufi Orders in Islam.* For a trenchant critique, see Ernst and Lawrence, *Sufi Martyrs of Love*, pp. 11–12.

3   For details on the history and practices of antinomian Sufi groups, see Karamustafa, *God's Unruly Friends*. Cross-cultural and historical studies on the polemics against Sufism in various Islamic societies are documented in the essays in De Jong and Radtke, eds., *Islamic Mysticism Contested*.

4   Ernst, *Shambhala Guide to Sufism*, p. xv.

5   A comprehensive account of Islamist movements is beyond the purview of this book. For a succinct overview of Islamism and related terms, see Hamid and Dar, "Islamism, Salifism and Jihadism." For more detailed studies of political Islam and Islamic fundamentalism, see especially Akbarzadeh, ed., *Routledge Handbook of Political Islam*; Akhtar, *Islam as Political Religion*; Cesari, *What Is Political Islam?*; Choueiri, *Islamic Fundamentalism*; El Fadl, *The Great Theft*; Euben, *Enemy in the Mirror*; Euben and Zaman, eds., *Princeton Readings in Islamist Thought*; Gould, "Toward a Theory of 'Islamist Movements'"; Hallaq, *The Impossible State*; Hamid, *Temptations of Power*; Lawrence, *Defenders of God*; Mahmood, *Politics of Piety*; Mandaville, *Global Political Islam* and *Transnational Muslim Politics*; Meijer, ed., *Global Salafism*; Nielsen, *Deadly Clerics*; Osman, *Islamism*; Roy, *The Failure of Political Islam*; Zaman, *Modern Islamic Thought in a Radical Age*.

6   Salafism (derived from the Arabic term *salaf*, or 'ancestors,' a reference to the early followers of the Prophet Muhammad and his companions) is a catch-all term for a diverse range of Islamist revivalist movements that emerged in the early twentieth century. Wahhabism refers to the official religious ideology of Saudi Arabia, based on the teachings of the eighteenth-century Arab preacher and activist Muhammad ibn Abd al-Wahhab (1703–1792). See Algar, *Wahhabism*; Commins, *The Wahhabi Mission and Saudi Arabia*; Crawford, *Ibn 'Abd al-Wahhab*; DeLong-Bas, *Wahhabi Islam*; Inge, *The Making of a Salafi Muslim Woman*; Menoret, *The Saudi Enigma*; Peskes, *Wahhabism*; Sells, "Wahhabist Ideology."

7   Ernst, *The Shambhala Guide to Sufism*, p. xiii. For the debates and contestations over Sufism in the context of modernity and colonialism, see also Dickson and Sharify-Funk, *Unveiling Sufism*, pp. 54–94; Rozehnal, *Islamic Sufism Unbound*; Sirriyeh, *Sufis and Anti-Sufis*.

8   *Jihad* literally means 'struggle.' The term has varied interpretations and applications in Islamic history. On Islamist militancy, terrorism, and *jihad*, see Ali, "Redeeming Slavery"; Cockburn, *The Rise of Islamic State*; Devji, *Landscapes of the Jihad* and *The Terrorist in Search of Humanity*; Gerges, *ISIS: A History*; Jalal, *Partisans of Allah*; Kepel, *Jihad*; Kurzman, *The Missing Martyrs*; Marranci, *Jihad Beyond Islam*; McCants, *The ISIS Apocalypse*; Rashid, *Jihad* and *Taliban*; Ullah, *Vying for Allah's Vote*; Wasserstein, *Black Banners of ISIS*. For a comparative study of global terrorist violence, see especially Pape, *Dying to Win*.

9   *Jihadi* militant attacks against Sufis are well documented in popular media outlets. See, for example, Callimachi, "To the World They Are Muslims. To ISIS, Sufis Are Heretics." A research database compiled by Esmael Mayar and David Damrel (no longer active online) detailed ninety-two Islamist militant attacks on Sufi and Shi'a shrines across the globe from 1995 to 2013. The authors also noted that local journalists' reports pegged the actual number of such incidences closer to two hundred. For a more comprehensive analysis, see also the database hosted by the University of Maryland, *Start: National Consortium for the Study of Terrorism and Responses to Terrorism* (http://www.start.umd.edu).

10 Safi, "Good Sufi, Bad Muslims." See also Mamdani, *Good Muslim, Bad Muslim*.

11 Aidi, *Rebel Music*, p. 47.

12 Ibid., p. 70.

13 http://www.rand.org/pubs/periodicals/rand-review/issues/spring2004/pillars.html.

14 http://www.rand.org/pubs/research_brifs/RB9251/index1.html. On the Gülen movement, see Hendrick, *Gülen*.

15 Aidi, *Rebel Music*, p. 74. Shaykh Hamza Yusuf (b. 1960) is a prominent American Muslim leader and the co-founder of Zaytuna College. For more on Yusuf and Zaytuna, see Korb, *Light Without Fire*. Nuh Ha Mim Keller (b. 1954) is an American Muslim convert, scholar, and teacher who now lives in Amman, Jordan. Shaykh Hisham Kabbani (b. 1945) is a Lebanese-American Sufi master and current leader of the Naqshbandi Haqqani Sufi Order of America. See chapter 7 for more on Kabbani and this global Sufi *tariqa*.

16 Ibid., p. 82. For a broader analysis of the US government's public relations media campaigns and the attempts to frame American Muslim identity, "diversity patriotism," and citizenship after 9/11, see Alsuntany, *Arabs and Muslims in the Media*, especially chapter 5, "Selling Muslim American Identity," pp. 132–162.

17 For an overview of the momentous geopolitical shifts in the Arab world in the early decades of the twenty-first century, see Anderson, "Fractured Lands." On the Arab Spring, see especially Bayat, *Revolution Without Revolutionaries*.

18 Walt, "The Unbearable Lightness of America's War Against the Islamic State."

19 For an overview of US foreign policy, militarism, and the 'war on terror,' see especially Bacevich, *America's War for the Greater Middle East*; Edwards, *After the American Century*; Johnson, *Blowback*; Khalil, *America's Dream Palace*; Mueller and Stewart, *Chasing Ghosts*; Scahill, *Dirty Wars*; Vine, *Base Nation*.

20 See, for example, the Pew Research Center's 2012 report and interactive map, "Controversies Over Mosques and Islamic Centers Across the U.S.A.": http://www.pewforum.org/2012/09/27/controversies-over-mosques-and-islamic-centers-across-the-u-s-2/

21 The rhetorical question "Why do they hate us?" was first used by President George W. Bush in an address to a joint session of Congress on September 21, 2001. For a full transcript of his speech, see http://edition.cnn.com/2001/US/09/20/gen.bush.transcript/. Fareed Zakaria echoed the phrase in a *Newsweek* magazine story published shortly after the attacks of 9/11, entitled "The Politics of Rage: Why Do They Hate Us?" (http://www.newsweek.com/politics-rage-why-do-they-hate-us-154345). The 'clash of civilizations' thesis was popularized by Samuel Huntington. See, for example, his best-selling book, *The Clash of Civilizations and the Remaking of World Order*. For trenchant historical critiques of this thesis, see Adib-Moghaddam, *A Metahistory of the Clash of Civilisations*; Lawrence, "Islam: Unbound and Global."

22 Echchaibi, "American Muslims and the Media," p. 123.

23 For scholarly research on public concerns about Islamist terrorism around the globe, see Poushter, "Extremism Concerns Growing in West and Predominantly Muslim Countries."

24 There is a growing academic literature on Islamophobia. See in particular Allen, *Islamophobia*; Bail, *Terrified*; Beydoun, *American Islamophobia*; Ernst, ed., *Islamophobia in America*; Esposito and Kalin, eds., *Islamophobia*; Gottschalk

and Greenberg, *Islamophobia*; Green, *The Fear of Islam*; Kumar, *Islamophobia and the Politics of Empire*; Kundnani, *The Muslims are Coming!*; Lawrence, "The Polite Islamophobia of the Intellectual"; Lean, *The Islamophobia Industry*; Love, *Islamophobia and Racism in America*; Qureshi and Sells, eds., *The New Crusades*; Sheehi, *Islamophobia*. The Center for American Progress has published two detailed reports that document the institutional architecture of Islamophobia in the United States: "Fear, Inc." (Ali, et al., 2011) and "Fear, Inc. 2.0" (Duss, et al., 2015).

25 Council on American-Islamic Relations, "Confronting Fear," pp. 35–41. For the growth of domestic anti-Muslim violence, see also Burke, "Threats, Harassment, Vandalism at Mosques Reach Record High" and Stack, "American Muslims Under Attack."

26 Cassidy, "FBI: Hate Crimes Against Muslims Up By 67 Percent in 2015."

27 For analysis of the systemic Islamophobia in the Trump administration, see Beinart, "The Denationalization of American Muslims" and Khizr Khan, "Attacks on American Muslims are un-American. Under Trump, They're on the Rise."

28 For updated data on incidents of Islamophobia in the US, see the Southern Poverty Law Center (https://www.splcenter.org/fighting-hate/extremist-files/ideology/anti-muslim); the "Mapping Islamophobia" project (www.mappingislamophobia.org); and *Huffington Post*'s database (http://testkitchen.huffingtonpost.com/islamophobia/). On hate crimes against Muslims in the wake of the 2016 presidential election, see Holpuch, Pilkington, and Goyette, "Muslims in Trump's America" and Morgenstein Fuerst, "Tracking Hate."

29 Pew Research Center, "U.S. Muslims Concerned About Their Place in Society, but Continue to Believe in the American Dream."

30 Said, *Covering Islam*. For analysis of Islam and Muslims in the contemporary US media, see also Alsultany, *Arabs and Muslims in the Media*; Echchaibi, "American Muslims in the Media"; Eickelman and Anderson, *New Media and the Muslim World*; McAlister, *Epic Encounters*; Pennington and Khan, eds., *On Islam*; Poole and Richardson, eds., *Muslims and the News Media*; Rane, Ewart, and Martinkus, *Media Framing of the Muslim World*; Shaheen, *Guilty* and *Reel Bad Arabs*.

31 Suliman, "Sufi Sect of Islam Draws 'Spiritual Vagabonds' in New York."

32 For an overview of Sufi history and practice, see especially Dickson and Sharify-Funk, *Unveiling Sufism*; Ernst, *The Shambhala Guide to Sufism*; Green, *Sufism: A Global History*; Knysh, *Sufism*; Schimmel, *Mystical Dimensions of Islam*. For encounters with living Sufi masters, see Lizzio, *Embattled Saints*; Sargut, *Beauty and Light*; Sugich, *Signs on the Horizons*. The following summary of Sufi beliefs and rituals is largely drawn from my own monograph of a contemporary Sufi order in Pakistan: *Islamic Sufism Unbound*.

33 Metcalf, "Introduction," pp. 9–10. For detailed studies on the role of *adab* in Sufi history, piety, and practice, see Chiabotti et al., eds., *Ethics and Spirituality in Islam*, and Rozehnal, ed., *Piety, Politics and Everyday Ethics in Southeast Asian Islam*.

34 Quoted in Schimmel, *Mystical Dimensions of Islam*, p. 99. On the life and legacy of the Prophet Muhammad, see Safi, *Memories of Muhammad*.

35 For translations and commentary on these early Sufi theorists, see Sells, *Early Islamic Mysticism*.

36 For a detailed discussion of each of these Sufi ritual practices, see Rozehnal, *Islamic Sufism Unbound*, pp. 173–225.

37 Jackson, "Knowledge of the Body," p. 337. Scholars in various academic disciplines have studied the role of the body in ritual practice. For an overview, see Bell, "The Ritual Body," in *Ritual Theory, Ritual Practice*, pp. 94–117; Csordas, ed., *Embodiment and Experience* and "Embodiment as a Paradigm for Anthropology"; Lock, "Cultivating the Body."

38 Kugle, "The Heart of Ritual is the Body," p. 42. For analysis of embodiment in Sufism, see Bashir, *Sufi Bodies* and Kugle, *Sufis and Saints' Bodies*.

39 The term 'discursive tradition' is borrowed from anthropologist Talal Asad. See "The Idea of an Anthropology of Islam," p. 14.

3. SUFISM IN THE AMERICAN RELIGIOUS LANDSCAPE

1 Lawrence, *Old Faiths, New Fears*, p. 38.

2 http://www.pewforum.org/2015/05/12/americas-changing-religious-landscape/

3 This term is borrowed from Wade Clark Roof and his book *Spiritual Marketplace*. On the generational shifts in the religious makeup and practices of Americans in the twentieth and now twenty-first centuries, see also Roof, *A Generation of Seekers*, and Wuthnow, *After Heaven, After the Baby Boomers*, and *The Restructuring of American Religion*.

4 Wuthnow, *America and the Challenges of Religious Diversity*, p. 286.

5 Bell, "Even at His Funeral, Muhammad Ali Wanted to Share His Muslim Faith With the World."

6 Nawaz, "Don't Let Madmen Like the Orlando Shooter Hijack Muhammad Ali's Legacy."

7 Hammer and Safi, "Introduction," p. 11.

8 Turner, "African Muslim Slaves and Islam in Antebellum America," p. 29. On the African-American Muslim experience, see the work of Curtis: *Black Muslim Religion in the Nation of Islam, Islam in Black America*, and *The Call of Bilal*. See also Abdullah, *Black Mecca*; Chan-Malik, *Being Muslim*; Diouf, *Servants of Allah*; Gomez, *Black Crescent*; Jackson, *Islam and the Blackamerican* and *Islam and the Problem of Black Suffering*; Knight, *The Five Percenters*; Marable, *Malcolm X*; Marable and Aidi, eds., *Black Routes to Islam*; McCloud, *African American Islam*; Taylor, *The Promise of Patriarchy*; Turner, *Islam in the African-American Experience*.

9 A full accounting of the long and complex history of Islam in America is well beyond the scope and scale of this book. For a summary of the historiography, see Leonard, *Muslims in the United States*. In recent years, a wave of groundbreaking new scholarship has pushed the field in new directions. For historical overviews, see Curtis, *Muslims in America* and GhaneaBassiri, *A History of Islam in America*. Recently published encyclopedias include Cesari, ed., *Encyclopedia of Islam in the United States*; Curtis, ed., *Encyclopedia of Muslim-American History*; Hammer and Safi, eds., *The Cambridge Companion to American Islam*. For revealing portraits of Muslim life in the United States, see especially Bayoumi, *How Does It Feel to Be a Problem?* and *This Muslim American Life*; Bilici, *Finding Mecca in America*; Cesari, *Muslims in the West After 9/11* and *When Islam and Democracy Meet*; GhaneaBassiri, "Religious Normativity and Praxis Among American Muslims"; Lawrence, *Old Faiths, New Fears*; Peek, *Behind*

the Backlash. For studies of American Muslim organizations, see Leonard, "Organizing Communities"; Moore, "Muslim Advocacy in America"; Nimer, *The North American Muslim Resource Guide*. On questions of Islamic authority, transnational networks, and American Muslim youth culture, see Grewal, *Islam Is a Foreign Country*. For analysis of American Islam and gender, see especially Chan-Malik, *Being Muslim*; Hammer, *American Muslim Women, Religious Authority and Activism*; Karim, *American Muslim Women*; Wadud, *Inside the Gender Jihad*. On the Shi'i community in North America, see Takim, *Shi'ism in America*.

10 Abdullah, "American Muslims in the Contemporary World," p. 65. See also Lawrence, *Old Faiths, New Fears*, p. 121.

11 Curtis, "The Study of American Muslims," p. 19.

12 Pew Research Center, "U.S. Muslims Concerned About Their Place in Society," p. 30.

13 Jamal and Albana, "Demographics, Political Participation and Representation," p. 98.

14 Lipka, "Muslims Expected to Surpass Jews." According to the Pew Research Center, Islam remains the world's fastest-growing religion. As of 2015, the global population of Muslims was approximately 1.8 billion. At current projections, the Muslim population will grow more than twice as fast as the overall world population between 2010 and 2050. In the second half of this century, Muslims will likely surpass Christians as the world's largest religious group. See Lipka and Hackett, "Why Muslims are the Fastest-Growing Religious Group."

15 After consulting a wide range of divergent polls from numerous organizations, I have opted to follow the 2017 Pew Research Center's survey in this brief demographic overview of the American Muslim community. For details, see Pew, "U.S. Muslims Concerned About Their Place in Society," pp. 5–29.

16 In the 2017 Pew survey, 'white' is a particularly fuzzy category that includes, for example, American Muslims who describe their race as 'Arab,' 'Middle Eastern,' or 'Persian.' Even the US census lacks a separate category for people of Middle Eastern and North African descent, prompting most Arab Americans to self-identify as 'white.' Given the absence of standardized (and nuanced) categories in polling data, it is extremely difficult to provide a detailed and accurate account of the racial and ethnic makeup of American Muslims.

17 Pew Research Center, "Muslim Americans: No Signs of Growth in Alienation or Support for Extremism." On American Muslim life in the aftermath of 9/11, see for example Cainkar, *Homeland Insecurity*, and Bakalian and Bozorgmehr, *Backlash 9/11*.

18 Grewal, *Islam Is a Foreign Country*, p. 33.

19 Ibid., p. 16.

20 Abdullah, "American Muslims in the Contemporary World," p. 76. On debates over religious authority and authenticity, see also Grewal, *Islam Is a Foreign Country*, pp. 33–42.

21 GhaneaBassiri, *A History of Islam in America*, p. 7.

22 Curtis, "The Study of American Muslims," pp. 25–26.

23 For reasons behind this general scholarly lacuna, see Webb, "Third-Wave Sufism in America," p. 86.

24 On the history and contemporary practice of Sufism in the West, see especially the edited volumes by Geaves, Dressler, and Klinkhammer, eds., *Sufis in Western Society*; Malik and Hinnells, eds., *Sufism in the West*; Westerlund, ed., *Sufism in Europe and North America*. See also Laude, *Pathways to an Inner Islam*; Sedgwick, *Against the Modern World* and *Western Sufism*. On twenty-first-century Sufism, see Dickson and Sharify-Funk, *Unveiling Sufism*, pp. 10–53, and Sharify-Funk, Dickson, and Xavier, *Contemporary Sufism*. For broader accounts of Sufism's place in Islamic civilizational history, see Green, *Sufism: A Global History*; Knysh, *Sufism: A New History of Islamic Mysticism*; Raudvere and Stenberg, eds., *Sufism Today*; van Bruinessen and Howell, eds., *Sufism and the 'Modern' in Islam*.

25 Hermansen, "In the Garden of American Sufi Movements," p. 169.

26 Webb, "Third Wave Sufism in America," pp. 87–91. See also Webb, "Sufism in America."

27 On the historical impact of Sufism on nineteenth-century American thinkers and writers, see Aminrazavi, ed., *Sufism and American Literary Masters*.

28 See Lavoie, *The Theosophical Society*; Prothero, *The White Buddhist*; Seager, *The World's Parliament of Religions*; Washington, *Madame Blavatsky's Baboon*.

29 See Roof, *A Generation of Seekers*.

30 GhaneaBassiri, *A History of Islam in America*, p. 365.

31 Dickson, *Living Sufism in North America*, p. 47.

32 Nawa, "American Sufi," p. 2. For more information on ISRA, see the organization's website: http://www.israinternational.com/

33 Hermansen's research on Sufism in the United States includes a number of important articles: "Common Themes, Uncommon Contexts"; "Global Sufism"; "Hybrid Identity Formation in Muslim America"; "In the Garden of American Sufism Movements"; "Literary Productions of Western Sufi Movements"; "South Asian Sufism in America"; "Sufism"; "Sufism and American Women"; "The Other Shadhilis of the West"; "What's American About American Sufi Movements?"

34 Hermansen, "In the Garden of American Sufism Movements," pp. 155–178. See also, "Literary Productions of Western Sufi Movements," p. 28. More recently Hermansen has posited a fourth category: 'post-*tariqa*' or 'quasi-*tariqa*' movements. Associated largely with the South Asian Deobandi, Tablighi Jama'at, and Barelvi movements, they are "somewhat removed from the Sufism of traditional orders" and "have little attraction for Americans and therefore they may also be considered transplanted forms of South Asian Sufism." See Hermansen, "South Asian Sufism in America," pp. 248, 257–262.

35 On the history of the traditionalist and perennialist movements, see Sedgwick, *Against the Modern World*.

36 Dressler, "Pluralism and Authenticity," p. 85.

37 Ibid., p. 87.

38 Ibid., pp. 88–89. In Sufi parlance, *baraka* is 'divine blessing.' On the trope of Sufi travel, see Hermansen, "Literary Productions of Western Sufi Movements," pp. 38–40.

39 Ernst, "Ideological and Technological Transformations of Contemporary Sufism," p. 244. For insights into contemporary Muslim youth cultures in multiple societies, see Herrera and Bayat, eds., *Being Young and Muslim*.

40 Green, *Sufism: A Global History*, p. 228.

41 Ernst, "Sufism, Islam and Globalization in the Contemporary World," p. 5.

4. NARRATING IDENTITY IN CYBERSPACE: INAYATI TRADITION AND COMMUNITY

1 The video was uploaded to both the order's new website (http://inayatiorder.org/our-new-name/) and YouTube (https://www.youtube.com/watch?v=u3xJPpjvfRQ).

2 For an analysis of this prayer and its meanings, see Sedgwick, *Western Sufism*, p. 166.

3 https://inayatiorder.org/hazrat-inayat-khan/

4 https://inayatiorder.org/noor-un-nisa/

5 https://inayatiorder.org/pir-vilayat-inayat-khan/

6 https://inayatiorder.org/pir-zia-inayat-khan/ The overview of Inayat Khan and his family lineage that follows is distilled from these web-page biographies, in combination with a variety of other scholarly sources.

7 *Hazrat*, *pir*, and *murshid* are all honorary titles for a Sufi master. A vast digital archive of Inayat Khan's writings is available online at: https://wahiduddin.net/mv2/index.htm?fbclid=IwARof8iP43Z29AcTFw3kJpTglWV5qLNu8lOOz2mlDON9kUva-zMYPkWf8TKU For details on the life, teachings, and legacy of Inayat Khan, see in particular his *Biography of Pir-o Murshid Inayat Khan* and *The Sufi Message of Hazrat Inayat Khan, Centennial Edition, Volumes 1–2*, as well as the edited volumes by Zia Inayat Khan: *A Pearl in Wine* and *Caravan of Souls*. Of the voluminous scholarly studies, see especially Dickson, *Living Sufism in North America*; Dickson and Sharify-Funk, *Unveiling Sufism*, pp. 40–48; Ernst and Lawrence, *Sufi Martyrs of Love*, pp. 140–144; Genn, "The Development of a Modern Western Sufism"; Graham, "Spreading the Wisdom of Sufism"; Hermansen, "Common Themes, Uncommon Contexts," "Literary Productions of Western Sufi Movements," "South Asian Sufism in America," and "Sufism"; Jervis, "The Sufi Order in the West and Pir Vilayat Inayat Khan"; Keesing, *Hazrat Inayat Khan: A Biography*; Mahmood Khan, "Hazrat Inayat Khan"; Zia Inayat Khan, "A Hybrid Sufi Order at the Crossroads of Modernity" and "The 'Silsila-i Sufian'"; Koszegi, "The Sufi Order in the West"; Rawlinson, *The Book of Enlightened Masters*, pp. 370–371, 543–552; Sedgwick, *Western Sufism*, pp. 156–171, 222–235; van Beek, *Hazrat Inayat Khan*; van Stolk and Dunlop, *Memories of a Sufi Sage*; Webb, "Third Wave Sufism in America," pp. 87–88. There are also two documentary films on Inayat Khan's life and teachings: *The Way of the Heart: The Life and Legacy of Hazrat Inayat Khan (1882–1927)* (www.cultureunplugged.com/play/7713/The-Way-of-the-Heart) and *Dervish* (https://www.youtube.com/watch?v=SoyxjP8LvAs&feature=youtu.be).

8 For a comprehensive overview of the Chishti order, see Ernst and Lawrence, *Sufi Martyrs of Love*. See also Kugle, *Sufi Meditation and Contemplation* and the definitive work by Nizami, including "Chishtiyya," *Tarikh-i mashayikh-i Chisht*, and *The Life and Times of Shaikh Nizam-ud-Din Auliya*. For an analysis of a contemporary sub-branch of the Chishti Sabiri Sufi order in Pakistan, see Rozehnal, *Islamic Sufism*. On the broader

history of Sufism in South Asia, see especially Schimmel, *Mystical Dimensions of Islam* (pp. 370–402) and the two-volume work by Rizvi, *A History of Sufism in India*.

9 Inayat Khan, *Biography of Pir-o Murshid Inayat Khan*, p. 111.

10 Sedgwick, "The Reception of Sufi and Neo-Sufi Literature," p. 185. Zia Inayat Khan describes his grandfather's teachings as a distinct form of "Occidental Sufism." In his words, "Inayat Khan's articulation of Sufism represents a hybridization of Indo-Islamic (specifically Chishti) and modern Western (specifically Romantic) intellectual canons. The result is a spiritual psychology that invokes theology to valorize the freedom and creativity of the human subject, and posits the development and expression of the personality as the *summum bonum* of existence" ("A Hybrid Sufi Order at the Crossroads of Modernity," pp. 339–340).

11 Sedgwick, *Western Sufism*, pp. 159–160.

12 As Hermansen documents, the land for Inayat Khan's tomb and shrine was donated by the famous Chishti-Nizami master, Khawaja Hasan Nizami (1878–1955), who had known him personally ("Common Themes, Uncommon Contexts," pp. 323–353).

13 For details on the life of Noor-un-Nisa Inayat Khan, see Basu, *Spy Princess*; Fuller, *Noor-un-nisa Inayat Khan*; and the 2014 film *Enemy of the Reich: The Noor Inayat Khan Story* (http://www.pbs.org/program/enemy-reich/). There is also a novel based on her life: Baldwin, *The Tiger Claw*.

14 Pir Zia issued this public declaration on Visalat Day, February 5, 2018. The full text is available at: https://gallery.mailchimp.com/fd8625857899793849a6f66bc/files/f9144c3b-324a-4c79-b602-96d6d9394bd1/Noor_Declaration_English.pdf. In the accompanying video, Pir Zia and Shaykh Mahmood Khan (Inayat Khan's nephew) confirm this announcement while reflecting on Noor Inayat Khan's life and legacy (https://www.dropbox.com/s/mm4t7452f7lwovh/Declaration%20Video%20%28Office%20of%20the%20Pir%29.m4v?dl=0).

15 For details on Vilayat Inayat Khan's life and teachings, see Dickson, *Living Sufism in North America*; Dickson and Sharify-Funk, *Unveiling Sufism*, pp. 47–48; Gowins, *Practical Sufism*; Hermansen, "Literary Productions of Western Sufi Movements," "South Asian Sufism in America," "Sufism," and "What's American About American Sufi Movements"; Zia Inayat Khan, ed., *Caravan of Souls*, pp. 73–76; Sedgwick, *Western Sufism*, pp. 222–235.

16 Zia Inayat Khan, "A Hybrid Sufi Order at the Crossroad of Eternity," p. 258. See also Zia Inayat Khan, ed., *Caravan of Souls*, p. 75.

17 https://inayatiorder.org/our-new-name/. See also Zia Inayat Khan, "A Hybrid Sufi Order at the Crossroads of Modernity," pp. 244–246; Sedgwick, *Western Sufism*, p. 231.

18 Dickson and Sharify-Funk, *Unveiling Sufism*, pp. 47–48.

19 Hermansen, "South Asian Sufism in America," p. 249; Sedgwick, *Western Sufism*, pp. 232–233.

20 Dickson, *Living Sufism in North America*, pp. 251–252, footnote 58. For a salient example of Pir Vilayat Inayat Khan's emphasis on Islam and Sufism, see in particular his book *In Search of the Hidden Treasure*.

21 http://launchingpad.hypermart.net/Sufi/vilayat.htm. I have personally visited the tombs of Inayat Khan and Vilayat Inayat Khan on several occasions. I am grateful to an anonymous reader, however, for reminding me of the spatial orientation between their two burial sites and the story behind these separate locations.

22 For details on Zia Inayat Khan, see Dickson, *Living Sufism in North America* and Hermansen, "South Asian Sufism in America," p. 250. In this article, Hermansen concludes: "Among the current following of the Sufi Order International [now 'the Inayati Order'] the Islamic or South Asian influence seems to be less than it was during Vilayat Khan's leadership in the late 1960s and 1970s." (p. 250). In this book, I argue precisely the opposite is true under Pir Zia's current leadership.

23 https://inayatiorder.org/pir-zia-inayat-khan/. For reflections on the teachings of Pir Rashid, see "Memories of Pir Rasheed" by Pir Scott Siraj al-Haqq Kugle, posted to Pir Zia's personal website on December 30, 2013: http://www.pirzia.org/memories-of-pir-rasheed/.

24 https://inayatiorder.org/pir-zia-inayat-khan/

25 http://inayatiorder.org/about/the-inayati-order/

26 http://inayatiorder.org/teachings/ten-sufi-thoughts/

27 https://inayatiorder.org/wp-content/uploads/2016/10/Ten-Sufi-Thoughts-Hazrat-Inayat-Khan-upd10.09.2016.pdf

28 http://inayatiorder.org/about/what-is-sufism/

29 http://inayatiorder.org/teachings/objects-of-the-order/

30 Dickson, *Living Sufism in North America*, p. 99.

31 Hermansen, "What's American About American Sufi Movements?," pp. 43–44. Hermansen notes that "the more perennial or New Age movements" like the Inayati Order tend to be less ethnically and racially diverse than other more traditional, global Sufi communities.

32 http://inayatiorder.org/teachings/prayers/; https://inayatiorder.org/event/jamiat-khas-annual-retreat-2018/

33 http://inayatiorder.org/teachings/objects-of-the-order; http://inayatiorder.org/programs/leadership-training; http://inayatiorder.org/programs/introductory-programs

34 http://sufihealingorder.org/

35 http://inayatiorder.org/executive-director-letter/

36 http://inayatiorder.org/about/our-lineage/

37 On the life and legacy of Nizam ad-Din Awliya', see especially Ernst and Lawrence, *Sufi Martyrs of Love* and Nizami, *The Life and Times of Shaikh Nizam-ud-Din Auliya*.

38 According to Genn, "Retreats at the Dargah of Hazrat Inayat Khan in New Delhi from 2003 to 2005 have been attended by Indian nationals, South American and Chinese *murids*, as well as Westerners from Australia, New Zealand, North America and Europe." See "The Development of a Modern Western Sufism," p. 275.

39 This image is one of a number of photographs from the 2012 'urs attributed to Karamat Hess and accessible via an online Flickr account: https://www.flickr.com/photos/93709313@No5/albums/72157633096521706.

40 http://inayatiorder.org/about/our-lineage/

41 http://inayatiorder.org/the-silsila/. The Inayati Order also claims a direct spiritual link to the Mevlevi Order, named for its eponymous founder, the famous Persian Sufi luminary, Maulana Jalal ad-Din Rumi (1207–1273). In a December 2017 Facebook post to the community on the occasion of the anniversary of Rumi's death, Pir Zia

outlined the spiritual genealogy of the "Mawlavi [*sic*] Silsila of the Inayati Order." (Facebook, "The Inayati Order," December 17, 2017).

42 In an important article, Pir Zia provides biographical portraits of each Sufi master in the Chishti lineage of the Inayati Order. The essay makes clear what the website only suggests: that the Inayati Order is first and foremost a Chishti Sufi lineage, strengthened via the authority of Sayyid Abu Hashim Madani to three other important Sufi *turuq* (Suhrawardi, Qadiri, and Naqshbandi). For details on the Inayati lineage, see Zia Inayat Khan, "The 'Silsila-i Sufian.'"

43 http://inayatiorder.org/our-new-name/. Rawlinson provides several detailed lineage trees that outline the links between the multiple organizations that all claim the legacy of Inayat Khan. See *The Book of Enlightened Masters*, pp. 544–546.

44 https://inayatiorder.org/centers/related-organizations/

45 http://federation-message-hazrat-inayat-khan.blogspot.com/

46 http://www.sufimovement.org/

47 http://www.ruhaniat.org/

48 http://sufiway.org/

49 http://www.soefi-contact.nl/

50 This distinction is made clear in a footnote on "The Inayati Order" link. It asserts that, "Among Sufis, lineages of spiritual teaching and practice often take their names from their founders. Thus, the lineages which trace their origins to Hazrat Inayat Khan are generally known as Inayati lineages. The Inayati Order is the name of the organization representing the Inayati lineage passed directly from Hazrat Inayat Khan to his son, Pir Vilayat Inayat Khan, and currently led by his grandson, Pir Zia Inayat-Khan" (http://inayatiorder.org/about/the-inayati-order/).

51 For website images of Pir Zia, see: http://inayatiorder.org/pir-zia-inayat-khan/; http://inayatiorder.org/about/teachers-guides/; http://inayatiorder.org/teachings/prayers/; http://inayatiorder.org/chivalric-rules/; http://inayatiorder.org/multimedia/.

52 Dickson, *Living Sufism in North America*, p. 186. The Qur'an asserts that Allah makes no distinctions between His prophets in multiple verses. See, for example, 2:186; 2:285; 3:84; 4:152.

53 Ibid., p. 194.

54 https://inayatiorder.org/news/

55 http://inayatiorder.org/executive-director-letter. The term 'matrix shift' was coined by Pir Zia's mother, Taj Inayat. Executive Director Jennifer Alia Wittman labels these moves "The Great Repositioning."

56 http://inayatiorder.org/board/

57 For the organizational flow chart of the Message Council, see http://inayatiorder.org/message-council/.

58 http://www.inayatiorder.org/organization/

59 This detailed report was originally uploaded to the website in late 2016. Although no longer available online, I downloaded a copy in December 2016.

60 http://inayatiorder.org/our-new-logo/

61 http://inayatiorder.org/welcome-to-our-new-website/

62 http://inayatiorder.org/welcome-to-our-new-website/

63 "2015 North American Annual Report," p. 9.

64 http://inayatiorder.org/digitalmedia/

65 Campbell, "Community," p. 57.

66 Cheong and Ess, "Introduction," p. xii.

67 http://w2.vatican.va/content/vatican/en.html; https://www.dalailama.com/

68 Cheong, "Authority," p. 82.

5. VIRTUAL PRACTICE: INAYATI RITUALS AND TEACHING NETWORKS

1 As Dickson aptly notes, "Although practitioners are free to follow whatever religious practices they choose, the spiritual progress of order members proceeds through a coherent path of spiritual training based on Chishti Sufi principles and methods" (*Living Sufism in North America*, p. 100). For a detailed analysis of Chishti Sufi rituals, see Ernst and Lawrence, *Sufi Martyrs of Love*; Kugle, *Sufis and Saints' Bodies*; Kugle, ed., *Sufi Meditation and Contemplation*; Rozehnal, *Islamic Sufism Unbound*.

2 http://inayatiorder.org/about/six-activities

3 http://theuniversalworship.org/

4 http://theuniversalworship.org/universal-worship-prayers/

5 http://theuniversalworship.org/services-celebrations/activities-universal-worship/

6 http://theuniversalworship.org/cherag-code-of-ethics/

7 http://theuniversalworship.org/services-celebrations/find-a-cherag-near-you/

8 In his chapter on Inayat Khan and the Sufi Movement, Sedgwick examines the parallels between Inayat Khan's morning prayer, *saum*, and *Surat al-Fatiha*, the opening chapter of the Qur'an. See *Western Sufism*, pp. 166–167.

9 http://inayatiorder.org/teachings/prayers/

10 For details on traditional Chishti *zikr* practice, *lata'if*, and the spiritual body, see Ernst and Lawrence, *Sufi Martyrs of Love*, pp. 27–34, 130–134; Kugle, "The Heart of Ritual is the Body"; Rozehnal, *Islamic Sufism Unbound*, pp. 184–201.

11 http://inayatiorder.org/teachings/purification/

12 http://inayatiorder.org/teachings/purification/

13 https://newrain.info/newrain-online/

14 For details on The Abode's history, layout, and myriad programs, see http://inayatiorder.org/centers/abode-of-the-message/; www.theabode.org/; www.sufiretreatcenter.com/. The Abode also maintains its own Facebook page, "The Abode of the Message."

15 http://www.inayatiorder.org/organization/message-from-pir-zia/

16 http://inayatiorder.org/official-moving-richmond/

17 Posted on August 14, 2016: http://www.inayatiorder.org/organization/

18 http://inayatiorder.org/we-are-a-movement-of-remembering/

19 https://inayatiorder.org/event/the-alchemy-of-happiness/

20 http://inayatiorder.org/message-pir-zia/

21 http://inayatiorder.org/staff/

22 Facebook post, "The Inayati Order," July 6, 2017.

23 https://inayatiorder.org/theastana/

24 http://www.inayatiorder.org/organization/message-from-pir-zia/. This message was posted to the Organization Blog on September 20, 2015.

25 "2015 North American Annual Report," p. 12. The document does not provide a detailed demographic breakdown of this global network of students.

26 https://inayatiorder.org/centers-worldwide-map/

27 Hermansen, "Literary Productions of Western Sufi Movements," p. 32.

28 http://inayatiorder.org/centers/

29 "2015 North American Annual Report," p. 12.

30 Ibid., p. 12.

31 http://inayatiorder.org/about/teachers-guides/

32 Dickson, *Living Sufism in North America*, p. 129.

33 http://inayatiorder.org/about/teachers-guides/

34 Hermansen, "South Asian Sufism in America," p. 264. In a separate study, Hermansen quotes a statement from a previous version of the order's official website: "Spiritual practices and service are fully integrated and initial attempts have been made to update the language of the teaching to include the feminine. Several of the women teachers in the Order have made rich contributions by developing practices that facilitate an awareness of, and a deeper identification with, the feminine aspect of the divine." See Hermansen, "Sufism and American Women," p. 2.

35 Dickson, *Living Sufism in North America*, pp. 154–155.

36 Facebook post, "The Inayati Order," December 17, 2017.

37 For details on the life and teachings of Khwaja Hasan Nizami, see Hermansen, "Common Themes, Uncommon Contexts"; Ernst and Lawrence, *Sufi Martyrs of Love*, pp. 114–118.

38 For broader discussions of women and gender in Sufism, see Buturovic, "Between the *Tariqa* and the *Shari'a*"; Cornell, *Early Sufi Women*; Elias, "Female and the Feminine in Islamic Mysticism"; Helminski, ed., *Women of Sufism*; Kugle, *Sufis and Saints' Bodies*; Murata, *The Tao of Islam*; Nurbakhsh, *Sufi Women*; Schimmel, *My Soul Is a Woman*; Shaikh, *Sufi Narratives of Intimacy*; Sharify-Funk, Dickson, and Xavier, *Contemporary Sufism*, pp. 186–244; Silvers, "Early Pious, Mystic Sufi Women"; Smith, *Muslim Women Mystics*.

39 http://inayatiorder.org/diversity-statement/. This link is no longer active on the order's website and has been replaced by a new page, "Inclusion Statement," which reads: "The Inayati Order welcomes you—in all your colors, ancestries, ethnicities, cultures, genders, sexual preferences, abilities, religious and wisdom traditions, and financial conditions. We affirm the oneness of humanity and of all beings. Toward our embodiment of this fundamental unity, we dedicate ourselves to the healing of the wounds in our shared humanity and to the fearless inquiry that this requires of us. We affirm this statement as being in deep alignment with our ideals of a living spiritual transformation." (https://inayatiorder.org/inclusion-statement/)

40 http://inayatiorder.org/we-are-a-movement-of-remembering/

41 http://leaderstraining.inayatiorder.org/

42 http://inayatiorder.org/inayati-leadership-training-spring-2017/

43 https://inayatiorder.org/event/jamiat-khas-annual-retreat-2018/; https://inayatiorder.org/event/inayati-order-leadership-spring-training-2018/

44 http://inayatiorder.org/programs/leadership-training/

45 https://inayatiorder.org/emergent-leaders-program/; https://inayatiorder.org/emergent-leaders-curriculum/

46 http://www.pirzia.org/the-esoteric-school/. Although this text appears on Pir Zia's personal web page, it is linked to the Inayati Order's official web page (http://inayatiorder.org/centers/related-organizations).

47 http://inayatiorder.org/programs/season-of-the-rose/

48 https://inayatiorder.org/programs/suluk-academy/

49 http://www.sulukacademy.org/en/discover/description-and-history. This web page was active until the fall of 2018. Following the move to the Astana, the program's location and format have changed.

50 http://www.sulukacademy.org/en/discover/description-and-history

51 http://www.sulukacademy.org/en/discover/programs

52 http://inayatiorder.org/we-are-a-movement-of-remembering/. According to Hermansen, "There is also a counter practice of 'secret' Western Sufi literature that is only shared with initiates. For example, the Sufi Order previously circulated a series of unpublished texts of Hazrat Inayat Khan known as *Gathas*, *Githas*, *Sangathas* and *Sangithas* exclusively among higher initiates. These were to be read as part of closed sessions and were kept only by leaders of local centers. At least some of these writings, the *Gathas*, were 'declassified' and published by the European branch of the Order in 1982" ("Literary Productions of Western Sufi Movements," p. 33). See also Sedgwick, *Western Sufism*, pp. 167–168.

53 http://www.sulukacademy.org/en/courses/graduate-studies

54 http://inayatiorder.org/programs/suluk-academy/

55 http://inayatiorder.org/programs/suluk-academy/, "Sample Daily Schedule."

56 https://inayatiorder.org/programs/suluk-academy/, "Dates."

57 https://inayatiorder.org/programs/suluk-academy/, "Pricing."

58 https://inayatiorder.org/login/

59 Posted to the Organization Blog on August 14, 2016 (http://www.inayatiorder.org/organization/summer-update-2016/).

60 http://inayatiorder.org/we-are-a-movement-of-remembering/

61 Facebook post, "The Inayati Order," October 22, 2016.

62 Ibid., February 15, 2017.

63 Ibid., August 9, 2017.

64 For a broader analysis of the interplay of vertical and horizontal pedagogy in a contemporary Sufi order, see Rozehnal, *Islamic Sufism Unbound*, pp. 150–153, 167–170.

65 Facebook post, "The Inayati Order," May 23, 2017.

66 www.gayanapp.org.

67 Helland, "Ritual," p. 37

6. BRIDGING THE DIGITAL AND ANALOG WORLDS: INAYATI SOCIAL ENGAGEMENT

1 http://kinshipactivity.org

2 These programs were detailed in a previous iteration of the Kinship web page which is no longer accessible.

3 http://www.hopeprojectindia.org/html/programs.htm

4 http://www.hopeprojectindia.org/html/store.htm

5 https://inayatiorder.org/knighthood/

6 http://inayatiorder.org/chivalric-rules/

7 http://inayatiorder.org/teachings/commentary-on-the-rules/golden-rules/

8 https://sufihealingorder.net/lineage-who-we-are

9 Ibid

10 http://inayatiorder.org/about/six-activities/. For a more expansive introduction to this philosophy, see Wilson, Bamford, and Townley, *Green Hermeticism*. Significantly, Pir Zia wrote the introduction to this collection of essays.

11 http://www.ziraat.org/indexORIG.htm

12 https://inayatiorder.org/events/

13 http://www.zenithinstitute.com/

14 http://www.zenithinstitute.com/faq/

15 https://www.youtube.com/watch?v=IjLEMCnviUo

16 https://inayatiorder.org/suluk-press/

17 Inayat Khan, *The Sufi Message of Hazrat Inayat Khan, Centennial Edition: Volume 1, The Inner Life*.

18 Facebook post, "The Inayati Order," July 13, 2016.

19 https://inayatiorder.org/inner-life-online-course/

20 https://inayatiorder.org/soul-whence-whither-online-course-pir-zia-inayat-khan/

21 https://inayatiorder.org/event/the-mysticism-of-sound-music-an-online-course-w-pir-zia-inayat-khan-friends/

22 Facebook post, "The Inayati Order," February 12, 2017.

23 The Zephyr Newsletter, Facebook post, "The Inayati Order," March 4, 2018.

24 Genn, "The Development of a Modern Western Sufism," p. 275.

25 http://www.sevenpillarshouse.org/pages/history/

26 http://www.sevenpillarshouse.org/pages/mission/

27 In June 2017, for example, Pir Zia hosted a group of Sufi teachers and musicians at a three-day event, "Sufi Celebration," at the Omega Institute for Holistic Studies, a prominent interfaith retreat center in Rhinebeck, New York, co-founded by Pir Vilayat in 1977 (https://inayatiorder.org/sufi-celebration-omega/). For details on the Omega Institute, see https://www.eomega.org/.

28 http://inayatiorder.org/programs/wisdom-of-the-prophets/

29 https://inayatiorder.org/event/wisdom-prophets-sufism-islam-sheikh-ghassan-manasra-sheikha-fariha-al-jerrahi-pir-zia-inayat-khan/

30 https://interland3.donorperfect.net/weblink/weblink.aspx?name=E117941&id=1

31 "North America Keynotes 2018."

32 https://inayatiorder.org/donate/

33 http://mailchi.mp/inayatiorder/happiness-a-sufi-giving-tuesday-2017

34 On the issue of religion in the context of American capitalist, consumer culture, see Lofton, *Consuming Religion*; Miller, *Consuming Religion*; Shirazi, *Brand Islam*.

35 Facebook post, "The Inayati Order," November 9, 2016.

36 Ibid., November 12, 2016.

37 Ibid., January 21, 2017.

NOTES | 231

39 Facebook post, "The Inayati Order," August 17, 2017. This statement was also posted on the Inayati website: https://inayatiorder.org/charlottesville-statement-pir-zia/.

40 https://inayatiorder.org/zephyr-march-2018/

41 https://inayatiorder.org/the-zephyr-october-2018/

42 Campbell, "Community," pp. 62–63.

43 Cheong and Ess, "Introduction," p. 12.

44 Godlas, "Sufism-Sufis-Sufi Orders"; Sedgwick, "Western Sufism and Traditionalism."

45 Hermansen, "South Asian Sufism in America," p. 264.

46 https://www.facebook.com/misha.kogan/videos/10213951837127241/. The quoted excerpt can be seen at 12:48. The video was recorded at the Sufi Healing Order Leadership and Shifayat's retreat held on October 19–22, 2017 at the Roslyn Retreat Center in Richmond, Virginia. The video was subsequently uploaded to Facebook by a participant. For a similar synopsis of Inayat Khan's legacy, see also Pir Zia's essay, "The 'Silsila-i Sufian," pp. 320–321.

47 Genn, "The Development of a Modern Western Sufism," p. 260.

48 Ernst and Lawrence, *Sufi Martyrs of Love*, p. 130. On the use of cyberspace by numerous other groups that claim the legacy of Inayat Khan, see also Ernst, "Ideological and Technological Transformations of Contemporary Sufism," pp. 241–242.

7. CONTEXTUALIZING AMERICAN CYBER SUFISM

1 Damrel, "Aspects of the Naqshbandi-Haqqani Order in North America," p. 115.

2 For a multidimensional account of the Bawa Muhaiyaddeen community in both the United States and Sri Lanka, see Xavier, *Sacred Spaces and Transnational Networks in American Sufism*. See also Dickson and Sharify-Funk, *Unveiling Sufism*, pp. 50–52; Geaves, "The Bawa Muhaiyaddeen Fellowship"; Korom, "Charisma and Community" and "Longing and Belonging at a Sufi Shrine Abroad"; Webb, "Negotiating Boundaries," "Third Wave Sufism in America," and "Tradition and Innovation in Contemporary American Islamic Spirituality."

3 On the historical roots of the Halveti Order, see Curry, *The Transformation of Muslim Mystical Thought in the Ottoman Empire*. The Jerrahi branch of the Halveti Order was established by Pir Nur ad-Din al-Jerrahi (d. 1721) in Ottoman Istanbul in 1704. For details on these two Halveti-Jerrahi branches in the United States, see Blann, *Lifting the Boundaries*; Corbett, *Making Moderate Islam*; Dickson and Sharify-Funk, *Unveiling Sufism*, pp. 10–15; Dressler, "Between Legalist Exclusivism and Mysticist Universalism" and "Pluralism and Authenticity"; Rausch, "Encountering Sufism on the Web." For an introduction to contemporary female Sufi teachers in the West, including Shaykha Fariha, see also Dickson, *Living Sufism in North America*, pp. 152–166; Sharify-Funk, Dickson, and Xavier, *Contemporary Sufism*, pp. 213–244.

4 On the history of Shaykh Amadou Bamba and the Muridiyya Order, see especially Babou, *Fighting the Greater Jihad*. For a comparative study of the West African Tijaniyya Order and its history in Senegal, see Seesemann, *The Divine Flood*. On

Senegalese and other African immigrant communities in the United States, see also Abdullah, *Black Mecca* and Kane, *The Homeland is the Arena*.

5 For a historical overview, see Weismann, *The Naqshbandiyya*. On the Naqshbandiyya in the West, see Damrel, "Aspects of the Naqshbandi-Haqqani Order in North America"; Dickson, "An American Sufism"; Dickson and Sharify-Funk, *Unveiling Sufism*, pp. 16–20; Nielsen, Draper, and Yemelianova, "Transnational Sufism"; Piraino, "Between Real and Virtual Communities"; Schmidt, "Sufi Charisma on the Internet"; Stjernholm, "A Translocal Sufi Movement."

6 For historical background, see Graham, "Shah Ni'matullah Wali" and Lewisohn, "The Nimatullahi Order." On the order in the West, see Lewisohn, "Persian Sufism in the Contemporary West" and Milani and Possamai, "The Nimatullahiya and Naqshbandiya Sufi Orders on the Internet."

7 For a sweeping overview of the life and legacy of Rumi, see Lewis, *Rumi—Past and Present, East and West*. On Rumi and the Mevlevi Order in the West, see Dickson and Sharify-Funk, *Unveiling Sufism*, pp. 29–39; Klinkhammer, "Sufism Contextualized"; Reinhertz, *Women Called to the Path of Rumi*; Sharify-Funk, Dickson, and Xavier, *Contemporary Sufism*, pp. 140–181; Somers, "Whirling and the West." There are myriad English renditions of Rumi's voluminous Persian poetry. See in particular the translations and commentaries of the epic *Masnavi* by Jawid Mojaddedi.

8 Tweed, *Crossing and Dwelling*, p. 60.

9 Ahmed, *What Is Islam?*, p. 297.

10 GhaneaBassiri, "Religious Normativity and Praxis Among American Muslims," p. 210.

11 Alan Godlas characterizes Sufi orders in the West according to the tripartite taxonomy "Islamic," "quasi-Islamic," and "non-Islamic" on his website: http://islam.uga.edu/sufismwest.html. As we have seen, Marcia Hermansen employs "hybrids," "perennials," and "transplants." See Hermansen, "In the Garden of American Sufism Movements," pp. 155–178.

12 Dickson, *Living Sufism in North America*, p. 5.

13 Eickelman, "Communication and Control in the Middle East," p. 38.

14 Echchaibi, "Post-Islamist Sounds," p. 16.

15 Hoover, "Religious Authority in the Media Age," p. 32.

16 Moosa, *Ghazali and the Poetics of Imagination*, p. 29.

17 Corbin, *Creative Imagination in the Sufism of Ibn 'Arabi* and *The Man of Light in Iranian Sufism*.

18 On dreams and visions in Islam and Sufism, see Hermansen, "Visions as 'Good to Think'"; Hoffman, "The Role of Visions in Contemporary Egyptian Religious Life"; Mittermaier, *Dreams That Matter*; Rozehnal, "Flashes of Ultimate Reality" and *Islamic Sufism Unbound*, pp. 176–184.

19 I am grateful to Professor Youshaa Patel who inspired this line of thinking in a conversation following an October 2014 public lecture at Lafayette College. Following a major software error that potentially exposed the data of hundreds of thousands of the service's more than 110 million users, on October 8, 2018 Google announced it would shut down Google+ for consumers by August 2019.

20 In 1965, Intel co-founder Gordon Moore noted that the number of transistors per square inch on integrated circuits had doubled every year since their invention. 'Moore's law' predicts this trend will continue in the future, an observation that is often used as shorthand to describe the exponential growth of computer technologies in general.

21 Garner, "Digital Trends" and Molla, "These Are the Companies Investing Most Aggressively in VR and AR."

22 For a particularly compelling (if unsettling) vision of the future of computer technologies, see Kurzweil, *The Age of Spiritual Machines*.

23 Campbell, "Introduction," pp. 3–4.

Index